Marks of an Apostle

Society of Biblical Literature

Semeia Studies

Number 53

MARKS OF AN APOSTLE
Deconstruction, Philippians,
and Problematizing Pauline Theology

James A. Smith

Marks of an Apostle

Deconstruction, Philippians, and Problematizing Pauline Theology

James A. Smith

Society of Biblical Literature
Atlanta

MARKS OF AN APOSTLE
Deconstruction, Philippians,
and Problematizing Pauline Theology

Library of Congress Cataloging-in-Publication Data

Marks of an apostle : deconstruction, Philippians, and problematizing Pauline theology / James A. Smith.
    p.   cm. — (Society of Biblical Literature Semeia studies ; v. 53)
Includes bibliographical references and index.
ISBN-13: 978-1-58983-172-8 (paper binding : alk. paper)
ISBN-10: 1-58983-172-1 (paper binding : alk. paper)
    1. Bible. N.T. Epistles of Paul—Theology. 2. Bible. N.T. Philippians—Criticism, interpretation, etc. I. Title. II. Series: Semeia studies ; no. 53.

BS2651.M375 2005
227'.606—dc22   2005021986

05 06 07 08 09 10 11 12   5 4 3 2 1
Printed in the United States of America on acid-free, recycled paper conforming to ANSI/NISO Z39.48-1992 (R1997) and ISO 9706:1994 standards for paper permanence.

For Mandy

Contents

Acknowledgments

I owe a great debt to the Department of Biblical Studies at the University of Sheffield for their contribution to this project. In particular, I wish to thank Professor David Clines for directing me toward Paul in the first place and Dr. Loveday Alexander for the rigor of her reading and the clarity of her insight. I am also indebted to Dr. Stephen Fowl (Loyola College) for providing invaluable perspective and methodological nuance in his reading of the first draft of this manuscript. Most important, I am grateful for Dr. Stephen Moore, whose encouragement and patience enabled me to find my way through a confusion of ideas, and whose keen insight provided a much-needed edge to my understanding of how this project needed to come together. In the end, however, there is no other person to whom this work is more indebted than my friend and partner in life, Mandy.

Abbreviations

AARTTS	American Academy of Religion Text and Translation Series
ABD	*Anchor Bible Dictionary*
AET	Abraham Malherbe, *Ancient Epistolary Theorists*
AJP	*American Journal of Philosophy*
ANRW	*Aufstieg und Niedergang der Römischen Welt*
AV	Authorized Version
BAGD	W. Bauer, W. Arndt, F. W. Gingrich, and F. W. Danker, *A Greek-English Lexicon of the New Testament and Other Early Christian Literature*
BDF	F. Blass, A. Debrunner and R. W. Funk, *A Greek Grammar of the New Testament and Other Early Christian Literature*
BECNT	Baker Exegetical Commentary on the New Testament
BNTC	Black's New Testament Commentary
BSac	Bibliotheca Sacra
BZAW	Beihefte zur Zeitschrift für die Alttestamentliche Wissenshaft
BZNW	Beihefte zur Zeitschrift für die Neutestamentliche Wissenshaft
CNT	Commentaire du Nouveau Testament
CPh	*Classical Philology*
DPL	*Dictionary of Paul and His Letters*. Ed. Gerald F. Hawthorn and Ralph P. Martin
ExpTim	*Expository Times*
FFNT	Foundations and Facets: New Testament
HNT	Handbuch zum Neuen Testament
HNTC	Harper's New Testament Commentaries
HTKNT	Herders Theologischer Kommentar zum Neuen Testament
ICC	International Critical Commentary
ICS	*Illinois Classical Studies*

Int	*Interpretation*
JAC	*Jahrbuch für Antike Christentum*
JETS	*Journal of the Evangelical Theological Society*
JHS	*Journal of Hellenic Studies*
JJS	*Journal of Jewish Studies*
JRS	*Journal of Roman Studies*
JTC	*Journal for Theology and the Church*
JTS	*Journal of Theological Studies*
LCL	Loeb Classical Library
LEC	Library of Early Christianity
LSJ	Liddell, Henry George, and Robert Scott. *A Greek-English Lexicon (with a Supplement)*. Revised by Henry Stuart Jones et al.
MeyerK	Heinrich August Wilhelm Meyer, *Kritisch-Exegetischer Kommentar über das Neue Testament*
MGWJ	*Monatsschrift für Geschichte und Wissenshaft des Judentums*
NA^{27}	*Novum Testamentum Graece*, Nestle-Aland, 27th ed.
NASB	New American Standard Bible
NCB	New Century Bible
NIBC	New International Biblical Commentary
NICNT	New International Commentary on the New Testament
NIDNTT	*New International Dictionary of New Testament Theology*, Colin Brown, ed.
NIGTC	New International Greek Testament Commentary
NRSV	New Revised Standard Version
NTC	New Testament Commentary
NTD	Das Neue Testament Deutsch
OCD	*Oxford Classical Dictionary*
OED	Lesley Brown, ed. *The New Shorter Oxford English Dictionary*
OLD	*Oxford Latin Dictionary*. Ed. P. G. W. Glare
RestQ	*Restoration Quarterly*
RevExp	*Review and Expositor*
RTR	*Reformed Theological Review*
SBLRBS	Society of Biblical Literature Resources for Biblical Study
SBLSBS	Society of Biblical Literature Sources for Biblical Study
SNTSMS	Society for New Testament Studies Monograph Series
SVF	*Stoicorum veterum fragmenta*. H. von Arnim. 4 vols. Leipzig, 1903–1924
TB	Theologische Bücherei

TDNT	*Theological Dictionary of the New Testament.* Ed. Gerhard Kittel
ThTo	*Theology Today*
TLG	Thesaurus Linguae Graecae
TNTC	Tyndale New Testament Commentaries
USQR	*Union Seminary Quarterly Review*
WBC	Word Biblical Commentary
WTJ	*Westminster Theological Journal*
WUNT	Wissenschaftliche Unterschungen zum Neuen Testament
WZUJ	*Wissenschaftliche Zeitschrift der Universität Jena*
ZAW	*Zeitschrift für die Alttestamentliche Wissenshaft*
ZNW	*Zeitschrift für die Neutestamentliche Wissenshaft*
ZThK	*Zeitschrift für Theologie und Kirche*

The Last Word First
An Introduction

The driving force behind this project is a question that has nagged me for many years: how can Paul, in Phil 1:18, say that he is able to "rejoice" in proclamation regardless of whether it is done in "truth" or in "pretext"? Of particular concern to me is that so few commentators seem to view Pauline studies as one of the few real strongholds of the historical critics into which critical theorists seldom dare to go. I am acutely aware of the hulking mass of Pauline studies and Pauline theology and of the volumes of brilliant work that those institutions have produced. So it is with great respect and admiration for those who have gone before me that I embark on this particular journey and dare to offer a critical squeak inside the cavernous halls of Pauline scholarship.

Philippians is used by Paul to create a sense of ease about his imprisonment and thus also about his gospel. He finds his impetus for this activity within the constraints of his social discourse. The following discussion presents Paul in terms of the Greco-Roman psychagogue as a means to understand the culturally constrained, cognitive procedures present to him. The immediate effects of this are the usual ones: Paul can only think and say what the language and structures of his culture allow. The implication is that Paul's "theology" can only ever be based upon a logocentric pre-text: the immanent features of his social discourse. Thus, the following discussion attempts to describe assumptions associated with the moral philosophers as the cultural pre-text for Philippians.

This then operates as the context for another activity: Phil 1:12–18a holds within itself a crisis, since Paul attempts to both affirm and deny the metaphysics of presence within re-citations of the gospel. The approach by commentators has been to gloss the problem with a hierarchy in which Phil 1:18 governs Phil 1:15–17, which only succeeds in exacerbating the problem, leading to yet another crisis. The book seeks to argue that the text itself appears to be written deliberately to create a point of undecidability in which the text deconstructs itself while leaving the ethical

1

imperative of proclamation unscathed. This then is shown to demonstrate that there is more going on in Philippians than is typically thought to be the case. Paul is using Philippians to secure his ideo-theological agenda at Philippi. This subtextual activity is first seen in the disclosure formula in Phil 1:12, which is at once an opening and a closing of the epistle's semiotic activity; it thus becomes (dis)closure. This veiled operation is then shown to work its way beneath the textual surface until appearing at Phil 1:18a, where Paul erases the essential lines of difference between truth (ἀλήθεια) and falsehood (πρόφασις).

1

The Marks of an Apostle
WRITING ABOUT PAUL

The Philippian Epistle may be taken to exhibit the normal type of the Apostle's teaching, when not determined and limited by individual circumstances, and thus to present the essential substance of the Gospel. Dogmatic forms are the buttresses or the scaffold-poles of the building, not the building itself. (Lightfoot 1953, ix)

Words block up our Path.—Wherever primitive men put down a word, they thought they had made a discovery. How different the case really was!—they had come upon a problem, and, while they thought they had solved it, they had in reality placed an obstacle in the way of its solution. Now, with every new piece of knowledge, we stumble over petrified words and mummified conceptions, and would rather break a leg than a word in doing so. (Nietzsche 1911, §47)

1. Introduction

Within Paul's letter to the Philippians there resides a crisis. Or perhaps it would be more accurate to say that a solution resides in Philippians and that this is precisely the problem. Paul expresses "splendid magnanimity" and "large heartedness" and "magnificent optimism," to list a few of the descriptions of scholarly surprise at his solution in Phil 1:18a: "whether by pretext or by truth, Christ is proclaimed."

At first glance, it appears that the solution in Phil 1:18a to the crisis stated in Phil 1:15–17 is of little consequence, confined to a small, forgettable section of the Pauline corpus and to an even smaller and less memorable section of Pauline theology. However, upon further investigation, it appears that the ease with which readers have dealt or not dealt

3

with this text is not representative of an ease with the semantic content of
the text itself but an ease with the art of glossing. To be sure, a number of
scholars have drawn attention to some of the peculiarities of this passage,
and many have confessed their surprise at Paul's comments, but most[1] fail
to take Paul "seriously."[2] The trend is rather to observe an apparent theological discord between Phil 1:15–17 and Phil 1:18a, and then quickly to
retool Phil 1:15–17 into a harmonized comment on what becomes in Phil
1:18 a flash of Paul's recently acquired magnanimity.

To excavate the "truth" or "meaning" of this text is to unearth a fracture within the unity of the historical excavation process, namely the
hermeneutical processes by which we prise from the text its "meaning" or
"significance." After having discussed the two kinds of preachers in
1:15–17, Paul then says, "What does it matter?[3] Except that in every way,
whether by[4] pretext (πρόφασις) or by truth (ἀλήθεια) Christ is proclaimed
and in this I rejoice."[5] The striking point is that Paul is willing to affirm or
even validate a gospel proclaimed through motives and intentions which
are inherently contrary to it: a gospel proclaimed in/by pretext (πρόφασις).

To state the thesis of this project, Paul writes the letter to the
Philippians in order to encourage them at a time when they themselves
were suffering for the faith that they had placed in Paul's message of
Christ, namely the gospel.[6] His own imprisonment served only to exacer-
bate their trials, since they could hardly take comfort in the knowledge.
Paul therefore attempts to head off any disillusionment that the
Philippians may have had toward the gospel which he had proclaimed
among them, and toward himself as one whose words are equal to his life

---

[1] These will be noted as the argument develops.

[2] On "seriously," see sec. 3.a.

[3] Unless otherwise stated, all translations from the Greek New Testament are
my own and are based on the NA[27]. Τί γάρ here functions as an exclamatory question. See the comments in BDF §299 (3): "What does it matter? or What difference
does it make?"

[4] While the locative tends to be the received rendering, it seems more appropriate to understand the dative as representative of the means, since it highlights
the process of proclamation: by means of truth or by means of pretext Christ is
proclaimed.

[5] Τί γάρ; πλὴν ὅτι παντὶ τρόπῳ, εἴτε προφάσει εἴτε ἀληθείᾳ, Χριστὸς καταγγέλλεται,
καὶ ἐν τούτῳ χαίρω. The text-critical issues here are minor: P[46], ℵ, A, and several
other uncials and minuscules support this text; whereas B omits πλήν, while D and
Ψ omit ὅτι. P[46] and bo[ms] insert ἀλλά before the clause καὶ ἐν κτλ. (clearly as a balance to the final clause). These are minor deviations; there is nothing that offers a
significant alternative to Paul's comment; more important, there is nothing that
seems to mitigate it.

[6] This is stated explicitly in the text (1:27–30) and is commonly noted by
commentators.

and deeds.[7] Paul does this by inserting a discourse into the situation which would cause the Philippians to understand the events in a way favorable to both the gospel he preaches and to himself as their spiritual leader. This power play is unearthed when we dig beneath the surface of the text of Phil 1:12–18, and of Phil 1:18 in particular. I would further suggest that the evidence indicates that Paul is perceiving the problem along the lines drawn by Greco-Roman moral philosophical ideals. That is, it appears that the Greco-Roman moral philosophical topic of flattery and friendship is operative here as a cohering factor in Paul's understanding of potential problems and in his attempt to resolve them.[8] Finally, I suggest that Paul performs a radical, critical maneuver, the effects of which ripple through the eventual production of Pauline theology.[9]

In this chapter, I begin the task by considering contemporary writing practices and their impact upon the way we write about Paul. Chapters 2 and 3 then pursue the necessary background information pertinent to understanding the context of this passage of Philippians. The goal of those chapters is to locate Paul, the Philippians, and the letter itself in their critical and social frameworks. The point of such an undertaking is not to present a definitive argument on all matters pertaining to these issues; rather, I have in view the attempt to demonstrate something of those *constraints* placed upon Paul which necessarily *precede* his thought and thus his writing. Finally, in chapter 4, I begin a rewriting of commentary on this text by attempting to follow the text down into its moments of impasse and allow its difficulties to operate within the commentary. The goal here is to show how commentary has failed to take Phil 1:12–18a "seriously" and has overlaid a problematic hierarchy onto the text, which glosses the real, undecidable problems of the text. In revealing that gloss and tracing the contours of the text as it deconstructs itself, we actually gain far more than we have lost.

---

[7] Greco-Roman philosophy was overtly ethical in nature (all philosophy was eventually *moral* philosophy) and as a result there was an emphasis on the psychagogic principle that a philosopher's deeds ought to match his words. For Seneca, "God" is an ever-present witness to our words and deeds (*Ep.* 83.1; *Vit. beat.* 20.5); for Musonius Rufus, the teacher's conduct should match the principles he teaches and demonstrate with his own body the lessons of his philosophy (82.28–30); and being good is the same as being a philosopher (104.36–37). See also Cicero *De Finnibus* 1.7.25; *Tusc.* 5.24–6; *Off.* 1.43.153.

[8] While there are numerous references in the moral-philosophical literature of the relevant period to the difference between flattery and frank speech, or between a flatterer and a friend, Plutarch has dedicated an entire discourse to it ("How to Tell a Flatterer from a Friend") and I use that discourse as paradigmatic.

[9] I discuss the ramifications of this in chapter 4.

2. Writing about Paul's Writing

While there are some micro-level[10] debates over such things as the identity of Paul's opponents and the nature of the Christ-hymn in 2:6–11, the macro-level interpretation of Philippians has not been something over which biblical scholarship has endured much angst. Philippians has rather been classified quite typically by the institution of Pauline studies. When discussing Pauline literature, the "great epistles"[11] or the *Hauptbriefe* (Romans, Galatians, 1 and 2 Corinthians), if not explicitly stated, lurk in the background as a dominant and delimiting force.[12] This "lurking" occurs not simply by virtue of the fact that the term both normalizes and marginalizes the respective Pauline texts, but also by virtue of the way in which that normalizing process writes itself into the *institution* of Pauline studies at the very point which provides the possibility of discussing Pauline texts as something in particular.

2.a. *The* Hauptbriefe *and the Construction
of a Pauline Point of Reference*

It is not my intention here to articulate a history of the interpretation of Paul. It is rather the case that I seek to consider the fact that some of Paul's writings are privileged in the discussion about "what Saint Paul really said." The problem of privileging in the Pauline epistles is hardly an obvious one, and I shall demonstrate later how it affects commentary on the way in which Phil 1:18 is either (re)presented as theology or forgotten altogether.

Let us note, to begin with, that the opening statement in Dunn's article on Romans in the *Dictionary of Paul and His Letters* claims that

> Romans is both the least controversial of the major NT letters and the most important. . . . It is most important as being the first well-developed

---

[10] By "micro-level" I refer to the fact that these are subsections of the letter's general theological interest and do not imply "insignificant" or "simple."

[11] For all practical purposes this privileging process started with F. C. Baur. He bases his own discussion, though, partly upon on Eusebius's history and analysis of the formation of the canon in which there were said to be two classes of Pauline epistles: the Homologoumena and the Antilegomena. "In the Homologoumena there can only be reckoned the four great epistles (*Hauptbriefe*) of the Apostle, which take precedence of the rest in every respect namely the Epistle to the Galatians, the two Epistles to the Corinthians, and the Epistle to the Romans" (1:246, 247).

[12] It is far more common these days for people to employ the phrase "undisputed epistles" and by that title to refer to Romans, Galatians, 1 and 2 Corinthians, Philippians, 1 Thessalonians, and Philemon. We note, however, that the title "undisputed" refers primarily to authorship and not perceived value. The idea of a "big four" remains a somewhat prominent feature on the noetic landscape of Pauline studies, both theological and historical.

theological statement by a Christian theologian which has come down to us, and one which has had incalculable influence on the framing of Christian theology ever since—arguably the single most important work of Christian theology ever written. (Dunn 1993, 838)

The question I entertain here is the degree to which the rather common working assumption that Romans is no less than "the single most important work of Christian theology ever written" influences our treatment of other Pauline texts. The study of the theology of Paul has traditionally privileged Romans in a way that is good neither for the study of Romans nor for that of Paul. The privileging of Romans has a good pedigree. Note, for example, F. C. Baur's own panoptical vision of Romans: "[O]nly from the standpoint of the Epistle to the Romans do we survey the rich treasures of the spiritual life of which the Apostle was the depositary and the organ" (2:308). Dunn calls Romans our "prompter and plumb line" (1998a, 26); Günther Bornkamm understands it to be "Paul's last will and testament" (1971, 88–96); Kümmel labels the epistle as "the theological confession of Paul" (1975, 312–13).

Calvin Roetzel offers a well-stated *caveat*. His contention is that "once Romans is established as the goal and quintessential expression of Paul's theology, then every other letter of Paul can be read as a preliminary or provisional statement of a Pauline theology that receives its most adequate expression in Romans. This letter then becomes the canon of Paul's mature theology" (93). An example of this is the classic centralizing of certain theological topics which subsequently place inappropriate demands on our reading of the Pauline epistles in general. Although there have been challengers,[13] historically, for the Protestant churches at least,[14] the predominant theological influence has been located in the treatment of justification by faith in Romans as the center of Pauline thought (Plevnik 1989, 461). This is quite clear in Bultmann's existential anthropo-theological reading of Paul as the founder of a Christian theology which refers not to a center as much as to a "basic theological position" which is "more or less completely set forth in Romans" (1951, 1:190). That position is, suggests Bultmann, the one which Paul developed as a response to his "conversion" to the Christian faith and subsequent rejection of salvation by human accomplishment, namely, justification by faith. Hence Bultmann's student Ernst Käsemann's synthesizing statement: "The epistle to

---

[13] Wrede had a somewhat indignant reaction to the way the Reformation had enculturated theology with justification by faith as the Pauline point of reference (122–23). Schweitzer argued that "by taking the doctrine of righteousness by faith as the starting point, the understanding of the Pauline world of thought was made impossible" and that the modern use of the doctrine was an "unconscious" adaptation (220); but see the whole discussion (219–26).

[14] "The tendency among Catholic scholars has been to identify the center in Pauline theology with Christ the Son of God" (Plevnik 1989, 462).

the Romans subsumes the whole of the preaching and theology of Paul under the one head—the self-revealing righteousness of God. In so doing, it undoubtedly gives to the unique Pauline message a nucleus and a name which bring its own peculiar nature into the sharpest possible relief against the background of the rest of the New Testament" (Käsemann 1969, 168).[15]

The problem here is primarily with the way Paul's letters, and Romans in particular, are thought to function. It is not with the answers theologians have produced,[16] it is rather with the questions being asked— not prior "theological" assumptions, rather prior assumptions about Paul and the nature of his letters. Hence the significance of Stanley Stowers's observation in the opening of his *Rereading of Romans*:

> Romans has come to be read in ways that differ fundamentally from ways that readers in Paul's own time could have read it. More than any other writing of earliest Christianity, Romans, especially in the West, came to bear the major economies of salvation. These systems of sin and salvation reshaped the frame of reference that determined the reading of the letter. (1994, 1)

The problem with privileging Romans is not a superficial one; after all, Romans is clearly a majestic epistle and a magnificent outworking of Paul's gospel, albeit in the terms of certain issues present to him during its composition. There is, therefore, a great need for us to consider the reality of a difference between what has come to be the normal or institutionalized way of reading Paul's letters and the way Paul would have expected his letters to be read. A good starting point for this discussion is Dunn's recent work, *The Theology of Paul the Apostle*.[17]

In a discussion on how we can move toward a theology of Paul (1998a, 23–26), Dunn posits a question which is not really a question at all

---

[15] Käsemann represents something of a climax for the "justification by faith" approach. See the rest of his chapter "The Righteousness of God in Paul" (168–82); see also his chapter "Justification and Salvation History in the Epistle to the Romans" (1971, 60–78). Käsemann notes that it has been observed that justification by faith is simply Paul's attack on Judaism; however, he then suggests that this is no reason to subordinate it to other Pauline theological concepts. In fact doing so, in Käsemann's mind, is to provoke schism between modern Protestantism and the reformation itself—insofar as the Reformation itself reflects a particular theology or interpretation of Paul (1971, 70).

[16] How could we question the skill with which the likes of Bultmann crafted ingenious responses to the questions presented to them?

[17] Dunn's status within the realm of Pauline studies, the proliferation and excellence of his writing and thinking on Paul, allows him to be used as representative of traditional Pauline studies. It should therefore also be noted that the subsequent focus on Dunn's work is really a focus on the institution of Pauline studies and not on Dunn in particular.

because the answer already is deeply etched into the cornerstone of institutional Pauline studies. Nonetheless, Dunn observes that "one final point needs to be decided before embarking on the enterprise, that is, where one should best locate oneself within the flow of Paul's thought in order to begin the dialogue with it." After a relatively short discussion, the answer is said to be easily made, "for there is one letter of Paul's. . . . And that is Romans." Now, this is perfectly legitimate in many respects; after all, as Dunn well states:

> [Romans] was written to a church which was not his own founding. It was written at the end of a (or, better, the) major phase of Paul's missionary work (Rom 15:18–24), which included most of the other undisputed letters. It was written under probably the most congenial circumstances of his mission, with time for careful reflection and composition. And, above all, it was clearly intended to set out and defend his own mature understanding of the gospel (Rom 1:16–17) as he had thus far proclaimed it and as he hoped to commend it both in Jerusalem and beyond Rome in Spain. In short, Romans is still far removed from a dogmatic or systematic treatise on theology, but it nevertheless is the most sustained and reflective statement of Paul's own theology by Paul himself. (1998a, 25)

However, a complex of assumptions has led Dunn to the same point to which many others have come and which I find to be problematic. To begin with, let us observe that Dunn's ultimate goal is "first of all . . . to get inside the skin of Paul, to see through his eyes, to think his thoughts from inside as it were, and to do so in such a way as to help others to appreciate his insight and subtlety and concerns for themselves" (1998a, 24). We may note here that Dunn's ultimate goal is indeed the ultimate goal of virtually everyone who approaches Paul, since it is well-noted that culture, time, and language conspire to create a significant, perhaps impenetrable, barrier between us and *understanding Paul on his own terms.* The fact that this is Dunn's primary "endeavor" exposes the problem with his attempt to provide a defense of Romans as *the means* for beginning this endeavor; that is, Dunn gets ahead of himself, putting the hermeneutical cart before the exegetical horse. Note for example the statement and question, "[O]ne final question needs to be decided *before* embarking on the enterprise. That is, where one should best locate oneself within the flow of Paul's thought in order to *begin* the dialogue with it" (1998a, 25, emphasis added). The problem terms are those italicized; they represent a rhetorical difference between a question of where Dunn says he wants to begin and the fact that this has already been decided and the conversation begun.

Dunn wants "to get inside the skin" of the apostle in order to locate himself in some Pauline *primordium,* and the suggestion is that Romans is the opening through which he plans to enter into that activity, but herein lies our problem. What Dunn actually attempts to "defend" is whether

Romans is a sufficiently stable text that represents a "statement of Paul's own theology by Paul himself" (1998a, 25). He does not defend Romans as the point through which he may enter into and begin to possess Paul's corpus. He in fact assumes it and thus makes a classic bid for (interpretive) power over the corpus, which is not a simple claim that "my interpretation is better than yours." By locating himself within the apostle as his hermeneutical starting point, Dunn seeks to rebuild Paul from the toes up, to precede other interpretations, and he spends 737 pages reconstituting someone/thing called "Paul the Apostle." There is an important and crucial difference here: it is not a given that the status of Romans as a stable text and its function as a privileged, primordial hermeneutical doorway are the same thing. That Dunn assumes or suggests that they are is a problem, since at the very point of real decision in this process, the point at which even Dunn thinks a reading of Paul is made possible, he glosses the most important question with a statement on the text's apparent relative lack of historical interest. We shall return to Dunn, but for now, with respect to commenting upon objects of criticism, we ask, What is the role of the gloss? or What is the role of concealment? Such suspicious queries are like Nietzsche's *Hinterfragen*,[18] but nonetheless necessary.

2.b. Hinterfragen

"When we are confronted with any manifestation which someone has permitted us to see, we may ask: what is it meant to conceal? What is it meant to draw our attention from? What prejudice does it seek to raise? and again, how far does the subtlety of the dissimulation go?" (1911, §523; also 1954–56, 1:1010–1279). So says Nietzsche, anyway. But do we think he has gone too far with his suspicion? Must we look at texts and see nothing less than sleight of hand? Freud, for his part, believes that he has observed in the Scriptures the most prestigious prestidigitation, nothing less than the Levitical legerdemain of the Hebrew Bible's ancient redactors, J.E.P.D. The redaction, the glossing, was a priestly act of mediation, a sanctified distortion, an act of biblical commentary, of replacement, of dominance, of power, and, Freud further observes, this "distortion [*Entstellung*] of a text is not unlike a murder. The difficulty lies not in the execution of the deed but in the doing away with the traces [*Spuren*]" (1951, 70; 1937, 411).

   Entstellung (distortion) is a fundamental concept for Freud and natu-

---

[18] *Hinterfragen* is translated in various ways. I prefer the idea of "suspicious" or "insidious questions." However, upon asking one of my German friends, Dr. Matthias Fechner, about Nietzsche's intentions here his delightful response was "I could imagine he meant questions which pierce the surface while creeping under the cover of conventional assumptions." In less philosophically charged contexts, the word is typically "examine; analyze."

rally became a technical term for later psychoanalysts. It is a reference to "the modification of forbidden thoughts, impulses, or experiences to make them more acceptable to the ego" (Goldenson 1984, 229), or "the disguising or modification of unacceptable impulses so that they can escape the dream censor" (Chaplin 1985, 134–35). The important point is that alteration *precedes* manifestation. For example, "[F]orbidden wishes are frequently expressed in disguised or symbolic form: The innocent act of walking upstairs is more likely to pass the censor set up by the superego than the guilt-laden act of intercourse which it represents" (Goldenson 1984, 229). Freud himself notes that he desires to bring into our understanding of his use of the term "distortion" "the double meaning to which it has a right. . . . It should mean not only 'to change the appearance of,' but also 'to wrench apart,' 'to put in another place.' That is why in so many textual distortions we may count on finding the suppressed and abnegated material hidden away somewhere, though in an altered shape and torn out of its original connection" (1951, 70).

Nietzsche's suspicion of "any manifestation which someone has permitted us to see" is bound up with Freud's "distortion." What Nietzsche suspects in a given manifestation is a prior distortion of something that *was* unsavory or "unacceptable" and thus was altered or disguised so as to sneak pass the censor, who would otherwise sound the alarm, and has *now* manifested itself as "acceptable." Indeed, Nietzsche's entire genealogical project is precisely the attempt to locate the points of what Freud calls "distortion" and demonstrate the dependence of current "acceptable" manifestations upon acts of distortion, that is, upon lies.

Is not biblical criticism very much "distortion," our commentary writing in particular? Does not the commentary seek to isolate difficulties and smooth them over so as to represent, or "manifest," the text as comprehensible and coherent? Does not the commentary seek to precede the text, to displace and eventually replace the text in favor of itself? Does not the commentary require, as Sontag observes, a "dissatisfaction with the work (conscious or unconscious)" (253), "conceal an aggression" toward the work, (251) manifest a desire "to replace it by something else" (253), invoke a "radical strategy for conserving an old text, which is thought too precious to repudiate, by revamping it" (251)? Is it not a classic manifestation of the Nietzschean will to power? It must surely be since, as has been claimed, "no critic can evade a Nietzschean will to power over a text because interpretation is at last nothing else" (Bloom 1986, 21). And yet it must surely also be Freudian "distortion," since, through acts of replacement, it "distorts" the ancient original. Could we go so far as to make the seemingly outrageous claim that it is "murder"? If so, of whom?

Plato complained (through Socratic citation) that writing can be read and reread by anyone while the "father" of the ideas represented in writing is absent. Plato's fear is of a loose, pubescent text in the hands of an oily interloper, who, replacing (and forgetting) the father, now couples with the text in order to produce new ideas, ideas dissimilar to the careful textual cultivation of the father. Says the paternal Socrates: "Every word, once it is written, is bandied about, alike among those who understand and those who have no interest in it, and it knows not to whom to speak or not to speak; when ill-treated or unjustly reviled it always needs its father to help it; for it has no power to protect or help itself" (*Phaedr.* 275E).[19] Socrates' desire is for paternal control over the text, and he suggests that the text, with a sense of its heritage, also desires to be controlled. The act of reading is thus represented as an act of paternal replacement, a violent act upon the text and the father, a patricidal act. The Socratic fear of patricide and the desire to possess and master drives the Socrates character to castigate the possibility of a loss of power over the text through what appears to him as the possibility of a bastard text,[20] a text that does not know its father, namely *writing*. Ultimately, however, the problem is the possibility of, indeed, the need for, commentary. Commentary seals the father's fate.

Commentary is an expression of this Nietzschean will to power; it seeks to replace the text with itself; it thus desires its own paternity over its readers. Commentary seeks to assist and guide, resolving aporiae, bridging gaps, translating the unacceptable into the acceptable; thus, commentary is this act of Freudian distortion. It therefore gives rise to Nietzsche's set of "suspicious questions": "What is it meant to conceal? What is it meant to draw our attention from? What prejudice does it seek to raise? and again, how far does the subtlety of the dissimulation go?" (1911, §523). Thus, Jameson devotes an essay to the need for "metacommentary," a "heightened and self-conscious" state in which "we observe our own struggles and patiently set about characterizing them" (4). It is to create a "translation" that is always aware of its inability to transport, "to carry to heaven . . . without death" (*OED*, s.v.); to see past the illusion "that there exists somewhere, ultimately attainable, some final and transparent reading" (Jameson 1988, 4).

To say it yet another way, commentary is an act of consumption and thus of destruction. The attempt to "bag" the text, to weigh and measure it, to tag it, and to comment upon it in the belief that we can mark out its territory is, at the same time, to transform it, since, to cite Herman Rapaport's summary of Trinh Minh-ha, "the approach of the Other prevents the real from being disclosed as merely something in itself" (98–103, 108). Or, to put it more simply, just as critics came to recognize that there is no such thing as mere history, we also recognize that no real thing can

---

[19] Phaedrus then, following Socrates' lead, goes on to announce that the written word (ὁ γεγραμμένος) is merely the "image" (εἴδωλον) of the "living and breathing" (ζῶντα καὶ ἔμψυχον) word (*Phaedr.* 276A).

[20] Plato has Socrates argue that only speech is the legitimate child (γνήσιος) and writing desires a father, but has no one to help it (*Phaedr.* 275E–267A).

ever be disclosed as merely something in and of itself. Metacommentary becomes, therefore, a prerequisite activity since "all thinking about interpretation must sink itself in the strangeness, the unnaturalness of the hermeneutic situation; or to put it another way, every individual interpretation must include an interpretation of its own existence, must show its credentials and justify itself: every commentary must be at the same time a metacommentary as well" (Jameson 1988, 5). But, is this even possible? Culler suggests, yes: "[E]ven if in principle we cannot get outside our conceptual frameworks to criticize and evaluate, the practice of self-reflexivity, the attempt to theorize one's practice, works to produce change, as the recent history of literary criticism amply shows" (Culler 1982, 154). Self-reflexivity, a form of suspicion about the self, another kind of *Hinterfrage*, is required if we are to progress. For now, we investigate some acts of "patricide."

"The writing of a commentary is a conspicuous (and sometimes dazzling) act of ministry to the church of Christ. But it is done inconspicuously"—so goes Eugene Peterson's description of commentary in his introduction to an invitational symposium on the writing of commentaries (1990, 386). And yet before the symposium even begins, it is already troubled by a description of commentary writing as both "conspicuous" (not hidden) and "inconspicuous" (hidden). Precisely what does Peterson mean by this? Well, commentary writing, which has now become institutional interpretation, is conspicuous in that commentaries have a visible life within the church. What is inconspicuous about commentaries is that "no one watches the commentator at work" (386). Peterson's concern here about the commentator's hiddenness is whether people get to know the "real" commentator or not, when the question should be whether the people get to know the "real" text.

These essays on commentary reveal little self-reflexivity and a good deal of totalization. Pheme Perkins displays a desire for commentary as "translation": "[L]ike translating, writing a commentary demands that one decide the meaning of every word and phrase" (395). The commentary provides "a framework for our field of vision. . . . Those who write commentaries do so because . . . we would like to enable other people to share our view" (398). F. Dale Bruner bypasses Perkins's slightly self-reflexive, though still paternal, phrase "our view" and goes straight to saying that commenting is "saying something about what *God* has said— responding ('what does God *mean* by this?!')" (399). Bruner recants a little later pointing out that "there is simply no such thing as coming to a text objectively" (400). But wherein lies the answer to the problem of interpretative subjectivity? It is not within increased independence, but within the increased dependence upon the "*communio sanctorum*" (400); that is, upon a text-forming community whose own communal patricide is held up as the real text simply because it is born of the community. Bruner quickly divests himself of his communal policing, though, and returns later in the essay to "the sheer delight . . . [of] rummaging in the thoughts and words of God" (401).

> Suddenly . . . a new idea occurs to him one day, *his* idea; and the entire blessedness of a great personal hypothesis, which embraces all existence and the whole world penetrates with such force into his conscience that he dare not think himself the creator of such blessedness, and he there-fore attributes to his God the cause of this new idea and likewise the cause of the cause, believing it to be the revelation of his God. How could a man be the author of so great a happiness? ask his pessimistic doubts. But other levers are secretly at work: an opinion may be strengthened by one's self if it be considered as a revelation; and in this way all its hypo-thetic nature is removed; the matter is set beyond criticism and even beyond doubt: it is sanctified. (Nietzsche 1911, §62)

Such a patricide is unworthy of us, the author-god is dead and we have killed him, and "who will wipe this blood off us?" cries Nietzsche (1910, §125). The response: "we will." But how? We must ourselves be-come gods simply to be worthy of such a crime (1910, §125)! That is, we must be able to engage in acts of (re)creation, and this is precisely what the commentary does and is.

2.c. *Two Exemplary Reasons for* Hinterfragen

Some acts of patricide are more subtle yet more aggressive than others. In his review of Dunn's *Theology*, Matlock obliquely observed that Romans is obviously not the only choice we must make in constructing a theology of Paul and that "a different choice would in turn bring different matters into prominence" (68). This is a simple comment to be sure, but the sim-ple fact of its legitimate possibility undermines the stability of Dunn's product and certainly calls into question the definite article employed in Dunn's title: "The *Theology of Paul the Apostle.*" This is especially true when Dunn himself alludes to the possibility of progression in Paul's thought (25), which naturally causes him to resist a synoptic approach to structur-ing Paul's theology which would produce a "mishmash—not the theology of Paul as he would have owned it at any particular time" (25). Romans is then said to be precisely this observable occasion in which Paul reveals his own theology, being "the most sustained and reflective state-ment of Paul's own theology by Paul himself. . . ." Hence the leading question, "[H]ow to write a theology of Paul, then? Paul's letter . . . to Rome is the nearest thing we have to Paul's own answer to that ques-tion. . . . Romans provides us with an example of the way Paul himself chose to order the sequence of themes in his theology" (25). Romans is the "mature theology of Paul" and we cannot do better than to use Romans as a "kind of template on which to construct our own statement of Paul's theology" (26).

The fact remains, however, that Romans remains as structured by its *oc-casional* reality as every other letter written by Paul. Yet Dunn contends that

Romans is special, having been written at the end of a major phase of Paul's missionary work, and probably under the "most congenial circumstances of his mission, with time for careful reflection and composition" (25). Certainly we can agree that Paul is probably already thinking of what he plans to do after he delivers the Gentile gift to Jerusalem, and even agree that perhaps a lot of the surface-level tensions are in fact removed during the writing of the letter. Yet Dunn himself acknowledges that Romans is a "defense" of Paul's understanding of the gospel (25). Consequently, the presence of this "defense" on the textual landscape of Romans should necessarily alert readers of Romans to the presence of a subsurface rhetorical agenda within Romans. The implication from Dunn is that the structuring forces of the rhetorical situation upon the form and function of the text are not really a factor in its reading, or at least not as much of a factor in Romans as elsewhere. I would venture to say at this point that it is precisely when the occasion of a letter, or its rhetorical situation, seems to be less intrusive that it is most capable of intrusion because it is less obviously so.

My point here is similar to the one made by Jane Schaberg in her commentary on Luke. It is precisely when things seem to be most congenial that they have the potential to be the most dangerous (275). Schaberg's name for this process is "seduction." The fact is, ideological or "interested" texts such as those found in the Bible, philosophy, and history are always doing something and they are never innocuous. The prudent hermeneutical posture to assume is thus one of suspicion, not a jaded expectation, rather a posture in which we suspect that in fact something else may be going on than what is immediately apparent. While it is not necessary to employ a hermeneutic defined by and cohering around "suspicion," I suggest that suspicion is a necessary part of the hermeneutical process.

For Ricoeur, suspicion is "the critical instrument of de-mystification," by which he means that it is the process through which one analyzes the product of socially discursive, illusory forces manifested within the individual but certainly originating prior to and thus enabling the thought of the individual. Ricoeur refers to this as "false consciousness," a term mainly derived from Marx, but, as he notes, easily applies to Freud and Nietzsche (205–6). The "hermeneutics of suspicion" is simply a way of reading so as to elicit certain forms of knowledge which were hitherto concealed. It is not meant to be a comprehensive hermeneutic, nor is it an attempt at totalization given that the nature of the form of knowledge uncovered is not necessarily "essential." Its function is rather a *part* of something which would *resemble* something like Schleiermacher's vision of a hermeneutical circle: "[K]nowledge always involves an apparent circle, that each part be understood only out of the whole to which it belongs, and vice-versa" (113).[21]

---

[21] The word "complete" is deliberately omitted from the beginning of this quote. This concept, however, is better stated by Heidegger (1962, 153) in whom

When Matlock presents Dunn with the observation that there is a lack of suspicion in his work on Paul (68–70), Dunn responds by asking if Matlock is suspicious enough of suspicion (1998b, 113). Dunn's perception of "suspicion" is therefore shown to be something more like linear, Cartesian doubt, rather than the genealogical, ideological, and illusional question of origins suggested by the Nietzschean, Marxist, and Freudian sense of suspicion catalyzed in Ricoeur's hermeneutics of suspicion (205–12). Dunn then goes on to state that he prefers the "old term 'criticism' which involves the attempt to take into consideration all that has gone into the making of the text . . . without excluding a *due degree* of *suspicion*" (1998b, 113–14, emphasis added). Who could ask for more? Well, the fact is that phrases like "due degree" in this statement belie an uncritical, worthy-of-suspicion "will to power" or totalizing force on Dunn's part that articulates rather nicely the conditions upon which much of traditional or "institutional" biblical studies is founded. This is indeed a delightful display of Nietzsche's idea of "micrological power," elucidated by asking the simple question, what is the actual content of the phrase "due degree"? Who decides where the boundaries for "due degree" are? At what point is the degree not enough and at what point is the degree too much? The answer is of course, Dunn decides, or rather the subtle, micrological forces which Dunn has failed to observe as founding the conditions upon which he constructs his own knowledge decide for him.

The way in which this will to power works itself out in an attempt to master "deviant" forms of inquiry is conveniently demonstrated for us in Dunn's response to Matlock, in which he points to Matlock's omission of specifying "the meaning or perspective or method implied [by suspicion]" (1998b, 113) and then proceeds to use the *very same word* in his critique of Matlock prefaced, however, by this empty and thus dangerous phrase "due degree." "Due degree" in Dunn's response becomes the locale from which ubiquitous, and thus "institutional," relations of power can operate in such a way so as to maintain proper surveillance over interpretive practices and thus also separate one set of interpretations from another. The most important feature of Dunn's power play is the fact that, to cite Dunn's own complaint, "the meaning or perspective or method is never spelled out" (1998b, 113).

What Dunn does here is not even slightly unusual; it is, in fact, quite the norm. Francis Watson, in his programmatic paper "The Scope of Hermeneutics," says that he is articulating a "view of hermeneutics as theoretical reflection on interpretive practice" (1997, 78). He qualifies this by suggesting that "contemporary theological hermeneutics must take as its main subject matter the distortions arising out of inappropriately drawn

---

we can already see the beginnings of hermeneutical suspicion, and then later worked out in Gadamer (1975, 235).

disciplinary boundaries, thereby mediating between the separated disciplines of biblical interpretation and Christian theology" (79). In his argument, he places a great deal of weight upon the final form of the biblical ("canonical") text, since "one of the tasks of theological hermeneutics is . . . to establish the reality of the canonical form of the texts, and to defend its integrity against interpretative practices that undermine it. Two such practices may be described as *archaeology* and *supplementation*" (76). Watson's citation of the word "archaeology" resonates with Foucault's, but of course as one follows Watson down through his excavation of the word, one finds that Watson has left Foucault at the surface.

Watson uses the Foucauldian term "archaeology" as a reference to getting back to "origins" (76). However, when Watson then says that the problem with this process is that it creates a situation in which the text is "no longer fit for its customary uses" (76) he fails to see that this is precisely the point of such a process and that "customary use" is exactly what is being called into question. That is, the whole idea of "customary use" is the potentially hegemonic concept that needs to be called into question; it is also a concept that attempts to represent a sense of stability and thus a sense of stable origins, and we want to know what the nature of that origin is *before* we talk about "customary use." As with Dunn's "due degree," we find that "customary use" is an empty and dangerous phrase which reserves for itself the determining principle of what is and what is not "customary."[22] Who decides what is customary? Watson does.

Watson uses another word in conjunction with "archaeology" that also resonates with French philosophy, namely the "supplement"—a word employed in Rousseau but that subsequently became the focus of Derrida's reading of Rousseau and conscripted for his own project. Watson has in view a slightly different version of his "archaeology" here, in that "supplement" refers to the *incorporation* of the socio-linguistic milieu of the biblical text into what we would presume to be the "customary" performance/use of the biblical text. In Watson's attempt to supplement the scope of hermeneutics he uses "supplement" in precisely the same way Rousseau used it and thus practically begs us to apply Derrida's subsequent deconstruction of Rousseau's *supplément*. Derrida's argument ends up demonstrating that by virtue of Rousseau's attempt to resign writing to be a "supplement" of speech he demonstrates the incompleteness of speech—the presence of a lack in speech, which of course for Derrida becomes the lack of presence—and that what was at one point only "supplementary" (in Rousseau's case "writing") shows itself to have always been essential to it. Thus by virtue of

---

[22] If indeed we did excavate Watson's phrase here we would find that "customary use" is *always* a use of the very origins that Watson prefers to suppress under the glossy, canonical final form.

the supplement, Derrida is able to implicate writing in the construction of speech.[23]

Nonetheless, "supplement" is innocent in Watson's view, because to "abstract the biblical texts entirely from their original environment would be to treat them docetically, as originating directly from above without the mediation of historically and culturally located human agency" (1997, 77). It becomes that *dangerous supplement*, however, when it "undermines the integrity of the biblical texts in their canonical form" (77). How is this so? Well, "the integrity of the text may be threatened by the *quantity* of the information with which it is supplemented" (77, emphasis added). Watson began with the assumption that the biblical text naturally needs to be culturally contextualized in some way, and anyone interested in what the actual writers were saying would want to strongly affirm that. When Watson subsequently looked into the biblical text and saw the world behind it, he was not prepared for what he saw: a vast, endless sea of context and thus also endless disruption to "customary use."[24]

The problem with context is that as different signifying, and thus iterable, units are perceived with respect to what may be called a focalizing event—the event which brings into existence a context around itself, as every perceivable event does—they appear to be in a given and immediate context of interpretation. However, the possibility of distinguishing between the event and its context, and of distinguishing between relevant and irrelevant contextual units, also enables new contextual units to be joined to them or to replace them in the break between event and interpretation. The result is that interpretation changes with new information. Again, the possibility of change nonetheless prevents closure from ever taking place, and this possibility is also continuous because context itself is continuous. Derrida makes a contextually relevant comment here; "no meaning can be determined out of context, but no context permits saturation" (1979, 81; similarly 1986, 18). That is, meaning requires a point of reference, but there can never be a final decision regarding what that point of reference might be, since "meaning is context-bound, but context is boundless" (Culler 1982, 123). Each time one demarcates the so-called relevant context, another context immediately appears along the borders of the demarcation. This new context was there all the time, but it becomes known through a process of differentiation brought into play by the line of demarcation. Thus, the context of any event is always beyond every description of it; thus, Watson's hope for a comfortable, delimited,

---

[23] Derrida's discussion of Rousseau's supplement may be found in Derrida 1976 (141–64).

[24] Hence Watson's earlier call for a defensive hermeneutic: the biblical text needs something "to defend its integrity against interpretative practices that undermine it" (1997, 76).

easy-to-handle context that sustains "customary use" is a hope relying on the success of rhetoric and not upon the nature of context at all.

Like Dunn's "due degree," we have in Watson's argument another dangerously empty structure, "quantity": "[T]he integrity of the text may be threatened by the *quantity* of the information with which it is supplemented" (77, emphasis added). The implication is that if you add *too much* you are a poor hermeneut, but if you add the *right amount*, you are a good one. Whence comes this knowledge of good and evil? The fact is that the empty structure is inhabited by Watson, who becomes the one who distinguishes between good and bad hermeneutics.

There is indeed a need for suspicion when it comes to thinking about Paul, namely because Paul's own significance has produced so much writing that it has become difficult to distinguish between the writing and Paul. Again, we do not need a suspicion for the sake of suspicion,[25] rather one that simply respects the fact that agendas develop, that history is ideologically "interested" and is never "pure." The tradition of writing about Paul's writing is a tradition that bears the interests of the writing parties.

2.d. *The Activity of Writing and "Interpreting" Paul*

It has long been observed that understanding Romans as a complete outlaying of Paul's theology is untenable (Kümmel 1975, 312), primarily because it does not actually include all of Paul's theology. The problem lies in the subtle shift from observing Romans as the outworking of Paul's thoughts on the gospel to using Romans as the occasion to observe what Paul is trying to *do*. There has been a fundamental hermeneutical failure to recognize the difference between function and information in the writings of Paul. The problem that this introduces to Pauline studies has been observed before (albeit in other terms); note Furnish's comment: "It is important to observe that the vast majority of works devoted to Pauline thought have sought to find its center in some particular *theological doctrine*. One must ask whether the diversity of proposals concerning that doctrinal center is not due at least as much to the character of Paul's thought and preaching as to the theological perspectives of Paul's interpreters" (1989, 335). What Furnish observes is a preoccupation with arriving at theology, or "information," and not with what Paul might actually be trying to achieve through his rhetoric. Note also Beker: "[W]e universalize . . . [the Pauline letters] and abstract them away from their immediacy into a set of propositions or doctrinal centers" (35).

In the attempt to renegotiate some of the impasses we have encountered in the study of Paul, it is becoming more common for scholars to

---

[25] Reading for the sake of suspicion alone is not to be considered as an invalid approach to the text, namely because the nature of language and communication affirms a multiplicity of readings. The fact is, however, that this is just one reading of many and holds currency only for like-interested parties.

focus on Paul's "theology" as the *result* of his apostolic activity and not as the starting point ("theologizing" rather than "theology"). For example, Roetzel attempts to understand Paul's thought not by trying "to plot a progressively rising trajectory in Paul's theology so much as . . . to get some idea of the way Paul's thinking emerged through conversations with his readers. Regarded in this way his theologizing is an interactive process, dynamic and flexible" (1999, 93). Thus also, P. Meyer suggests that "instead of assuming most of the time that Paul's 'theology' or 'convictions' are the *resource* or starting point *from* which he addresses the issues placed before him, may one rather, as a kind of 'experiment in thought,' think of them more consistently as the end-product and result, the *outcome* to which he arrives in the process of his argument, his 'hermeneutic,' or his 'theologizing'" (1995, 697).

Engberg-Pedersen takes it to the next step (whether consciously or not). That is, he argues for this very thing, namely Paul's theologizing as "dynamic and open-ended," a "symbolic universe *in the making*, not a fully worked out, static, and final one" (1993, 106). Thus he comes close to a functional approach to Paul when he argues that "whatever system we shall be able to discover in his letters will lie not in a fully worked out set of ideas but rather in Paul's *handling* of his theological conceptions in the different situations he is addressing" (1993, 106). It is the reference to "handling"[26] that is of interest here. The goal of Engberg-Pedersen's argument is to put forward a case for a more dynamic and less static view of Paul's theology. However, in so doing, he (along with the others attempting to do the same thing) necessarily shifts the emphasis from product to process. That is, he moves from a focus on the traditional search for pure information to a focus on how that information is produced.

The contention in this project is that once the focus has been removed from an already-established Platonic structure (e.g., Engberg-Pedersen 1993, 107), and fixed back onto Paul's dynamic activity as a letter writer, we are then free to advance in our understanding of Paul's thought. The particular argument here is that we must continue along the lines established by those who see Paul as a "theologizer" rather than a theologian, but not stop with that observation. That is, when Paul's "activity" comes to the fore of our analyses, our attention is naturally drawn to what he sought to achieve by virtue of that activity; furthermore, only by incorporating the goals of Paul's "theologizing" may we understand more fully the content of that "theologizing." In other words, if we are to be concerned about theology, then let us be concerned with a theology that arises out of the functional effects of a text rather than amputating the rhetoric at the level of the text.

It is the preoccupation with "theological doctrine" that has clouded the fact that Paul was a man in history trying to achieve a very specific set

---

[26] On which Engberg-Pedersen himself places emphasis.

of goals and that his writings were written as a *means* of reaching those goals. It is the gradual realization that we cannot sustain such a preoccupation that causes Engberg-Pedersen to sigh with relief that "scholars have gradually come to realize that in addition to the manifest meaning of Paul's statement as *importing information* and responding to the particularities of the letter situation at the level of direct communication, these statements have a number of functions that are more indirect, but no less important for that" (1994b, 258, emphasis added). He further suggests that "functional aspects of Paul's statements are also part of the meaning of these statements simply because Paul is engaged in a specific communicative act between particular people" (1994b, 259). I would suggest that it is only *after* we discern the *function* of Paul's texts can we even begin to consider issues of significance or "theology."[27] I would in fact suggest that a teleological (though not necessarily eschatological) approach to Paul's writing gives us the coherence we need to create an integrated approach to Paul's writing in general. I would further suggest that while Romans and the rest of the *Hauptbriefe* have been useful sources for thinking about Paul's thought, their academic treatment has in fact distracted us from the fundamentally important issue of what Paul himself was trying to do. Finally, it should be noted that a glaring problem in contemporary hermeneutics is the lack of appreciation for what the writers of antiquity were thinking when they themselves put texts together. It appears that ancient writers may have been more attuned to what their texts were intended to *do* as opposed to what they were intended to *mean*.

3. Writing Performance as Logocentric Citation: Cite-Seeing with Derrida and Austin

Language is given its value by virtue of its operation as the means by which we encounter and articulate "reality." Language resides "above" us as a system prior to and thus structuring our experiences and "below" us as a system reinforced by our collective use of it. As a collective, we use language to describe and prescribe our social realities and thus to make language a social construct; its most important function is to enable us to achieve our social goals. That is, the social nature of language is a *performative* one. Thus Berger and Luckmann note that language is basically referenced by our "pragmatic motive." "Language originates in and has its primary reference to everyday life; it refers above all to the reality I experience in wide-awake consciousness, which is dominated by the pragmatic motive (that is, the cluster of meanings directly pertaining to

---

[27] Since I affirm that content and function are in a reciprocal relationship, I therefore agree with Engberg-Pedersen when he states that "the meaning of a Pauline letter should be construed as a sort of conglomerate resulting from the interaction in it of *all* the different types of 'saying and doing' that are active in Paul's statements" (1994b, 259).

present or future actions) and which I share with others in a taken-for-granted manner" (Berger and Luckmann 1967, 38).

A highly operative factor in the ancient perception of what a letter was doing was a sense of how the letter was appropriate for the particular set of social realities present to the letter's writer and reader. Critically attending to the function of a letter is necessarily attending to the rhetorical situation which gives occasion for the letter in the first place. The implications for this are similar to those found in the speech-act theory of J. L. Austin.[28] The primary feature applicable here is the observation that the direction of critical interest is reversed. Typically, intentionality is accounted for by assuming that "the meaning of a text be grounded on what is *in the text*" (Patte 1988, 90). That is, the final point of critical analysis is the text. Speech-act theory, however, sees the final point of critical analysis as the social realities impacted *by the text*; "thus studying a text as a speech act involves taking into account *something which is not in the text*, and yet is a part of the communication of meaning by that text" (Patte 1988, 90).

It is important to clarify that what is not in view, for Austin, is simply any impact occasioned by the text. He rather has a sense of a performance realized by the text through the previously existing structures (social norms and institutions) which are understood and utilized by the speaker. The point is that it is not the text *alone* or the thing/person being impacted *alone*, rather, that these are a part of the performance of a larger communicative structure. Thus, Austin has not marginalized the material text, he has simply erased the traditional boundary around it in order to consciously incorporate those features of which it is necessarily a part.

Speech-act theory is a helpful voice to include in the chorus of biblical criticism. It is perhaps prudent at this point to lay out Austin's basic thoughts on the matter, and then to introduce Derrida's reading of Austin. Yet before that, let us restate the problem of the thesis in terms appropriate to Austin: Why is it that Paul seems to think that an utterance spoken in a "non-serious" mode (pretext) has the same value as one spoken in a "serious" mode (truth)? This is a problem because the philosophical opposition between the serious and non-serious use of linguistic acts, as articulated by Austin, seems so fundamental to a theory of meaning, primarily because the notion of authorial intention, the possibility of a text meaning only what the author intended it to mean, is put in question. Yet, as we closely follow the textual contours of Philippians, we find that the traditional concept of the relationship between an author's intention and the text is indeed undermined.

---

[28] Wittgenstein had already observed that language had a performative quality (I: 491, 493, 498; II: ix–x).

3.a. *Reversal and Displacement in Derrida and Austin*

As I shall argue later, both Paul and Derrida rewrite the difference between serious and non-serious utterances. But how far does this relationship go? In one simple move, Paul does away with the hierarchical structure altogether, whereas Derrida makes a few more preliminary and duly cautious moves. Derrida initiates, or intervenes with, a reversal and displacement of the two opposites. The hierarchy of the oppositional structure non-serious/serious is reversed so that it becomes serious/non-serious, showing the serious to be a special case of, or derived from, the non-serious. The hierarchy is then displaced to become (non)serious. For his part, Paul presents the two modes of speech in Philippians as in opposition, but also pragmatically suspended from canceling each other out, displacing them in the Derridean sense.

This displacement is one side of a two-sided, yet single, deconstructive move: reversal or "re-placing" and displacement. Reversal is the overturning or inverting of hierarchical oppositions (speech/writing to writing/speech), and is an "indispensable phase" of deconstruction (Derrida 1981a, 6). Derrida finds justification for this action in terms of the "violent" nature of hierarchies. That is, since one side of the philosophical binary opposition suppresses, marginalizes, governs the other, Derrida sees no reason not to re-introduce (by reversal or replacing) the suppressed element back into the discourse allowing, momentarily, the governed to govern (1981b, 41). Reversal on its own, however, is rather pointless since it leaves the problem of violent hierarchies in place; thus, *dis*placement of the hierarchy is also a necessary part of this single but structured/stratified process. Displacement prevents the hierarchy from operating, it "intervenes," "disorganizes," "neutralizes" the hierarchy. It suspends the two elements, intervening in the production of yet another violent hierarchy (1981b, 41–42). Thus, the process of deconstruction is one whereby binary opposites are rewritten through a process which Derrida terms "bifurcated writing" (1981b, 42), so as to allow both to operate in the text, albeit in mutually excluding acts as each opposite continuously effaces and is effaced by the presence of the other. Deconstruction must therefore, through this bifurcated writing or

> double gesture . . . double science . . . practice an *overturning* of the classical opposition *and* a general *displacement* of the system. It is only on this condition that deconstruction will provide itself with the means with which to *intervene* in the field of oppositions that it criticizes, which is also a field of non-discursive forces. . . . Deconstruction does not consist in passing from one concept to another, but in overturning and displacing a conceptual order, as well as the non-conceptual order with which the conceptual order is articulated. (1986, 329)

It is also important to note here that Derrida's desire for deconstruction is not born of malice. Derrida understands his use of Heidegger's *Abbau* and

Destruktion as not referring to a destruction, and characterizes his relationship to the texts he deconstructs as "loving jealousy and not at all . . .
nihilistic fury" (1985, 86–87). In fact, Derrida actually sees deconstruction
as a positive and "not a negative operation" (1988, 3).

3.b. *Austin's Deconstruction of Constative/Performative*

To inscribe Derrida's point, we must note Austin's own deconstructive behavior which Derrida mimics in a classic display of deconstruction. In his
well-known book *How to Do Things with Words*—an outworking of the
William James Lectures—Austin attempts to account for the meaning of
utterances when he discusses his distinctions among locution (actual utterance), illocutionary force (the performance of the utterance), and
perlocution (the consequences of illocutionary force) (1976, 98–108).[29] As
Culler points out, Austin makes similar moves to those of Saussure. In the
same way that Saussure sought to account for acts of signification, his *parole*, by describing the system which makes *parole* possible, his *langue*
(7–17), Austin poses a system of speech acts to account for illocutionary
force (Culler 1982, 111). But Austin's arguments are also in the vein of the
later Wittgenstein. Both Austin and Wittgenstein sought to untie the
knots that logical positivism had tangled, not only around meaning and
language but also around the very investigation of meaning and language. Indeed, Austin is specifically contrasting his work with the logical
positivists when he suggests that "it was for too long the assumption of
philosophers that the business of a 'statement' can only be to 'describe'
some state of affairs, or to 'state some fact,' which it must do either truly
or falsely" (1). Such a program did not provide much, if any, space for the
philosophical or critical discussions of aesthetics, religion, and ethics,
which were thought to contain an "emotive meaning as opposed [to] cognitive or scientific meaning, and were held therefore as unamenable to a
(further) philosophical assessment" (Cavell 1995, 50). Austin disagreed
with the idea that if an utterance did not come under the category of
"statement"—that which can be verified either truly or falsely—then it
was somehow less rational.

After pointing to the dogmatic practice of Western philosophers to exclude anything that was not classed as "statement," Austin set about
developing an argument for a distinction between what he termed the
"constative" and the "performative," and then later for a deconstruction
of the distinction.[30] However, during the course of the lectures, or, in our
case, the re-citation of the lectures in book form, Austin repeatedly comes

---

[29] Austin also presents a discussion on the distinction between meaning and
force, since there is already a question about the relationship of meaning and
force set up in this description of his goals.

[30] For the distinction see Austin 1976, 1–4; but 135–47 for the blurring of the
distinction.

up against the problem—of which he was not unaware (91, 146–47, 152; Bearn 1995, 4–5)—of not being able to draw effectively a line of distinction between performatives and constatives. The trouble lay in the fact that the distinctions kept disappearing, since either one of the oppositions could/would masquerade as the other (Bearn 1995, 4–5).[31] Thus Bearn comments, somewhat nihilistically, that Austin "determined to strip the masks from the masqueraders . . . found behind each mask another one," as "the distinction between constatives and performatives vanished twice, finally disappearing into a hall of illocutionary mirrors" (Bearn 1995, 23, 5).[32] Yet Derrida sees within these points of impasse the promise of Austin's work, characterizing it as an "analysis that is patient, open, aporetic, in constant transformation, *often more fruitful in the recognition of its impasses than in its positions*" (1986, 322, emphasis added).

Performatives are utterances which cannot be described as simply true or false; rather, there is only a performance—a particularly interesting perspective in light of Derrida's own desire to suspend the hierarchical forces operating within binary oppositions. In this case, the opposing structure true/false is suspended from causing new hierarchical striations to arise within utterances.[33] An example of a performative performing is the minister officiating at a marriage ceremony saying, "I name you husband and wife." The minister's words are an official act and are a part of the action of marrying. Such an utterance conforms to Austin's two conditions for performatives: "A. they do not 'describe' or 'report' or constate anything at all, are not 'true or false'; and B. the uttering of the

---

[31] Bearn does not include the possibility that Austin came to see that a blurring of the distinction, a deconstruction of the two opposing categories, was in fact an appropriate conclusion to the project.

[32] Bearn's article is concerned with analytically defending the basic premise of Derrida's "Signature, Event, Context." The article suggests that Bearn relies on a success/failure oppositional structure remaining intact in the argument of "Signature, Event, Context," whereas it seems to me that such a structure is precisely the sort of structure upon which Derrida is not relying and indeed is interested in deconstructing in "Signature, Event, Context." Since Bearn's entire article presumes this structure, it ends up being a logocentric overlay which exposes the contours of the surface argument of "Signature, Event, Context" but which glosses over the cracks in which Derrida's argument really takes place.

[33] For a discussion on the relationship of performative statements to the true/false structure, see Austin 1976, 9–11. He uses a quote from Euripides' *Hippolytus*, ἡ γλῶσσ᾽ ὁ μώμοχ᾽, ἡ δε φρὴν ἀνώμοτός, which he translates "my tongue swore to, but my heart (or mind or other backstage artiste) did not," to imply a metaphysical disjunction "between saying and intending" (Cavell 1995, 62). Interestingly, Cavell, in an essay generally suspicious of Derrida's "Signature, Event, Context," points to the fact that this "classic expression," as Austin calls it, is also cited in both Plato's *Symposium* and *Theatetus*, as well as in Aristophanes' *The Frogs*, thereby highlighting the operation of citationality or iterability. For Derrida on the suspension of hierarchical forces, see Staten 1984, 114.

sentence is, or is a part of, the doing of an action, which again would not *normally* be described as, or as 'just,' saying something" (1976, 5). That is, performatives do things; they are in themselves actions and not reports of actions or of a given state of affairs. According to the philosophers against whom Austin wrote, such utterances did not have the same rational value as "constative" statements, which report on actions or a given state of affairs.

Austin further suggests that constatives, namely "historical references" (6 n. 2), are merely abbreviated forms of performatives (135–36). That is, a constative is supposedly a statement in which one describes a state of affairs. For example, the statement "my computer is made by Compaq" is a constative statement on the surface, but Austin shows that it is really an abbreviated performative statement *implying* a performative verb, such as "I affirm," or "I tell [you]."

By moving away from the positivistic notion that statements are only valid if they state a fact or describe something, Austin began to dismantle the metaphysical structures ensnaring the Western philosophy of language—inadvertently deconstructing the traditional philosophical hierarchy that privileged constatives over all other kinds of statements ("pseudo-statements"; 2, 3). He demonstrates, on the one hand, that the opposite is actually the case ("reversal"), insofar as these constatives are dependent upon or derived from the category of pseudo-statements, or his "performatives." On the other hand, he prevents a new hierarchy from developing ("displacement"), by preventing the true/false opposition from participating in the illocutionary force of performatives by showing that constatives are a special case of performatives. Thus, Wolfgang Iser was later led to call for a general doing-away with these structures and to "replace ontological arguments with functional arguments, for what is important to readers and critics alike, is what literature *does*, and not what it *means*" (1978, 53). Iser maintains an oppositional dichotomy between meaning and function here, which may not be altogether confluent with his own desire for a functional approach, but the point is that Austin opened up a crack in the wall that many have tried clambering through in order to escape the oppression of the metaphysical in language and the question of meaning.

3.c. *Derrida's Deconstruction of Austin: Serious/Non-Serious*

But Austin, like Saussure, in offering a critique of the logocentric moves typically made by Western philosophy, and upon which traditional Western philosophy relies—acts of excluding and privileging elements of binary oppositions which thereby create violent hierarchies—does not himself move beyond logocentrism; rather, he (necessarily) stays within it. Every critique of logocentrism will, at the same time, rely upon it; "even a theory based on difference does not escape logocentrism but finds itself appealing to presence, not only because some concepts of analysis, demonstration, and objectivity involve such reference but also because in order to identify differences responsible for meanings one needs to treat some meanings as if they were given, as if they were somewhere "present" as a point of departure" (Culler 1982, 110). And we find that Derrida affirms this when, in preparing to argue his case against Austin's text, he says that "I must take as *known and granted* that Austin's analyses permanently demand a value of *context*, and even of an exhaustively determinable context" (1986, 322, first emphasis added). That is, in order for Derrida to critique an argument he must acknowledge that there actually is an argument that can serve as the point of reference for a deconstruction of the text. Thus, Derrida does not himself claim to be beyond the problems of logocentrism. He necessarily works within logocentric structures in order to critique them. This has been a common misconception of Derrida. Lionel Abel thinks that because Derrida uses logic to question truth and logic, his deconstructive project is consequently invalidated. But, as Sherwood points out, Abel's criticism is ironic since "by exposing the double logic at work in Derrida's texts . . . [he affirms] with him the universality of deconstruction" (153–54). This is a part of the reason why deconstruction always employs the existing structure of the text to operate, and why Derrida is always having problems with his critics not remaining within the text (1976, 24; 1985, 86–87).

Derrida discusses Austin's *How to Do Things with Words* in "Signature, Event, Context" and, in the second section of the essay, deconstructs the difference between serious and non-serious, the original and the citation. Derrida repeats or mimics Austin's attack on logocentrism. That is, Derrida rigorously pursues the logic of Austin's text in its own terms, which causes his own argument to mimic or cite the turns of Austin's text as he pushes the logic of that text to its limits.[34] "The movements of deconstruction do not destroy texts from the outside. They are not possible and effective, nor can they take accurate aim, except by inhabiting those structures. . . . Operating necessarily from the inside, borrowing all the strategic and economic resources of subversion from the old structure" (1976, 24). Indeed, "deconstruction is . . . an activity of reading which remains closely tied to the texts it interrogates, and which can never set up independently as a self-enclosed system of operative concepts" (Norris 1982, 31). We could summarize Norris by saying that deconstruction is a part of, or participates in, the text and is not a discussion *about* the text. The deconstructive argument is often the same argument operating within the text, and is performed in terms of the text, which is to say that it takes place within the text, but in order, as Culler says, "to breach it" (Culler 1982, 86). Interestingly, in an exchange with Searle, who criticized

---

[34] "Derrida drives Saussure's project to its ultimate conclusions and seeing where those conclusions work to challenge the project's conventional premises" (Norris 1982, 30).

Derrida's reading of Austin, saying that Derrida was not being true to Austin's text, Derrida points out that Searle is not offering a serious critique because he does not work within the terms of the text. In contrast, note that in the course of Derrida's reply to Searle, *Limited Inc*, Derrida eventually cites Searle's argument in its entirety.

Insofar as Derrida does this, it could be said that he produces a text more "true" to Austin's text than Austin's own. He does this by first affirming and stabilizing the argument of the text through a discussion (and praise) of what Austin was attempting to achieve, but then he goes beyond Austin and shows the way in which the logic of this same text undermines that argument. That is, Derrida shows how Austin's text exceeded him, not to poke fun at Austin, but to demonstrate a problem of language, to demonstrate that language escapes our attempts to tether it to our intentions and the presence of our conscious will to communicate. It is the nature of language to have within it opposing forces and aporiae arising from within the opposition of those forces, problematizing a text's assertions, turning those assertions against themselves. And these are what Derrida brings to light in his reading of Austin, again, not to show Austin's failures, but those within philosophical discourse in general, since "the reading must always aim at a certain relationship, unperceived by the writer, between what he commands and what he does not command of the patterns of the language that he uses" (1976, 158). Thus, deconstruction leads to exposing a problem, not with an author's logic, but with the logic of the relationship between what an author does have control over and that which an author does not, that is, a problem within the logic of language itself.[35]

For Derrida, the discourse of Western metaphysics has always relied on a system of exclusion and the establishment of hierarchies; he thus notes: "[T]his is not just one metaphysical gesture among others, it is the metaphysical exigency, that which has been most constant, most profound and most potent" (1998, 93). The history of truth, according to Derrida, has been a history of maintaining the illusion created by this kind of oppositional exclusion and suppression; indeed, he says, it has been "the condition of the very idea of truth" (1976, 20). For example, Derrida argues that

> the privilege of the *phonè* [the practice of exclusion] does not depend upon a choice that could have been avoided. It responds to a moment of *economy* (let us say of the "life" of "history" or of "being as self-relationship"). The system of "hearing (understanding) oneself speak" [*s'entendre parler*] through the phonic system . . . has necessarily dominated the history of the world during an entire epoch, and has even produced the idea of the world, the idea of world-origin, that arises from the differ-

---

[35] See Johnson's comments in the "Translator's Introduction" of Derrida 1981a (xv).

ence between worldly and the non-worldly, the outside and the inside, ideality and nonideality, universal and nonuniversal, transcendental and empirical. (1976, 7–8)

In this comment, Derrida portrays the structure which has been laid over Western perceptions of reality and consciousness, and in so doing indicates a problem inherent to that structure: that the economies of life, history, and perceiving oneself are dependent upon a set of oppositions for which the point of reference can be the phenomenon of *s'entendre parler*, the perceived ability to hear and understand oneself speak with no mediation. Since they are based on oppositions, such as presence/absence, this economy has been one of an illusion in which one element in the oppositional structure has been suppressed. It is an economy of exclusion. Moreover, this has not been an unavoidable structuring of philosophical discourse because these economies were founded—if I may be permitted to allude to an origin of sorts—on privilege and suppression.

Austin's deconstruction of the constative/performative opposition—showing that the previously privileged constatives were a special class of the previously excluded, or marginalized performatives—is an insightful critique of the logocentric structures operating within philosophical discourse by virtue of his reversal and displacement discussed earlier. However, Derrida shows that Austin himself excludes or marginalizes non-serious language and privileges the serious. Derrida then proceeds to demonstrate, in the manner of Austin, that the serious is a special category of, or parasitic upon, the non-serious, thereby displacing the oppositional structure set up by Austin through revealing the mutual contamination of the two opposites. To say that the serious ends up as a special case of the non-serious sounds like the results of one of Zeno's *reductio ad absurdum* paradoxes. But Derrida is not saying that everything is non-serious, or that reality is not real, or even, with respect to Austin, that intentionality does not exist. In fact, Derrida is quite sober about the necessity to accept such things as necessary. It is only when one attempts to base an entire philosophical system on these oppositional structures and upon language conventions that a problem arises (note Norris 1982, 110).

> Above all, I will not conclude from this [the general graphematic structure of every "communication"] that there is no relative specificity of the effects of consciousness, of the effects of speech (in opposition to writing in the traditional sense), that there is no effect of the performative, no effect of ordinary language, no effect of presence and of speech acts. *It is simply that these effects do not exclude what is generally opposed to them term by term*, but on the contrary presuppose it in dyssemtrical fashion, as the general space of their possibility. (Derrida 1986, 327, emphasis added)

Thus, and again, Derrida does not say everything is non-serious, but only that the effects of the serious or the non-serious do not exclude what has been traditionally opposed to them. He is not out to debunk intention or meaning altogether, rather to show what the discourse about them has excluded and suppressed throughout the last twenty centuries of philosophy. Derrida believes there has been a veil laid over philosophical discourse so that we might not look intently at that which was failing, and even today that same veil remains unlifted because it is only removed in the transcendental signified. Or perhaps it is more accurate to say that this very discourse—the traditional philosophical discourse of the West— has simply ignored, in regular, regimented, and regulating fashion, certain phenomena of language and communication, thereby creating an illusion of realism. And this illusion has been put into service as a governing norm by which the oppression of the other—the marginalized, the different, whether in society, philosophy, or in theology—has received validation, and by which the failures of this discourse have been hidden.

3.d. *Derrida's Deconstruction of Austin: Iterability, Citationality, Convention*

At issue in Derrida's essay is the iterable, or repeatable, nature of signs, which naturally brings to the fore two other important issues: intentionality and context. "Intentionality" is discussed because if signs can simply be repeated anywhere, they are structured in such a way so as to deny the possibility of a total presence of intention in the (re)iteration of those signs. The relationship between iterability and intention harks back through the ages to Plato's comment that writing bastardizes speech, which is another way of saying that the moment of the sign is the moment which marks the death of the author. The fact of a sign forces an irreconcilable space between the writer and the written. Thus, the sign never really belongs to the author; it is an escapee of his consciousness via the tyrannical passage of time and irreconcilable spacing. As sure as one moment is eternally divided from the next, the evolution of consciousness from presence to iterable sign eternally divides *signum* from *homo significans*. "Context" is introduced because the iterability of signs naturally opens up the possibility of a boundless context, insofar as a chain of signifiers can be continually repeated, reiterated, cited in new circumstances. It is important to note here that the ability of a sign to be repeated, reiterated, cited in new circumstances is also that which enables it to signify in the first place; thus, iterability is not a mere secondary significance of the nature of signs, as if the citation were somehow less than or even other than the supposed origination. This underlies Derrida's argument in "Signature, Event, Context."

As previously mentioned, Austin argues that he will not consider nonserious utterances because they are "void" and "parasitic upon . . . normal use"; therefore, "performative utterances, felicitous or not, are to be understood as issued in ordinary circumstances" (1976, 21, 22). With this utterance, Austin thus banishes the non-serious to the same philosophical fringe where he found performative utterances wandering before he carried them off to fame and fortune and, supposedly, to live happily ever

after at the center of philosophical discussion. But Derrida finds the difference created between normal and abnormal use, the serious/non-serious
opposition, to be ripe for deconstruction. Specifically, he finds that *the
same structuring forces which afford the possibility of the abnormal or the non-serious are the very same which make possible normal or serious signification*: the
structuring forces of iterability. "A writing that would not be structurally
legible—iterable . . . would not be writing" (1986, 315).[36] If a series of marks
(aural, ocular, tactile) do not have within them the structure of repeatability they cannot signify, or we could say that they cannot constitute a form
of communication.[37] Thus, says Derrida, for writing to be writing or communication to be communication, it "must be able to function in the
radical absence of every empirically determined addressee in general.
And this absence is not a continuous modification of presence; it is a break
in presence, 'death,' or the possibility of the 'death' of the addressee, inscribed in the structure of the mark" (1986, 315–16).[38] The iterability of the
mark—that which enables a mark to function as a sign, to function socially
or intersubjectively—is that structure mentioned earlier which enables
the separation of *signum* from *homo signifiens*.

Another aspect of Austin's work leading to Derrida's deconstruction
of it is that Austin puts a lot of weight on convention (social iterability) in
order for his performatives to work properly. Convention for Austin is
normal or "appropriate circumstances" (1976, 13–14). The notion of convention, however, takes us back to iterability, since convention is
ritualistic or ceremonial, a structure of repetition, recognizable, and performative only because of this repetition. Convention also raises the
question of the difference between original and copy since it finds its possibility as copy or citation. If Austin questions the validity of the
non-serious or cited performative he finds himself in some contradiction
in his approval of convention, which is itself a citation, a non-original.
This possibility caused by the copy is the possibility caused by the iterability of the mark. At the very beginning, what makes an original possible is
this structure of the iterable mark of signification. Thus, within the original is already the copy, that is, the structure of the copy. This then
naturally leads to a blurring of the distinction between original and copy,
a displacement and ultimately a deconstruction of the hierarchical structure that has opposed them to each other.

While maintaining his displacement of a true/false judgement of utterances, Austin employs what he calls "the doctrine of the *Infelicities*" to
account for the "unhappy"—that is, neither true nor false, just "un-

---

[36] Derrida here uses the name, or paleonym, "writing" in the sense of archewriting. On paleonymy see also Derrida 1986, 329; 1981b, 71.

[37] On the structure of experience in general, see Derrida 1986, 318.

[38] Derrida does not mention the "addressee" here to evoke a discussion of the
reader.

happy"—circumstances in which a performative goes wrong (1976, 14). Austin offers six rules that govern the happy functioning of the performative; a violation of any one of the rules will see unhappy performative results (14–15). However, the fact that Austin acknowledges the possibility of the performative's failure is one thing, but, as Derrida argues, Austin does not acknowledge or investigate the *consequences* that the possibility of failure has upon our understanding of language performance and communication in general.[39] If there is a possibility of failure, then failure becomes a necessary part of the structure of the performative, because, as a *possibility*, it is *always* possible; thus, Derrida asks, "What is a success when the possibility of failure continues to constitute its structure?" The success/failure structure of the performative is, therefore, considered to be "insufficient or derivative" (1986, 324).[40] That is, that which enables the success of the performative is also that which causes its failure. There is, therefore, a structuring of language *prior* to the very function that Austin analyzes, yet Austin does not consider it. Moreover, this structuring already distances the presence of intention from any utterance to the effect that Austin's argument—that there be a context of an appropriate sincerity, or seriousness in the frame of the utterer's mind—is displaced (14–16).

All communication relies on iterability, even if only for the very basic fact that an addressee must recognize the identity of the marks, or "arche-marks"—any structure of differentiated and thus iterable marks—in order then to decode them (Derrida 1986, 317–18). The notion of "death" is used by Derrida to communicate a sort of absolute disjunctive effect of the structure which iterability introduces into language. On one level, the marks which constitute, for example, the material aspect of the gospel, the marks of the apostle Paul, continue to have effect by virtue of their iterability even after Paul's death and, most importantly, have always contained within them this possibility as an inherent quality of their structure. On another level, and one that Derrida is most interested in, the marking of the mark marks the death of author or reader because it marks the "essential predicate" to all communication: absence (1986, 314). Derrida posits two hypotheses to account for this essential predicate:

> 1. Since every sign . . . supposes a certain absence . . . it must be because absence in the field of writing is of an original kind if any specificity whatsoever of the written sign is to be acknowledged. 2. If, perchance, the predicate thus assumed to characterize the absence proper to writing were itself found to suit every species of sign and communication, there would follow a general displacement: writing no longer would be a species of communication, and all the concepts to whose generality writ-

---

[39] For Derrida, this is the point at which Austin's project was doomed to fail.

[40] "Derivative" in the sense that it is derived from another, necessarily prior system or structure.

ing was subordinated (the concept itself as meaning, idea, or grasp of meaning and idea, the concept of communication, of sign, etc.) would appear as noncritical, ill-formed concepts, or rather as concepts destined to ensure the authority and force of a certain historic discourse. (1986, 314–15)

Derrida's point here is not to say that writing is not communication, rather that writing could be held up as the genus of communication and not a species, not subordinate (hence "displacement") in some way. And again, not writing per se but writing as a reference to a structure, a structured absence. This writing-as-a-reference-to-structure is often referred to by Derrida as "archewriting." Furthermore, "to write is to produce a mark that will constitute a kind of machine that is in turn productive, that . . . [an author's] future disappearance in principle will not prevent from functioning and from yielding, and yielding itself to, reading and rewriting" (1986, 316).

Derrida's argument against Austin's banishing of the non-serious is based on this prior structuring process of iterability, which intrudes upon all communication with a measure of absence, thereby causing a general displacement of the opposition of what one could consider to be the original/serious/present to the copy/non-serious/absent. I say "displacement" because the metaphysical assumptions which had privileged the former categories over the latter are neutralized by locating within the former group the very structure which was said to cause the latter group to be treated as inferior. This structure of absence is the force that allows the mark to "constitute a kind of machine" which can be set in operation, or turned on, without the presence of the one who assembled it; that enables the mark to produce effects in the general nonpresence of the author,

for example the nonpresence of . . . [the author's] meaning, of . . . [the author's] intention-to-signify, of . . . [the author's] wanting-to-communicate-this, from the emission or production of the mark. For the written to be written, it must continue to "act" and to be legible even if what is called the author of the writing no longer answers for what he has written . . . whether he is provisionally absent, or if he is dead. (1986, 316)

4. Summary

Writing abut Paul's writing (or commentary in general) has been a critically problematic endeavor when the attempt is made to comment upon transcendent meaning. Due to this critical problem, we are in need of some "insidious questions" to evaluate the glossing behavior of traditional commentary (Jameson's "metacommentary"), *and also of ourselves* with acts of self-reflexivity. Romans (and the *Hauptbriefe* in general) has been privileged by contemporary critics in a way that marginalizes what was privileged by the writers of antiquity. The contemporary imbalanced focus on texts as informational or constative, over against functional and performative, gives rise to an imbalanced treatment of the Pauline epistles. What I would like to suggest as something of a correction to the asymmetrical arrangement within the Pauline corpus is that we generate a reading of Paul based on the performative function of the text rather than information contained within it, but not to the exclusion of information. However, in considering language as performative, we also encounter language as iterable. We further find that the issues of performance and iterability are located within our analysis of Phil 1:12–18. Derrida has demonstrated that all language, in order to perform/mean anything, must be iterable; thus, all language must be radically separated from its origins by the spacing inherent within its iterability. We find, then, that the two cited iterations of the gospel in Phil 1:12–18 are implicated in this dilemma through their being described as πρόφασις and ἀλήθεια respectively.

It is necessary for any discussion concerning Paul to be guided by our understanding of the nature of texts in general, and the functional nature of ancient texts in particular. The panoptical privileging of Romans as the Pauline point of reference is plagued with a disproportionate focus on significance over function. In general, I would suggest that we can attain a far greater sense of coherence in Paul's texts, and greater social product, if we think in terms of function and performance over significance. This discussion is usually a "theological" discussion, as the title of the article in the *Dictionary of Paul and His Letters* testifies: "The Center of Paul's *Theology*" (Martin 1993), as opposed to, for example, "the center of Paul's *activity* or *mission* or *work* or *life*" and so forth. The term "theology" in Martin's title is parallel to such terms as "thought," "mind," and so forth, in that they all represent a priority of significance and a certain metaphysical arrangement that suggests some one-to-one, continuous metaphysical correspondence between text and meaning.

While theology and meaning are needed and indeed desired, they necessarily are the products of a process more deferred than that suggested by the sort of theology which places the analysis of Paul in a questionable position by establishing a prior structure to the very process of asking the questions about Paul. That is, before the questions are even asked, they are already problematic. In view of this, Furnish comments that "if the advances made in Pauline studies over the past forty years are to prove worthwhile, they must result eventually in some new models according to which 'Pauline theology; can be analyzed and presented" (1989, 338).[41] Why? Primarily because the old models were "developed largely as topics of 'systematic theology'" (1989, 338). Furnish continues, "[T]he real challenge for interpreters of Paul's thought lies just here: to find ways of respecting the situational and dialogical character of his theology without

---

[41] While the idea of yet another "model" is somewhat problematic, given the plethora of models with which we are presently faced, the need for development is certainly a reality.

abandoning the attempt to understand its most fundamental convictions and its most pervasive concerns" (1989, 338). The possibility for the "new models," which Furnish understands to be necessary, is slightly problematized by the way Furnish issues his challenge. That is, the duality of Furnish's challenge may lead to reinscribing within the structure of the attempt to rise to the challenge the force of the "old model." I say "may" lead because I also see within Furnish's challenge a genuine possibility of a new model.

The challenge is not really about achieving one or the other of the two foci of "situational and dialogical character," and "fundamental convictions and pervasive concerns." The challenge, of course, is to achieve them both at the same time. Again, I would suggest that functional readings of Paul's texts are going to achieve this goal much more efficiently than readings which focus on information. This will be the case since reading for information or significance (the "old model" focus on the ontological qualities of Paul's texts) is unable to reconcile two differing positions of invariant significance found within the one writer. This wreaks havoc with the ontological, or ideal, categories desired by this approach. The tactic is rather to privilege one of the positions (usually on the basis of some historical-critical argument which is affirmed by some and denied by others) and on that basis to dismiss the other as "non-normative"—more commonly phrased as "un-Pauline."

Reading for the functional performance of Paul's letters will attempt to locate within Paul's letters overarching purposes of which those letters are the manifest means through which he attempts to realize those purposes. Such an approach maintains our focus on what Paul was trying to do to his readers, what actions he was trying to perform by writing what he wrote. It reminds us that Paul's texts are of this world and that they represent a person who, like all such people, was seeking to promote his personal ideology, but necessarily within the confines of a particular social discourse.[42] This is not to separate Paul's activity from his beliefs about God; the point is rather that Paul's ontological beliefs are naturally an integral feature of his ideology. It is just that the activity of asking about Paul's beliefs concerning God, his theology, his sense of how the ontological realm is classified is different from asking about what Paul was trying to do in this "logocentric" world. In order to begin that process, we must take stock of the historical and social and philosophical location of Paul, the Philippians, and the letter. We now turn to that task in the following two chapters.

---

[42] By "social discourse" I refer to the complex of norms, expectations, assumptions, values, and so forth which a given society or cultural group shares.

2

The Historical Context of Paul, the Philippians, and the Letter

1. Introduction

In this chapter, I seek to contextualize Paul, the Philippians, and the letter in terms of their historical location. I shall focus on the historical situation of the letter itself and the particular circumstances Paul finds himself in when he writes. In view here are the historical-critical issues of literary integrity, provenance, purposes, character, the nature of Paul's imprisonment, as well as the nature of Paul's opponents, all of which go to assist our appreciation of the rhetorical situation[1] behind the creation of this particular discourse.

2. The Historical Situation of Philippians

The authorial authenticity of Philippians is not under consideration here, since it is no longer a significant issue in contemporary criticism. However, it is worth noting that while the authenticity of Philippians currently enjoys a scholarly consensus, it has not always had the privilege.[2]

---

[1] A "rhetorical situation may be defined as a complex of persons, events, objects, and relations presenting an actual or potential exigence which can be completely or partially removed if discourse, introduced into the situation, can so constrain human decision or action as to bring about the significant modification of the exigence" (Bitzer 1968, 6:13).

[2] F. C. Baur's suspicions are treated fully in Baur 1878–76, 2:45–64 . They are also summarized in an 1849 *Theologische Jahrbücher* essay: "What appears suspicious to me in the Philippian epistle may be reduced to the following three heads:—1. The appearance of Gnostic ideas in the passage, ii, 6–9. 2. The want of

2.a. *Literary Integrity*

Inquiring as to the purpose of Philippians implies a certain singularity and thus tends to assume the epistle's literary integrity. It is not the purpose of this project to account for the epistle's integrity or lack thereof.[3] The issue has had its various advocates for both sides since 1803, when Heinrichs suggested a juncture at 3:1–2 representing an "exoteric" letter (1:1–3:1a; 4:21–23) to the church and an "esoteric" letter (3:1b–4:20) to closer friends (H. A. W. Meyer 1885, 6). There was (and still seems to be) some thought that it really began in the sixteenth century with a comment made by Le Moyne based on an observation concerning Polycarp's epistle to the Philippians, in which Polycarp referred to Paul's own epistolary activity toward the Philippians with the plural ἐπιστολάς (Le Moyne 1685, 343; Koperski 1993, 599). However, it seems that the trend of attributing the division to Le Moyne has been more myth than fact, since it appears that Le Moyne's thinking has been misrepresented (Cook 1981, 138–42). This of course is also in view of the fact that Polycarp's use of the plural suddenly becomes remarkably uninteresting when compared to other Greek writings (Lightfoot 1953, 69 n. 1; Gnilka 1968, 6 n. 23).

The argument derived from Polycarp is based on the idea that when he wrote to the Philippian church, he seems to have referred to a plurality of Pauline letters sent to them (ὃς καὶ ἀπὼν ὑμῖν ἔγραψεν ἐπιστολάς) (3:2). Lightfoot has prepared an impressive disputation against taking Polycarp's ἐπιστολάς to be a reference to more than one letter (138–42). He cites texts from three different periods[4] in which the plural ἐπιστολαί is in the vicinity of the singular ἐπιστολή and both refer to the same letter.[5] The upshot of his argument is that using ἐπιστολή in the plural does not compel one to read it as a reference to more than one letter. The function of the plural, he suggests, is that it is employed to refer to "a missive of importance" when used in the prose of a given letter. That Polycarp may refer to his own letter is, as Lightfoot further points out, not confluent with the humble tone of his letter. Lastly, Lightfoot reminds us that if

---

anything distinctively Pauline. 3. The questionableness of some of the historical data" (cited in Baur 1875–76, 2:45 n. 2).

[3] For more comprehensive discussions on epistolary integrity, see the major commentaries; also see in particular Dalton 1979; Furnish 1964; Garland 1985; Gnilka 1968; Jewett 1970b; Koester 1961–62; Mengel 1982; Pollard 1966; Rahtjen 1959–60; Reed 1997; Russell 1982; Swift 1984; Watson 1988.

[4] Thucydides 8.51; Josephus, *Antiquities* 12.10–11 (227–28); Alciphron, *Ep.* 19 (2.4) 1, 3.

[5] See also the following list of examples in which the plural form (typically ἐπιστολάς) is employed as a reference to a specific letter: Euripides, *Iph. taur.* 589, 767; *Iph. aul.* 111, 314; Thucydides 1.132.5; 4.50.2; Polybius, 5.43.6; Lucian *Am.* 47; Julian, *Ep.* 70; 1 Macc 5:14; 10:3, 7; 11:29; 12:5. Note that ἐπιστολαί in Esth 3:14 is probably a translation of the singular noun כְּתָב (Lightfoot 1953, 141).

there were more than one epistle known to Polycarp and the church at Philippi, it is hard to explain why it may be that this was the last word on their existence; furthermore, it appears that Polycarp's pupil, Irenaeus, is aware of only one epistle.[6] However, the basis of the more recent question regarding the literary integrity really proceeds along the lines suggested by Heinrichs, namely a perception of an apparent rupture in the epistle's unity at Phil 3:1, where the phrase τὸ λοιπόν seems to suggest that Paul is about to close the epistle, but instead of closing, 3:2 begins a new subject.[7]

The tradition of integrity is a strong one and is in fact becoming more commonly held. All extant copies of Philippians and all references to the epistle, so it appears, assume the epistle's integrity. The manuscript tradition has no argument against the epistle's integrity. P[46], the principal manuscript, is dated as early as the second to third centuries.[8] Note also the point made by Aland and Aland that the "transmission of the New Testament textual tradition is characterized by an extremely impressive degree of *tenacity*. Once a reading occurs it will persist with obstinacy" (Aland 1989, 291). The implication is that the fact we have no textual variants suggesting a redacted text is problematic from a transmission perspective (see further Silva 1992, 21–27). While this proves little, it demonstrates a good degree of plausibility that the epistle is a single unit. It is important then to note that Loveday Alexander added further plausibility to the epistle's literary integrity through her demonstration that the problematic word (τὸ) λοιπόν functioned in at least some "family letters" as a simple conjunction rather than a closing formula (1989, 96–97).[9] Λοιπόν also appears in 1 Thess 4:1 and is typically translated the same way ("finally"), yet is nowhere near the end of the epistle. Alexander further cites two other family letters. The first is an early-second-century letter, "Sempronius to Gaius, His Son" (P. Mich., 191, Winter 1927), in which λοιπόν is employed clearly in the body and not the salutation and is translated by Winter as "in the future" (Winter 1927, 245–46). The second is a citation from the "Letter from a Prodigal Son."[10] Here λοιπόν clearly occurs

---

[6] See also more recent arguments against the suggestion in Aland 1979, 349–50. Aland notes the simple point that the very same Polycarp who wrote the plural ἐπιστολάς in 3:2 seems to operate under the assumption of a singular correspondence (ἐπιστολή) in 11.3: "*derselbe Polykarp 11,3 vom Brief an die Philipper im Singular spricht*" (1979, 349).

[7] Lightfoot accounts for this by postulating that just as Paul was about to say again the thing that was no trouble to say again, he was interrupted and reminded of some bad circumstances (1953, 69).

[8] Note the relatively recent attempt to redate P[46] to the late first century by Young Kyu Kim.

[9] My comments here are derived from Alexander's article.

[10] Archive no. 846 in the Berlin Koeniglichen Museen (III.), in Deissmann n.d., 128–29, fig. 26.

in the mid-body of the letter and is translated by Deissmann as *Im übrigen*, "besides," "as to the rest," or "furthermore" as the English translation has it (Deissmann n.d., 177). Of course, the significance of this is that the function of the word has been understood in a way not necessarily confluent with generically parallel literature, and insofar as this is true, has been ill-used as a means for rupturing the epistle's integrity.

In this project, I shall be writing with the understanding that the epistle is probably a literary unit.[11] Even if this assumption is incorrect, it does not affect the objectives of this project in any significant way. The reason for this is simply that none of the suggested separate letters breaks up the first chapter, or Phil 1:12–18a in particular. Those who advocate a redacted epistle typically understand the redaction to have taken place along one of two lines: the two-epistle redaction (Gnilka 1968, 10; Friedrich 1990, 128), and the three-epistle redaction (Collange 1979, 6, 8–15). Our passage falls into perhaps the longest unquestioned fragment, namely Phil 1:1–3:1(a).[12]

2.b. *The Purposes of Philippians*

The "purpose" of Philippians here is a reference to those functions which the epistle attempts to perform. There is a slight difference between the occasion of an epistle and the purpose(s) of an epistle. The occasion of Philippians is probably as simple as Epaphroditus's return to Philippi (Phil 2:25–30). Given this occasion, Paul now has an opportunity to perform some other necessary tasks. Critically speaking, the purpose of Philippians enjoys no scholarly consensus, although the variations are relatively minor ones. Furthermore, it is quite rare for someone to claim that Philippians has a single purpose; most scholars prefer to speak of the purposes (plural) of Philippians. That is, most scholars refer to a number of circumstantial complexes which caused Paul to perceive an exigence requiring an epistle, rather than to one single circumstance. Kümmel, for example, after listing four of the more obvious functions, notes that "the reasons for writing this very personal letter are so numerous that its origin[13] is readily understandable" (Kümmel 1975, 324). Even a recent study of Philippians by G. Peterman that tends toward a single purpose understands that purpose to be in conjunction with another more encompassing purpose.

---

[11] For further discussion, see the following select bibliography: Dibelius 1937; Garland 1985; Lohmeyer 1964; Kümmel 1975; O'Brien 1991; Reed 1997; Watson 1988.

[12] For discussions on the breakdown, see the comprehensive lists compiled by Reed (1997, 127–30).

[13] It seems to make more sense to translate *Entstehung* (rendered here as "origin") as "formation" (see Kümmel, Feine, and Behm 1965, 232).

The major functions generally understood[14] to be the complex of purpose behind Philippians are (1) to respond to their gift, (2) to allay fears of his own welfare, (3) to warn of false teachers ("opponents"), and (4) to exhort them to be steadfast and unified in the face of conflict (e.g., O'Brien 1991, 35–37). The first two of these are generally contextualized in terms of an intimate relationship between Paul and the Philippians.[15] The latter two suggested purposes reflect the general tone of Paul's apostolate that pervades all of his letters.

Given this relatively standard list, it is necessary to supplement the discussion with an overview of an important recent study by Peterman, who suggests that the primary purpose for writing was to contextualize the gift. Furthermore, for the purposes of this book, we must consider two other "purpose" elements within the epistle that clearly speak to the activity Paul is attempting to perform upon the Philippians, namely reassurance, and the creation of Christ-centered *phronēsis*.

2.b.i. The *"gift."* Peterman's hypothesis is that the primary purpose of Philippians is to contextualize the gift (Phil 4:10–20) in an overarching theological structure which helps the Philippians understand the significance of their generosity in terms of Paul's mission. The distinctive nature of the thanks section in 4:10–20 has given occasion for some to see it as a separate ("thank-you") letter entirely.[16] Beare, who is somewhat typical, generates this hypothesis on the basis that "it is inconceivable" (to Beare) that Paul would have waited "some months" to send off his thanks for the gift which Epaphroditus had delivered. Thus he dismisses Scott's suggestion (1959, 9–11, 121) that Paul had sent an earlier letter as well as the one we find in Philippians as "quite untenable." Precisely why this is less tenable than his own position he does not say. While Beare's inability to conceive the delay as normative may reflect a valid problem, it has to be weighed against the overarching problems associated with the redaction hypothesis in general. If the latter proves to be incongruent with the extant evidence, then it really comes down to a matter of our having to alter our expectations of normal behavior in the Greco-Roman world. Whether or not *we* can conceive that a certain ancient act is adequately polite is not

---

[14] Even when the epistle is partitioned, these typically emerge as the major functions of what would be the extant Philippian correspondence. For example, when we translate Collange's three partitions into terms of purpose, the letters produce the same categories as stated above. See Collange 1979, 6, 8–15, and note that the above-stated fourfold purpose is stated virtually everywhere: example discussions are Kümmel 1975, 323; O'Brien 1991, 35–38.

[15] On the intimate character of Philippians, see sec. 2.d. below

[16] See, for example, Beare's commentary, which was *one of* the earliest publications suggesting the partition (1959, 4, 150).

a basis for criticism.[17] Indeed, with reference to Beare's argument, and any other argument about the position and nature of the thanks in 4:10–20, it is only on the basis of such work as Peterman's that we can make claims as to the appropriateness or inappropriateness of Paul's expression of gratitude in Philippians.

Peterman's much-needed work explores the social conventions of gift-giving in the Greco-Roman world. He sees the Philippians' gift as adhering to the structure of Greco-Roman norms of social reciprocity associated with the establishment and maintenance of friendship (see Peterman 1997, 88). Clearly, early Christians adopted established social structures to carry on their basic activities. Thus, when it comes to the gospel, one of Peterman's main points is that the structures of reciprocity are employed to the effect that the Philippians are partners in the gospel with Paul by virtue of their gift-giving. Peterman understands this social convention and its relationship to the gospel to be so deeply connected that he suggests that virtually the entire letter is a prelude to the offering of thanks in 4:10–20: "In a sense, 1:1–4:9 are prolegomena to the response of 4:10–20" (103).

Peterman's argument is appreciated because it combines social realities with certain Pauline ideals, specifically his attention to the spread and development of the gospel. The only criticism to offer is that it seems Peterman gives the balance of the emphasis to the "thanks" section as opposed to the gospel. It seems preferable to say that the epistle is yet another attempt by Paul to promote his gospel; one of the ways he achieves this in Philippians is by recognizing and explaining the Philippians' participation in the gospel. This is necessary since there are other issues that do not fit into Peterman's reconstruction of an epistle that is nine parts prolegomena. Thus while the kind of reading Peterman has produced for Philippians is appreciated, the problem is that social reciprocity alone requires us to diminish the significance of topics within Philippians which have greater moment for Paul and his ministry in general.

2.b.ii. *Reassurance.* It is a position of this book that the activity of reassurance in Philippians is used in two different ways.[18] Thus, a discussion on whether the viability of reassurance is a feature of Philippians in general, and of our text in particular (Phil 1:12–18), is naturally warranted. The idea of reassurance involved in this letter is implicated in the formally rhetorical category of ethos (ἦθος). John Marshall has attempted to explicate Paul's development of ethos in Philippians. He argues that Paul is not

---

[17] Apparently independent of each other, no fewer than four authors suggested the 4:10–20 partition: Beare in 1959, Schmithals in 1957, Müller-Bardorff in 1957/58, and Rahtjen in 1959/60.

[18] See the discussion in ch. 4, sec. 3.

really aware of the actual situation at Philippi, and thus his ability to develop appropriately the logos and pathos aspects of a formal rhetorical unit is hampered. As a result, Paul is forced to rely more heavily on the remaining rhetorical element, ethos, which is developed within the speech unit. Marshall suggests that the primary way in which this is achieved is the usual one: identification with the audience. This is necessarily going to be achieved in, though not confined to, the early stages of the epistle. We find that Phil 1:3–11 does that very thing as Paul expresses his strong personal affection for the Philippians.[19]

Ralph Martin has put the case for reassurance forward in oblique but certain terms. He contends that "Paul's picture of the Christian life is at odds with the sectarian viewpoints, and this explains the undertone of firm resistance to their ideas and practices which runs like a thread through this letter in all its chapters" (1976, 34). What Martin is referring to here is the fact that there were obvious features of Paul's present condition as well as the present condition of the Philippians which contradicted normal assumptions of truth, success, and so forth. Paul's imprisonment, for example, does not immediately present itself as a great success story in the Greco-Roman world—nor, for that matter, does the suffering of the Philippians. Martin believes that these ostensibly negative points are being exploited by Paul's opponents in favor of "a presentation of the believer's life in terms of triumphalism and present glory" (1976, 34). Thus, Martin's suggestion is that Paul is creating a discourse in Philippians designed to "supply a rationale for the Christians in time of persecution" (1976, 34), that subverts the discourse being presented by the opponents, and that reassures the Philippians that all is well with the gospel and its adherents.

More specifically, however, in her research on Hellenistic letter forms, Loveday Alexander has demonstrated that the formal structure of the epistle itself suggests that the central reason for writing is all about reassuring the Philippians concerning Paul's situation (1989, 95). The argument is made on the basis that a "disclosure formula" (γινώσκειν δὲ ὑμᾶς βούλομαι), subcategory of what John White calls "informational formulas," signals the primary reason for writing (Alexander 1989, 92). Disclosure formulas seem to contain four standard features: a verb of desire such as θέλω (here βούλομαι); a verb "to know" in the infinitive (here γινώσκειν); the party addressed (in accusative, here ὑμᾶς); the information to be known (often announced by a ὅτι-clause, as is the case here) (Mullins 1964, 49).

Alexander begins her argument by demonstrating that Philippians subscribes to the formal structure of the Greco-Roman "family letter" (90,

---

[19] That the opening section, the thanksgiving period in particular, reflects Paul's demonstrations of personal affection is everywhere attested in the commentaries; e.g., Fee 1995, 72–74; O'Brien 1991, 53–55.

93–96),[20] or more generally what Koskenniemi terms a *Verbindungsbrief* (Alexander 1989, 93; Koskenniemi 1956, 107)—a letter intended primarily to convey information, usually between family members. What is important for the argument is that family letters seem to focus almost entirely on this exchange of information which, Alexander implies, leads to "strengthening" family ties (see further Alexander 1989, 95). Importantly, within that formal structure, Alexander locates reassurance as a common feature of these letters, pointing to the fact that, within at least two of the family letters discussed (see also White 1986, 102, 104B), the disclosure formula "marks off this section as the information-bearing focus of the letter" (1989, 92). Considering Philippians in these terms, when we add this focus to the more general features of the family letter, we end up with a letter "with the primary purpose of strengthening the 'family' links between the apostle and the Christian congregation in Philippi" (1989, 95). On the basis of the formal structuring of the letter, the "real business" of the letter is therefore said to be the "exchange of news and reassurance" (1989, 95).

> It seems clear that the letter is not written to inform the church that Paul is in prison . . . but to reassure them that the situation is "all right" in three ways: *first* because "what happened to me has really served to advance the Gospel" (1:12–18); *second*, because death, if it should come, is not to be feared (1:19–23); and *third* and slightly contradictorily, because Paul will probably soon be released anyway (1:24–26). (1989, 95)

2.b.iii. *Christ-centered phronēsis.* According to Meeks, "this letter's most comprehensive purpose is the shaping of a Christian *phroēnesis* [*sic*], a practical moral reasoning that is 'conformed to [Christ's] death' in hope of his resurrection" (1991, 333). Meeks has in mind that Philippians presents its readers with "models to think from" (1991, 333); thus, it provides a way for the Christian community to engage issues of internal unity and harmony, and external hostilities (1991, 333–34). Meeks is entirely correct; the only problem, however, may be the fact that Meeks has not carried the role of the proposed *phronēsis* far enough.

Stephen Fowl, in his essay "Christology and Ethics," encounters Alexander's formal analysis of Philippians, and while citing agreement on the need for such formal study, suggests that "too heavy a reliance on this formal analysis" may prevent the appropriate amount of attention being paid to the "moral and theological work Paul's accounts of his own situation and his expressed desires for the Philippians are meant to do" (1998, 141). Fowl then cites Wansink to lend support to his position. Wansink's

---

[20] For a long discussion of Philippians as a "letter of friendship," see the introduction in Fee 1995, 1–24; White 1972, 121–22; Stowers 1991, 107–14; 1986, 60; Kennedy 1984, 422; Mullins 1964, 44–50.

assumptions about formal analyses, however, locate them within a dis-
continuous relationship between the theology of a text and the structure
of a text. For his part, Fowl agrees that "attention to formal analysis may
be quite significant in resolving some interpretive debates regarding
Philippians"; he nonetheless also suggests that "such analyses will [not]
do much to advance discussions about the relationships between the
christology of 2:6–11 and the moral demands Paul makes in the epistle"
(141).

While Fowl and Wansink both warn against the perils of privileging
formal structure, they also set up formal analysis as somehow other than
the theology of a text. It is possible that the idea of separating the formal
structure from theology is a problematic one. In Wansink's account, the
formal analysis of the epistle, while making some contribution, does little
more than provide details about structure; he then describes the results of
formal analyses in the subjunctive mood, but shifts to the indicative when
he suggests that there "*is* much more at stake" than what formal analysis
suggests (1996, 106, emphasis added). However, it is not the design of formal analysis to take the place of further, theologically orientated analysis;
it is rather the case that the formal analysis is necessarily a part of that
study by virtue of providing a critical "starting point."[21] That is, one cannot have a christology of Philippians that is not in dialogue with the
material means by which that christology is formed and presented; thus,
the formal analysis of an epistle is always a part of any theology generated by that epistle.

After (rightly) pointing to the "potential pitfall of too heavy a reliance
on . . . formal analysis," Fowl states:

> Unlike the standard family letter, at least one of the main points of "busi-
> ness" of Philippians is Paul's attempt to get the Philippians to view
> things—such as Paul's imprisonment, God's activity in Christ, and the
> experiences of Timothy and Epaphroditus—in such a way that they
> themselves will be capable of thinking and acting in particular ways.
> (1998, 141)

This is clearly an accurate assessment of the situation. However, it is precisely due to the information provided by the formal analysis of the
epistle—that reassurance is its "real business" (Alexander 1989, 95)—that
we are able understand the nature of how Paul works to elicit the sort of
ethical responses Fowl sees within the text. Fowl himself points out that
by creating a change in the way the Philippians "view things," Paul will
then generate an ethical response. My suggestion is that reassurance is really quite a fundamental feature of the rhetorical ethos required to make

---

[21] See Alexander's survey and discussion in 1989, 88, in which she briefly describes the role formal analyses play in how we understand the general movement of the epistle.

the proposed necessary changes in the way the Philippians "view things." In fact, it is this sort of rhetorical operation that is the subject of my later discussion of the opening in Phil 1:1–11, and the (dis)closure of Phil 1:12, in which I suggest, among other things, that Paul is seeking the development of a certain hermeneutic which would enable them to "view things" the way Paul wants them to.

In an earlier work, Fowl, albeit independently, comes to the same phronetic orientation of Philippians as Meeks. Fowl presents the Christ hymn's operation in terms of an "exemplar." The story of Christ in Phil 2 is said not to be designed as a means by which an orthodox christology is related, nor is it even designed to present a model for imitation (since a Philippian Christian could hardly be required to imitate the exaltation suggested in Phil 2:9–11; 1990, 80). It rather serves to present a concrete situation from which the Philippians derive actual situational parallels regarding their own lives and consequently know how to act in those situations (see further 1990, 92).

Meeks and Fowl both present a perspective on Philippians which is confluent with the goals of this book. My only point of difference with them is that where they see a Christian ethic focused on the salvation of the self (both the personal self and the local ecclesial self), I see a Christian ethic which, while based on this personal and communal salvation, extends to the larger pragmatic operation of the respective ministries of Paul and Christ. As Fowl, for example, proceeds through his discussion of the relationship of the hymn to the earlier (Phil 1:27–2:5; 1990, 85–92) and later stages (1990, 98–101) of the epistle, the Philippians are everywhere said to be exhorted to a higher ethic (steadfast unity, heaven-based corporate sense of activity, worshiping in the spirit, boasting in Christ and not the flesh) with a view to when "Christ will transform their bodies of humiliation into the body of his glory" (1990, 101; note also Meeks 1991, 333, 335). It is clear that Paul does in fact exhort the Philippians to such ethical activity. The only problem I have with this is that it suggests that the ethic presented to the Philippians is not entirely descriptive of the actual ethics of Paul himself, nor of Christ, for that matter.

The Christian *phronēsis*, and its subsequent ethic, presented here, while rightly located within the self, remains within the confines of the ecclesial group and does not represent the thinking and practice portrayed by the simple and concrete situations of both Paul and Christ: Paul is willing to subordinate his interests *for the greater benefit of others* (Phil 1:21–24), Christ is willing to subordinate his interests *for the greater benefit of others* (Phil 2:5–11). This "greater benefit" is nothing short of the reconciliation of humanity, which is abbreviated by Meeks (1990, 333) and Fowl (1990, 89) as *personal* salvation or resurrection. I therefore assume that *some* soteriological reference is being made by the Christ hymn, in contrast to Fowl who contends that "there is no specific indication that when Christ took on a human body it was for the purpose of ultimately freeing

humanity from its subjection" (1990, 89). Though there is clearly no indication on the poetic level of the hymn itself, surely in the context of
Philippians (e.g., Phil 3:7–11) Paul has this very thing in mind, or, at the
very least, it is not absent from Paul's mind as he narrates the Christ story
in Phil 2. Indeed, given the ease with which Fowl extends the ethical ramifications of the hymn to the other passages, is it not equally reasonable to
extend the soteriological ramifications of the other passages to the hymn?

Proclamation, in the view of this book, is the means by which that
"greater benefit" is actualized by Paul and the church, and thus is the ultimate ethical goal that Paul has for himself and thus also for his churches
(the later conclusions of this book bear out the potential viability of my argument). Thus, with respect to the presentation of the purpose by Fowl
and Meeks, I would argue that proclamation is the *ethical point* of the
Philippians' ability to "deploy their knowledge [*phronēsis*] of the gospel in
concrete situations in which they find themselves" (Fowl 1998, 145).
However, Fowl continues this sentence in a way that, as mentioned, potentially abbreviates the ethical imperative: "so that they will be able to
live faithfully" (1998, 145). The problem lies with the content of "live faithfully." What I would add to this is that to "live faithfully" extends beyond
the sense of personal unifying activity and personal redemption (see Fowl
1998, 148), and into the larger Christian responsibility envisaged and exemplified by Paul throughout his ministry and, in Philippians,
exemplified by the stories of both Paul and Christ, namely *active* participation in God's overarching process of advancing the gospel.

The argument of this book takes its leave from the assumption that
the real business of the epistle is to reassure, and then proceeds to describe the role proclamation plays in the attempt to reassure.[22] The
subsequent exegetical impact of this on Philippians is that the issue of
Christian proclamation, which I understand in a fairly general way to be
the attempt to further what God sought to achieve through the whole
Christ story, is a subtle but substantial one. In general, it is a shift away
from the focus on personal benefit to a focus on personal responsibility
not just to the local church but to the greater mission of the gospel, since
for Paul "*everything* is subordinate to the preaching of the gospel"
(O'Brien 1991, 117, emphasis added).

Such a reading of the immediately surrounding text would look
something like the following: Paul's shame (1:19) would be a reference to
his inability to allow God to work through him to bring about his greater
purposes (O'Brien 1991, 114)—achieved through the proclamation of the
gospel. When Paul then goes on to elaborate on the relative value of life
and death (1:21–26), he concludes that he should subordinate his own

---

[22] For example, I later suggest that the sort of *phronēsis* found in Philippians is
a hermeneutic Paul is attempting to give the Philippians to deal with certain kinds
of conflict.

personal interests to those of the Philippians. He does not do this just because they are great people, but because the ministry of the gospel must be furthered among them, and Paul is subordinate to what he perceives to be God's greater interests. Thus Paul presents an example of what is necessary for God's ministry to operate in this world, the subordination of one's own interests to God's.

Paul's subsequent exhortation in 1:27–30 is an attempt to get the Philippians to subordinate their own interests to God's. Indeed, O'Brien contends that this exhortation "stands as a rubric to the whole section 1:27–2:18, *with the subsequent admonitions and statements expanding and explicating what is involved in living worthily of the gospel*" (1991, 146).[23] This whole section (1:27ff.) begins with an interesting adverb, "only" (μόνον), which delimits the verbal activity (BAGD, 528) of "conduct"; thus, Barth argues that the real concern of the Philippians is to be the "*rectus cursus*," namely "the *prokopē* (advance) of the Gospel or the faith" (Barth 1962, 45). The verb "conduct" (1:27) is here used by Paul not simply as a reference to membership in a heavenly commonwealth, but also to the responsibility that they actually have to do things. Here those things are to result in the progress of the gospel, and they do those things in an actual social/civic context.

The contrary interests of that context mean that in order for the gospel to progress, a "struggle" (ἀγών) develops in the same way that it has for Paul in his own attempt to advance the gospel. Thus the Philippians are exhorted to conduct themselves "in a manner worthy of the gospel"; such conduct would be manifested when they "stand in one spirit, with one mind (ψυχή), striving together for the faith of the gospel."[24] The *point* of standing and striving together is to promote the faith of the gospel in the context of a struggle (ἀγών) against the same kind of opposition Paul experiences for the same reason;[25] thus, by so standing and striving, Paul's followers "show that their goals are the same as his own," namely the general progress of the gospel (O'Brien 1986, 226).

As Paul continues the discussion of the exhortation to conduct oneself worthily of the gospel in 2:1–16, he begins with a series of particular conditions expressing his belief that what is necessary for the Philippians to achieve what he wants them to achieve is already present among them.

---

[23] With respect to the ethical outliving of the importance Paul places on the gospel, O'Brien's reading of "gospel" in Philippians is largely confluent with my own. Apart from his commentary, note also the whole discussion in O'Brien 1986.

[24] Taking the genitive of the phrase τῇ πίστει τοῦ εὐαγγελίου to be one of origin results in the translation "the faith which is based on the gospel" (O'Brien 1991, 152); as appositional, the result is "the faith that is the gospel" (Fee 1995, 167).

[25] On the ἀγών motif in Philippians as a reference to a struggle for the progress of the gospel, see Pfitzner 1967, 82–129, 191–95.

Importantly, when in 2:2 he comes to the apodosis of the series of pro-
tases, in 2:1, the last phrase completes the structure with a focus on this
Christian *phronēsis*: "thinking the same" or "intent on one purpose" (ἔν
φρονοῦντες). That purpose or intention, in this reading, would naturally
be the proclamation or progress of the gospel. The particular Christian
phronēsis Paul has in view is one which enables the Christians to create
within them a set of conditions that enables the gospel to progress. This
phronēsis is one in which the Philippians understand that they need to
subordinate their own interests to the progress of the gospel. Paul then,
in 2:6–11, presents the story of Christ who did this very thing. He subordinated the privilege of his heavenly state to the soteriological needs of
humanity, which, of course, is the gospel in that it represents God's overarching goal in human history.

The subsequent exhortations (2:12–18) turn to how the gospel is more
specifically worked out in the lives of the Philippians themselves. Paul's
sense of the progress of the gospel cannot be tied to proclamation alone;
it must also carry with it the outliving of the gospel after it has been accepted—that is, after proclamation. Furthermore, the church's
responsibility to advance God's purposes through proclamation necessarily includes creating the conditions for progress as well, which is enabled
by Paul's focus on internal cohesion; hence Meeks's comment that "the
emphasis in Paul's paraenesis . . . is not upon the maintenance of boundaries, but upon internal cohesion" (Meeks 1983, 100). Thus, the sort of
phronēsis we find in Fowl and Meeks is clearly a necessary part of achieving what God wants to achieve. That is, God wants to provide salvation,
but the (post-messianic) goal *and* means of that salvation is the same: people are the goal and people are the means.

Finally, this duality is not exactly foreign to the whole concept of
gospel. It is apparently operative within the word εὐαγγέλιον itself.
Becker has presented εὐαγγέλιον as a term which carries both a kerygmatic concept and an active concept of proclamation (1976, 2:111). This is
based on his prior argument that the New Testament usage of the term is
derived from the Greek and not from the Hebrew sense (which tended to
focus on the act more than anything else), or LXX usage (which separated
the action from the content and weakened the meaning). He notes that,
in the Greek usage, the term maintained a sense of its original usage,
namely a confluence of the act of bringing good news and the good news
itself (1976, 2:108–9).

2.c. *Provenance*

The issue of provenance remains a somewhat significant issue in our critical appreciation of Philippians. For the purposes of this book,
provenance has a tangential role in the later discussion on Phil 1:13, when
Paul points to contextualizing information about his circumstances that
has spread throughout the "whole praetorium" (ὅλῳ τῷ πραιτωρίῳ).

However, it should be noted that while I take τὸ πραιτώριον to be a reference to the imperial guard in Rome, my later argument is based on the *communication* of information and not upon the specific audience to whom that information is conveyed.

It appears to me that the weight of the evidence rests with the traditional position that Paul wrote Philippians from a prison[26] in Rome. This appears to be the case primarily because it is entirely confluent with the external evidence[27] and none of the internal evidence is against it; indeed, it is wholly compatible with it. Furthermore, the frequently presented alternatives (Caesarea[28] and Ephesus)[29] simply require a more strained reading than Rome. While it is beyond the scope of this book to provide a comprehensive discussion of that matter, I shall outline the basic issues and where I stand on them.

On historical issues such as this, the most appropriate path to follow is to begin by stating the basic data upon which there is general and necessary agreement: (*a*) Paul writes from a prison (Phil 1:12–14, 17); (*b*) the imprisonment probably poses a threat to Paul's well-being or even life (Phil 1:20–30); (*c*) there is a "praetorium" (τὸ πραιτώριον) with which he has contact (Phil 1:13); (*d*) there are some Christians in the purview of Paul's imprisonment ministry who are specifically labeled in Phil 4:22 as being "out of Caesar's household" (ἐκ τῆς Καίσαρος οἰκίας); (*e*) there has been correspondence and travel between Paul and the Philippians (Phil 2:26; 4:18); (*f*) Epaphroditus, a Philippian envoy, is presently with Paul (Phil 2:25); (*g*) Timothy is presently with Paul and about to be sent to the Philippians (1:1; 2:19). Unfortunately, all of these data are used in various ways to demonstrate the veracity of the respective hypotheses.

For example, an Ephesian provenance is typically presented on the basis of the suggested problem that Philippi was too far from Rome to account for the proposed number of correspondences (as many as seven)[30] between the two cities to occur within a reasonable time frame.[31] Once the problem of correspondences versus time frame is established, and subsequently solved by the suggestion of an Ephesian provenance, since

---

[26] Thus also, with the vast majority of scholars, I hold that the phrase τὰ κατ᾽ ἐμέ is a reference to Paul's imprisonment, as opposed to Paul's revelation (made from non-Roman prison) that he is a Roman citizen; see Collange 1979, 9–10.

[27] The Marcionite Prologues state that the epistle was written from Rome (Grant 1946, 19).

[28] Initially suggested in 1799 by H. E. G. Paulus (Kümmel 1975, 328).

[29] Initially suggested by H. Lisco in 1900 (Hawthorne 1983, xxxviii). On Corinth as an option, see a full discussion of the issues in Hawthorne 1983, xl–xli.

[30] Four journeys before the letter, and three proposed journeys, see Kümmel 1975, 325.

[31] Suggested by Adolf Deissmann (n.d., 229 n. 1; 230–31; 1957, 17, and the listed bibliography), but for a slightly different version of the journeys see Collange 1979, 15–19; 119 n. 2.

Philippi is a lot closer to Ephesus than Rome, the agreed data is swiftly squared with the Ephesian hypothesis. Thus, the proposed visit by Timothy would fit well with the fact that he is known to the Ephesians (based on Acts 19) and appears to agree with Acts 19:22, that Paul sent Timothy and Erastus into Macedonia while "he himself stayed in Asia for a while." The reference to the Καίσαρος οἰκίας works with Ephesus as well, since "according to the prevailing usage" the term should be understood not as a reference to the imperial family or their relatives, but to the members of the imperial civil service, the *Familia Caesaris* and their attendants (BAGD, 557; also Lightfoot 1953, 171–78; Dunn 1978; Deissmann n.d., 230 n. 3). The presence and traveling of Epaphroditus fits just as, or even more, easily into the Ephesian hypothesis as it does the Roman.

Thus the Ephesian hypothesis appears to make use of most of the data generally agreed upon just as well as the Roman hypothesis does. The problem is this: the Ephesian hypothesis requires extending the historical references beyond the natural or most simple reading of the text. In particular, the reference to τὸ πραιτώριον, while applicable to a Caesarean provenance, and of course to a Roman provenance, applies to Ephesus only under the most strenuous reading for the simple reason there does not appear to have been a πραιτώριον at Ephesus. F. F. Bruce and B. Reicke make some extremely helpful points here. To begin, the use of a Latin loanword (*praetorium*) signals technical usage. Furthermore, the word refers to "the headquarters of the praetor, more particularly the commanding officer's headquarters in a military camp" (Bruce 1981, 263–65; 1989, 11). In Rome, it is a specific reference to the emperor's guard; outside Rome in the empire at large, it was a reference to the headquarters of the governor of an imperial province who had military forces at his disposal (1989, 11). Bruce further states that "there is no known instance in imperial times of its use for the headquarters of a proconsul, the governor of a senatorial province such as Asia was at this time" (1989, 11).[32] However, due to some inscriptions near Ephesus bearing reference to a member of the praetorian guard (*praetorianus*) there is the natural assumption of the presence of a praetorian guard itself. However, Bruce notes that the "*praetorianus* mentioned in three Latin subscriptions was a *former* member of the praetorian guard who later discharged police duties as a *stationarius* on a Roman road in the province of Asia" (1989, 12; Reicke 1970, 283).

The crucial data provided by Bruce and Reicke demonstrate the strong unlikelihood of an Ephesian provenance or, as Hawthorne has it, "the fatal flaw in the Ephesian imprisonment hypothesis is that is entirely built upon conjecture" (xxxix). Even though much of the data do in fact fit, if they cannot all fit, then we are left with having to look elsewhere.

---

[32] Reicke notes that the governor of Ephesus was at the time "not a propraetor, but rather a proconsul" (1970, 283).

Rome, of course, resolves any difficulty of locating a πραιτώριον, but so does the only other viable option, Caesarea. Adding to the difficulty of discerning between Rome and Caesarea is the fact that the main problem cited against a Roman provenance, that it is too far from Philippi, is also true of Caesarea. However, I once again point to the fact that the external data supports Rome—none of the internal evidence is against it—so what would cause someone to elect Caesarea over Rome?

Essentially, the difference is one of the interpretation of the cumulative effect of certain "small" data (while ignoring the most important piece of information). For example,[33] (a) there was a πραιτώριον at Caesarea (note the comment in Acts 23:35). (b) There is a specific reference in Acts 23 to a Caesarean imprisonment. (c) Acts 24:27 suggests a sufficient amount of time (two years), despite the distance, for a number of correspondences between Caesarea and Philippi to take place. (d) The reference in Phil 1:7 to an ἀπολογία could possibly refer to a situation in which Paul has already given a defense, and thus κεῖμαι in Phil 1:16, on Hawthorne's reading, would suggest that Paul lay in prison in spite of the earlier ἀπολογία (xli); importantly all of this squares well with the Acts 24:24–27 account of Paul at Caesarea. (e) The strong tone of the polemic in Phil 3:2–6, if the object is taken to be Jewish opposition and not Judaizers, fits well with the account in Acts 21:37–26:32 of a bitter battle going on at Caesarea between Paul and his Jewish opponents. (f) The reference in Philippians to a desired visit from Paul (Phil 2:24), and his confidence that he would be released (Phil 1:24–26; 2:24), works with the statements in Romans (Rom 15:28) that Paul desired to get to Rome and then move west into Spain, rather than to go from Rome back eastward. All this amounts to a cumulative effect that suggests a strong viability for a Caesarean provenance.

However, in spite of that strength, it simply does not match the cumulative effect of the very same data when they are applied to the traditional provenance, Rome, not to mention the failure to deal with the most problematic assumption: (a) while there was unquestionably a πραιτώριον in Rome, the reference to a πραιτώριον outside of Rome (as with Caesarea)[34] is not a reference to the personnel of a governor but to the governor's residence itself (Reicke 1970, 283). In Rome, however, it was a reference to the personnel making up the imperial bodyguard (Reicke 1970, 283), while the Acts 23:35 reference, τῷ πραιτωρίῳ τοῦ Ἡρῴδου, easily bears this sense of a governor's residence as opposed to personnel. Furthermore, and most important, Phil 1:13 clearly refers to a group of people among whom this information has been spread and not

---

[33] Largely taken from Hawthorne, who offers a recent and comprehensive argument in favor of a Caesarean provenance (1983, xli–xliv).

[34] Πραιτώριον is used in the Gospels in precisely this way; see Matt 27:27; Mark 15:16; John 18:28, 33; 19:9.

to a building; thus, this point alone counters the viability of the Caesarean hypothesis. (*b*) There is a specific reference to a Roman imprisonment in Acts. (*c*) Acts also suggests two years for a Roman imprisonment (Acts 28:30). (*d*) The reference to an ἀπολογία in Phil 1:7 does not require a previous specific defensive speech. Note that while the term does have a technical legal usage for a courtroom defense (BAGD, 96; O'Brien 1989, 69; Silva 1992, 54), as in Hawthorne's reading, "the language does not appear to be exhausted by reference to the trial proceedings" (O'Brien 1989, 69; note Silva 1992, 8, 54). Apart from the connotative breadth of the term, the simple *possibility* that Paul is referring to a future trial, and not one that has passed is, again, a perfectly viable option (O'Brien 1989, 69). (*e*) The suggestion that the reference in 3:2–6 is to Jews remains debatable—in this book I support the hypothesis that they are in fact Judaizers.[35] (*f*) The confidence represented in Philippians that Paul expected to be released is a matter I also discuss later. In short, Rapkse has been able to demonstrate that it is entirely reasonable for Paul to have expected to be released. The suggestion of a postimprisonment visit to Philippi in Phil 2:24 is not problematic. The problem is based on the fact that when Paul wrote Romans he imagined that, when he eventually arrived there, he would then go on to Spain. However, we recognize that the plain historical reality of the situation is that Paul did not get to Rome by the means imagined while writing Romans. The situation has already changed enough to suggest the possibility that Paul's plans themselves had been, at the very least, altered. Hawthorne clearly overstates his response to such a possibility when he suggests that "to assume that Paul later changed his mind and made plans to return east from Rome would be a most perplexing assumption, and one entirely without foundation in fact" (1983, xlii). Furthermore, Hawthorne argues that going west "loomed extremely large in his [Paul's] thinking because he believed that there was no more place for him to work in the east" (xlii). Hawthorne's vigorous denial of this possibility rests upon the rather tenuous foundation of Rom 15:20, 23, 24. The use of Rom 15:20 to support this argument is problematic, since work done at Philippi could hardly be a reference to "another man's foundation." Romans 15:23–24 simply points to the fact that Paul has done what he wanted to do in the east, not that he did not ever want to go back there. They certainly do suggest, however, that Paul desired to move his mission westward to Spain. The question to be asked here is whether with a number of years of prison under his belt, and various forms of support from Philippi during that imprisonment (Epaphroditus, and the "gift"), it would not be conceivable that Paul would go and spend some time with them before heading off once again. One can hardly argue that when Paul penned Romans, he was figuring into the equation what appears to have been a four-year prison term. In

---

[35] See the discussion in sec. 4 of this chapter.

short, things have changed enough to warrant the *possibility* of altered plans. That there is no announcement of changed plans in Philippians, as Carson, Moo, and Morris expect (1992, 320), is hardly a basis for suggesting there was no change of plans.

One last point on this matter needs to be made. It is that of the proposed journeys, since these are typically used to suggest the presence of internal evidence that is against the external. The matter comes down to two different sets of issues: the first is the historical-critical issue of how many trips the text suggests were made between Paul and Philippi, the second is the plain historical matter of the distance between the two points and the time it would take to cover the distance. A generous reading of the number of journeys allows for seven journeys: one to alert the Philippians that Paul is in jail; a second to send Epaphroditus with a gift; a third for the Philippians to hear about Epaphroditus's illness; a fourth for Paul and Epaphroditus to hear about the concern of the Philippians. The letter is then thought to suggest three more trips: two journeys for Timothy to get to the Philippians and then to return (Phil 2:19), and a third journey for Epaphroditus to get back to Philippi (Phil 2:24).[36]

The only question is whether it is possible to make these trips within the required time frame of a Roman imprisonment that has the only external evidence in favor of it. The answer is that it is most certainly possible for the following reasons. Concerning a mainly land-based journey, through the major routes of the Via Appia and the Via Egnatia, the distance is "more than 700 miles" (Brown 1996, 495), whereas a sea-based journey "would be over 900 miles" (Lightfoot 1953, 38 n. 1). The distances of the possible individual legs for a land journey are carefully laid out by Lightfoot (1953, 38 n. 1) using references and cross-references from ancient writers. He then arrives at the conclusion that it would take about a month to travel one-way between Rome and Philippi.[37] As to a sea journey, though it was a greater distance, it would have been covered in less time (Lightfoot 1953, 38 n. 1; Reicke 1970, 284). Pliny lists the time frames of several sea-based trade journeys to and from various points around the Mediterranean, Egypt, and Europe, all of which are done over remarkably short periods (19:3–4).[38] The swiftness of the journeys in Pliny reflect what may have been *possible*, though any sea-based journey from Rome

---

[36] So, for example, Carson, Moo, and Morris 1992, 318. However, just why the final journey of Epaphroditus needs to be accounted for in the time frame is unclear, since the time required would be subsumed by the time it would take Timothy to get there and back.

[37] On the rate of travel by foot, see Ramsay's detailed discussion (1912, 386). Ramsay sees that an average of 17 Roman miles (15–16 contemporary miles) per day would be normal. While this would have been a base level of speed, other forms of travel in varying combinations would naturally alter the travel time.

[38] While Pliny's lists reflect swift travel, they are only cited here as a means of referencing possibilities for travel. Note Reicke's comments (1970, 284).

to Philippi would naturally include land components in varying degrees. Nonetheless, a sea-based journey would have been quicker than the one-month land journey.

What all this amounts to is that the slower journey time, around a month, and a generous reading of the number of journeys, seven, do not enable the internal evidence to present us with any chronological conflict. Furthermore, as Silva points out, this is really a "pseudo-problem," and it remains "very difficult to understand why this argument against a Roman origin continues to be taken seriously. The matter should be dropped from any further consideration. If we do so, however, then the *only* clear argument against the traditional view disappears" (Silva 1992, 7).[39]

2.d. *The Intimate Character of Philippians*

The intimate character of Philippians cannot be easily discarded from the evaluation of its general function. Indeed, it is a position of this book that intimacy plays an important role in how we ought to understand what is going on in Philippians. The tone of intimacy is naturally set by the introduction and thanksgiving period. Thus, I refer to O'Brien's comments that Paul's introduction is "unusually earnest" (1986, 216), and that "the expressions in vv. 7 and 8 show a depth not plumbed elsewhere" (1991, 72–73; also Fee 1995, 93–95; Martin 1976, 67). Beare, referring to letter C of a partitioned/redacted Philippians (Phil 1:1–3:1; 4:2–9, 21–23), claims that "it is perhaps the most intensely personal of all Paul's letters" (1959, 25; see 52). Indeed, this "impression of intimacy and cordiality is echoed by all commentators, and forms the most noticeable characteristic which distinguishes Philippians in the Pauline literature" (Martin 1987, 45). For example, Vincent sees the letter as having a generally positive and "happy" mode: "The pervading tone of the letter is imparted by Paul's strong personal attachment to the church" (1897, xxxiv). Lightfoot claims that "the Philippian church was bound to the Apostle by closer ties than even the Thessalonian. . . . But in the epistle to the Philippians the Apostle's commendation is more lavish, as his affection is deeper" (1953, 66). For Deissmann, Philippians is "the most gracious of all St. Paul's writing" (n.d., 230). Müller observes that the qualities of the letter "all bear a very personal stamp, and make it—to a measure surpassing any other letter of the apostle—*a letter*, the effusion of the heart to a Church he loved" (1991, 20–21). Coming from a Greco-Roman perspective, Stowers notes that while there are no generically pure letters of friendship in the New Testament, Philippians bears out the "commonplaces and language from the friendly letter tradition" (1986, 60); he later notes that "the letter is . . .

---

[39] For more detailed discussions on the matter, see the following: O'Brien 1989, 19–26; Bockmuehl 1998, 25–32; Hawthorne 1983, xxxvi–xliv (and his bibliography); Reicke 1970; Lightfoot 1953, 30–46; Silva 1992, 5–8; Kümmel 1975, 324–32; Carson, Moo, and Morris 1992, 319–21; and most of the major commentaries.

densely packed with the motifs of friendship" (1991, 107). Philippians would, however, remain "intimate" regardless of its generic features. For example, a rhetorically obvious feature is that the asymmetrical power structure, so overt in the patron-client language of the other Pauline letters, is muted in this epistle.[40]

Even with such generic influences in place, the language goes beyond their requirements. The use of "joy" terms (χαρά and χαίρω) is comparatively concentrated in Philippians, employed fourteen times in Philippians and only thirty-six times throughout the rest of Paul's work (Silva 1992, 12). In conjunction with a list of other words indicating intimacy and oneness, there is a high concentration of συν-prefixed words, indicating Paul's perception of their partnership: συγκοινωνός (1:7); συναθλέω (1:27; 4:3); σύμψυχος (2:2); συγχαίρω (2:17, 18); συνεργός (2:25; 4:3); συστρατιώτης (2:25); συμμορφίζω (a reference to fellowship with Christ, 3:10); συμμιμητής (3:17); σύμμορφος (3:21); σύζυγος, συλλαμβάνω (4:3); συγκοινωνέω (4:14).

3. Paul's Immediate Context

There is no disputing that the epistle is surrounded by suffering on the part of both Paul and the Philippians. Philippians 1:27–30 indicates that Paul was under the impression that the Philippians were experiencing suffering. Paul himself, we believe, was writing from prison since he refers to himself as having "bonds" (δεσμοί) in 1:7, 14 and, of course, to his intercourse with the Praetorian Guard in 1:13.[41]

On the details of Paul's imprisonment, I accept the argument of Brian Rapske (1994, 174–91) that Paul's imprisonment was relatively light and that he enjoyed a degree of freedom due to an expectation on the part of the Roman officials that his hearing would go in his favor, and that they expected him to be released. Furthermore, Rapske's argument corroborates claims made by Paul in the Philippians (1:24–26; 2:24), to the effect that Paul himself expected to be released. Rapske's argument, while obviously suggestive of the fact, does not require that Paul was released in contradiction to the tradition. His argument only holds that the Roman officials' estimate of the situation was that Paul would be released. Given the little we know of Nero, one could hardly require him to be consistent with this estimate. Nonetheless, considering (1) that it was the Jews who were bringing a case against Paul and their unfortunate reputation, and (2) that the *litterae dimissoriae* would have counted the case thus far in Paul's favor (182–89), and, finally, (3) that if the account in Acts is anything

---

[40] For a discussion on patron-client language, see Saller 1982, 8–39, especially the discussion on the language of reciprocity and social roles (22–26); see also Bockmuehl 1998, 34–35.

[41] On the nature of the Praetorian Guard and the letter's provenance, see the above discussion in sec. 2.c.

to go by (27:9–44), Paul would have easily gained a rather healthy reputation among the Roman guard, then we can agree that Paul would have stood a good chance of gaining an expected release.

This of course is in some contrast to the deliberation going on in Phil 1:20b–24, which suggests that any expectation on Paul's part was qualified in his own mind by the fact that he was still in prison and subject to the whims of the Roman judiciary. That is, while all seemed to bode well for his release, he nonetheless contemplated death as a real possibility. There is, of course, the possibility that Paul was contemplating suicide, which at the time was not entirely repulsive and often honorable. Craig Wansink has suggested the interesting possibility that Paul employs the language of voluntary death so as to indicate that he does indeed have a choice and that it is to go against what he desires ("to depart and be with the Lord," 1:23) for the sake of the Philippians and thus to offer himself as an example to the Philippians (125).[42]

These expectations on Paul's part are interesting because, in fact, Paul represents himself as being somewhat in control of his outcome. Phil 1:20–25 basically states that it is better for Paul personally if he dies and goes to be with the Lord; however, to remain alive would result in "fruitful work." Thus Paul finds a dilemma: Is it better to die or to remain alive? He says that he is hard-pressed between the two options; he prefers to die (1:23) but in the end sees that it is better for the Philippians that he should remain alive (1:24). For this reason, he then says, "[B]eing confident of this [that it is better for the Philippians], I know that I will remain and continue with you all." Most commentators reject the idea that Paul had an actual choice, because it is very difficult to imagine that, given his circumstances, he could have. However, a lot of problems develop from this because Paul does seem to suggest that he does have a choice. He suggests that he has two options and that one of them is better for him (1:23); of the two, he does not know which one to choose and thus has nothing to make known (καὶ τί αἱρήσομαι οὐ γνωρίζω, 1:22) but that he has settled on one of the choices, to continue living since this is better for the Philippians (1:24–26). The significant aspect of this is that Paul actively subordinates the power of the Roman government to the power he endeavors to construct with respect to his apostolic role.

Just what Paul means by καὶ τί αἱρήσομαι οὐ γνωρίζω is under some dispute. It could be a reference to a part of the conditional sentence in which the apodosis would be introduced by the καί,[43] or a separate sentence or independent clause that would locate the introduction to the

---

[42] On the possibility of suicide, see in particular Droge and Tabor 1992, 168–83; also Droge 1988, 263–86; 1989, 14–21.

[43] Clearly a problem, often noted by those who elect this reading, such as Lightfoot 1953, 92.

apodosis at τοῦτό μοι.[44] Furthermore, do we take οὐ γνωρίζω in its typical
New Testament usage and translate it "I do not make known," since
γνωρίζω is understood in its twenty-five other New Testament occur-
rences to mean "make known" or "reveal,"[45] or do we read it this once as
"I do not know" (BAGD, 163; Silva 1992, 83–84; Fee 1995, 144–45)? Lightfoot notes that while the former view here is typical of New Testament
Greek, the latter is typical of classical Greek (1953, 93).

It seems that the best way to deal with this is first to reject the reading that suggests Paul knew something but refused to reveal it, the
"causative" reading ("I do not make known"; e.g., Vincent 1897, 27–28;
Kennedy 1903, 428; Hendriksen 1962, 77 n. 56), and then to accept that
Paul is representing *rhetorically* the fact that he has experienced a genuine
dilemma even though he has already decided upon a choice and resolved
his dilemma (1:23–26). Thus, however one wants to translate οὐ γνωρίζω,
that Paul does make it known or appear to know what choice he will
make must be taken into consideration, and what we actually have stated
in the text must have precedence in determining how we read οὐ γνωρίζω
over word studies and extrabiblical parallels.

It is surprising that there appears to be no one who has emphasized
the fact that this phrase is a *rhetorical* reconstruction of Paul's experience
rather than the actual experience itself, the resolution of which is stated in
1:23–26. For this reason, the argument over whether Paul meant "I do not
know" (Lightfoot 1953, 93; BAGD, 163; Fee 1995, 144–43),[46] or "I do not
make it known" (Vincent 1897, 27–28; Kennedy 1903, 428; Hendriksen
1962, 77 n. 56), is really a pointless one since it assumes that Paul is actually in the midst of a struggle, when it appears that the struggle is over.
The language Paul uses to express his situation in this section (Phil 1:21–
26) is a reinforcement of a certain discourse which claims power for itself
above all other powers. In so doing, Paul seeks to affirm the power of the
gospel message, so central to his discourse, and which his followers, in
this case the Philippians, have adopted. If Paul is seen as impotent against
the Roman state, so does his discourse and, thus, so does the gospel
message.

One significance of Rapske's point is that one would assume that the
Philippians would also know how the land lay regarding Paul's imprisonment, that is, that they may have known the estimation of the Roman

---

[44] Also seen as a problem since it assumes an ellipsis of a predicate (με?) in the
protasis; so Lightfoot 1953, 92; Silva 1992, 83.

[45] Or "declare" (O'Brien 1991, 127–28); also see the discussion in Vincent 1897,
27–28.

[46] Fee seems to have misread O'Brien saying that "some of these [interpreters]
suggest "I cannot tell" in a less colloquial sense, of his *not being able* to reveal it"
and cites "esp. Lohmeyer and O'Brien" (Fee 1995, 145 n. 28), when in fact O'Brien
is clear that while such a reading cannot be excluded, it is not the one he chooses
(1991, 127–28 n. 66), note also his translation (1991, 116).

officials. If so, it may speak to why Paul mentions nothing about his personal circumstances and points only to the well-being of the gospel.[47] Many scholars already have pointed out various reasons for Paul's omission of his *personal* circumstances. These reasons generally come under a common and expected umbrella, namely that, for Paul, the gospel is of the highest importance and thus entwined in, or even more important than, his own personal circumstances.[48]

If the Philippians were under the impression that Paul expected to be released, in keeping with Rapske's suggestion of the Roman officials' estimate of the situation, then perhaps there was no real need for Paul to go into too much detail unless there were some new development of his situation. In spite of this, it is still difficult to imagine why Paul, who is generally held to have had a close relationship to the Philippians, did not mention anything, unless of course he understands his epistle to be functioning on a level other than simply personal communication, that he had some other, greater rhetorico-theological or etho-poetic purpose in mind. Indeed, this is one of the claims I wish to make in this book: While Paul's letter is ostensibly a communication-letter (*Verbindungsbrief*), it nonetheless attempts to subvert any questioning on the part of the Philippians that there may have been something wrong with Paul and/or his gospel.

Paul is in prison. His freedom to act as he wills has been removed. He is a man who believes he has a divine commission but who has been forced into submission by an earthly power: the collision of two power structures. Yet he converts his prison to a locus of the gospel's power. He inverts the situation and represents his weakness all the more as strength. He turns impotence into power. He engages in creating a new (sub)version of his circumstances (τὰ κατ' ἐμέ, 1:12). Through his epistle, he engages in an attempt to invert the normal expectations of Greco-Roman culture so that his readers are given the "correct" lens through which they must read his circumstances; that is, they are being persuaded to read τὰ κατ' ἐμέ, *the way Paul wants them to read them.*

Being in prison would have been a conventional stroke against Paul's reputation.[49] "Regardless of why prisoners found themselves in prison, their mere presence there often was seen as pointing to unscrupulous,

---

[47] Paul's omission of his personal circumstances has caused some surprise among scholars (Collange 1979, 51).

[48] Among the many, see Collange 1979, 51; O'Brien 1991, 91; 1986, 219, 220, 222; Martin 1976, 70–71 (who also believes that there is a "tantalising obscurity about these verses"); Fee 1995, 108 ("to reflect on how his imprisonment has furthered the gospel *is* to reflect on his life!"; correctly, he adds that Paul probably expected Epaphroditus to fill in any other details).

[49] See the excellent and comprehensive discussion on the relationship between shame and prison in Rapske 1994, 283–312.

immoral or illegal activity. . . . Regardless of whether one was actually guilty of any crime, imprisonment in itself was seen as a reason for shame" (Wansink 1996, 135). What Wansink has in view here is that the previously established social construction of the prison was of such a nature that entering into prison meant entering into a previously established category of shame existing within the minds of those within the society. Not only did one feel a sense of shame by virtue of the social value, but everyone else automatically and perhaps unconsciously imputed shame to that person by virtue of that set of social assumptions.

It is commonly held that Greco-Roman society, particularly among the educated classes, operated on an economy of honor, the acquisition of which was "a constant social tug of war, a game of social push and shove" (Malina and Neyrey 1991, 29). Imprisonment was one of the fastest ways to lose honor and incur shame; equally fast was the public flogging. Both together, as in Paul's case at Philippi, were a devastating blow to any honor held by the subject.[50] Rapske shows that not only is honor removed from the subject of a prison sentence, or beating, or some other humiliating punishment, those closely associated with the subject were in danger of losing honor as well (Rapske 1994, 291–95). For this reason, it was rather common for people to abandon anyone suffering the shame of prison and quite remarkable when they did not (Wansink 1996, 133–45). What is most significant in Rapske's work is not the prison-shame scenario but the intensity of it and its lingering effect on the subject's social status if he or she should be freed. As to the question of whether Paul would have been alive to these social concerns, one would simply ask how could he not be? Shame and honor was the real currency of the Greco-Roman world, and "Paul would have known that imprisonment, like exile, strained and changed the relationships between people." Having himself imprisoned others, "he would have been conscious of the fragility of relationships between those in prison and those outside" (Wansink 1996, 133; Rapske 1994, 298).

Paul's first move to compensate for his problem is, of course, to invoke a sort of martyr principle: Paul is in prison for the sake of the gospel. Since this is true, it is an effective way for Paul to maintain his apostolic economy, insofar as his followers, those over whom he is positioned as a spiritual father or leader, continue to maintain both the social and spiritual structures which govern their relationship to Paul. However, a prolonged imprisonment could easily take its toll on such an economy, since it could be perceived that the divine power surrounding the apostle Paul was either no longer active or that perhaps there was some

---

[50] For an excellent discussion on this, see Rapske 1994, 283–312. Note that he discusses in some detail the circumstances of Paul's beating and incarceration at Philippi.

discrepancy between his claims of the gospel's power and the fact that he remains in prison.

The Philippians, according to the Acts narrative,[51] have already experienced a Paul in prison (Acts 16:22–26); however, on that occasion he was freed by a σεισμός, yet remained in prison along with the other prisoners, which led to the conversion of the jailor as well. The important development in this story, however, is the honor-shame issue associated with Paul's beating and then incarceration in stocks in the inner prison. Most important, Paul's public and thorough humiliation also publically disgraces the gospel that he had been preaching, along with those with whom he had associated.

Paul's experiences at Philippi, according to Acts, are an example of this tug-of-war for honor. As mentioned, Paul is "publicly" (δημοσία) shamed in Philippi. The next morning—one assumes it was relatively early since it is to be done in "secret" (λάθρα contrasting δημοσία, Acts 16:37)—the city officials try to eject Paul from the city and have the matter finished. The result of this would have been to affirm their position as men of power in Philippi who can shame others at will and to secure Paul's public shame in Philippi. Paul has other ideas. He is clearly aware of the problem that this secret expulsion poses for him and the gospel's progress in Philippi, and therefore refuses to leave the prison in secret and thus to maintain or even validate his shame (Acts 16:35–37).

Paul's response is to indicate that his shaming was the result of an error on the part of the city magistrates; specifically, he points to a lack of due process (ἀκατάκριτος)[52] in his being railroaded directly to a public flogging and to a night at the pleasure of the Roman government. Paul has the Philippian magistrates in a rather awkward position, which they confirm by virtue of their subsequent actions. It appears that they also assumed that the trial of Paul and Silas was less than desirable, and that rather than risk a challenge and then possible failure and subsequent personal condemnation under Roman law, they were willing to shame themselves to some lesser degree by agreeing to the demands of Paul, the previously shamed prisoner. Paul and his entourage now get a *public* escort by the city magistrates, yet Paul is not so easily dispatched. He uses this honor-building process to its fullest and goes to Lydia's house to meet the church before he leaves. The honor-shame struggle is over; scars are marked on both sides.

It would be wrong to claim that Paul felt that his honor was fully re-

---

[51] The reliability of Acts is a subject far too vast to deal with in this book. For discussions on the historicity of Acts, see Hemer 1990. For the relationship of Paul to Acts, see Roetzel 1999.

[52] Paul was not claiming that it was illegal for the magistrates to mete out the stated punishment on a Roman citizen (Rapske 1994, 299–300), against Tajra 1989, 28; see the summary in Rapske 1994, 301–2.

stored at this point (so Rapske 1994, 298). It is clear, from 1 Thess 2:1–2, that Paul maintained some indignation regarding the episode. In his letter to the Philippians, Paul refers to his experiences rather obliquely. In Phil 1:20 there is the possible reference to, or at least a resonance with, the shame of his experiences at Philippi: "according to my eager expectation and hope, that I shall be shamed (αἰσχύνω) in nothing." Philippians 1:29–30 is more explicit: "for to you it has been given on behalf of Christ, not only to believe in him but also to suffer (πάσχω) on his behalf, having the same sort of struggle (ἀγών) you *saw* in me and now hear to be in me." The point here is that Paul is sensitive enough to the dishonor and shame of public humiliation and imprisonment for it to linger around in his mind and to surface in his subsequent writings (see 1 Thess 2:2; 2 Cor 7:5; 11:23–27). Paul's extended imprisonment (at least two years in Caesarea, Acts 24:27), culminating in his voyage to Rome and subsequent imprisonment for at least another two years (Acts 28:30), is easily another occasion for Paul to feel the pressure of social shame, even if he hopes against it (Phil 1:20). As with the Philippi episode, however, Paul is not going to allow shame to take him so easily, and thus he represents his circumstances in a positive light (Phil 1:12–18).

In further connection to the Philippi episode and the shame-honor issue, it would be correct to assume that there was enough material in this event for the church to make something good of it. Paul was now well-known in Philippi, more so than perhaps he would have been had he visited the city without incident, and there was always that puzzling spectacle of the magistrates escorting them out of the city for the church's spin doctors to play with. The incident at Philippi would have been rather powerful testimony to communicate around Philippi; it certainly would have been woven into the fabric of the nascent church's understanding of its identity.

It is also worth noting the frequently observed fact that one of the "we" passages in Acts ends when Paul leaves Philippi the first time (Acts 16:11–13; 17:1; 20:1–7) and picks up again when he returns. Assuming that the "we" passages are not literary devices, it would seem that this indicates that Luke stayed on in Philippi. Luke is the one who communicates the prison story in Acts, and he is also the one who, it seems, stays on in Philippi. It was obviously an important event, and Acts shows that Luke knew just how to narrate the story to generate the best effect. If Luke is left in Philippi, then one would expect him to integrate the story into his evangelistic work with the church. Even if Luke did not remain in Philippi, such a story would become well-known and an integral part of the church's identity. If so, that Paul is once again imprisoned, for at least four years, must have presented some challenge to the impression generated by stories of what would now be classified as "divine favor" shown to Paul while experiencing conflict in Philippi. Where is this divine favor now? Was it ever there?

4. The Philippians in the Context of Conflict

While Philippians presents conflict occurring on a number of fronts, the conflict represented in Phil 3 seems to have evoked the most academic interest.[53] The state of scholarship regarding the identity of Paul's opponents in Phil 3 has not changed a great deal since Gunther's investigation into the subject revealed no less that *eighteen* different positions being put forward (1973, 2). A more recent contribution is by Bateman, in which he conflates an older suggestion that the opponents were both Judaizers and Gentile Christians, and suggests that they were Gentile Judaizers.

It is not my purpose here to deal with all the various suggestions, but the major trends are worth noting. Paul does not indicate that these opponents are necessarily in Philippi; instead, it appears he is simply warning the Philippians of a potential or impending threat (Fee 1995, 9). Almost all of the positions concerning identity incorporate Jews or proselytes of some description. That we are dealing with Jews of some sort is obvious (to most) from the various points made in the earlier part of Phil 3.[54] What clouds the issue is that as we get to the end of the chapter there is a less-definable group mentioned: "enemies of the cross" and so forth. Are they the same group or are they different? At least since Lightfoot's 1869 commentary (143–44, 155), and as recently as Robert Jewett (1970a, 362–90, esp. 378–87), many have observed that the two passages in Phil 3 seem to indicate two different kinds of opponents: 3:2–6 reflects a more Jewish opponent and 3:18–19 reflects a more Antinomian/Libertine-Gnostic opponent. Rather than attempt to encompass the two under one theory—a task which Jewett believes requires too much energy (1970a, 362)—some have decided that it makes more sense to divide them into two groups.

Jewett, who is representative, has preempted a challenge to his argument when he prefaces it with a long discussion of the character of the Philippian church that ends up claiming that the Philippians had a desire for "perfection," which formed the basis of the disparate appeal of the two groups: on the one hand, some felt they could find perfection in cir-

---

[53] The issue of identity is the dominant issue in the scholarly discussion of conflict at Philippi. This issue is, however, beyond the scope of this book. The interest in this book is the fact of conflict and the determining elements that outline the problem sufficiently. For more detailed discussion on the subject, see Gunther 1973, 2; although not recent, he lists eighteen variant perspectives on the opponents. See also Klijn 1965; Holladay 1969; Jewett 1970a; Grayston 1986; Tyson 1976; Schmithals 1972, 65–122; Tellbe 1994; O'Brien 1991, 26–35; Silva 1992, 9–10; Hawthorne 1983, xliv–vii.

[54] Paul's references to circumcision and his word play on κατατομή to slander those who value it, along with his account of his own Jewish heritage, all strongly suggest that we are dealing with Jews of some sort.

cumcision; on the other hand, others felt they could achieve it though an "exalted spiritual self-consciousness" (1970a, 387). This last phrase of Jewett's is suggestive of how far from the actual evidence within the text he has strayed, since it bears little resemblance to anything Paul actually says. Jewett is following good historical practice by reading in the negative (following the hints and tips from Schmithals and Köster) and builds his argument upon the assumption[55] that the phrase "enemies of the cross" in Phil 3:18 is closely paralleled to 1 Cor 1:17, which he suggests "refers to a gnostic denial of the soteriological significance of the cross," but which actually says, "For Christ did not send me to baptize, rather to evangelize, not with sophistic speech, in order that the cross of Christ may not be made empty (κενόω)." From this, Jewett builds his arguments for the existence of a second, libertinistic group in Phil 3. It seems that, with respect to Jewett's complaint, more energy is spent on the two claims necessary for his position: that "enemies of the cross" refers to Gnostics and that the Philippians had a desire for "perfection," which formed the basis of an attraction to two opposing theologies.

Another question that raises itself is whether those references that are clearly Jewish are aimed at Judaizers requiring some obedience to the law or simply Jews preaching their pre-Christian theology in an effort to proselytize. As to the latter, Gnilka observes that nowhere (unless this is the exception) does Paul write against Jews who are posing a threat to the church (1968, 211; 1965, 260–64). While this argument from silence does not prove much, it demonstrates certain trends. The text itself seems to bear out that we are dealing with Judaizers, since Paul's argument within the text seems to make more sense when understood in reference to Judaizers as opposed to just Jews (also O'Brien 1991, 33). The brief mention of the kinds of circumcision suggests that what is at stake is not Judaism versus Christianity, but whether (some?) Jewish rites apply to Christianity. On the one hand we have an actual circumcision given the label κατατομή, by which Paul redirects the sign of circumcision as "sign of the covenant" (Gen 17:11) simply to be a sign *of circumcision*, to signify the thing itself rather than a metaphysical covenant. On the other hand we have a circumcision that is not an actual circumcision given the label περιτομή, the intended signification of which is entirely metaphysical or, as Paul would say, "spiritual" and therefore "real." The function of the label κατατομή only works if actual, physical circumcision is being given value by those so labeled. When Paul then makes the claim that the Philippians are the (true) circumcision because[56] they worship God *in*

---

[55] Suggested by Schmithals 1957, 331–32.

[56] The phrase in Phil 3:3, οἱ πνεύματι θεοῦ λατρεύοντες καὶ καυκώμενοι ἐν Χριστῷ Ἰησοῦ καὶ οὐκ σαρκὶ . . . , is in a causal relationship to ἡμεῖς γάρ ἐσμεν ἡ περιτομή, insofar as the former explains the basis for the latter.

spirit, his point is not to introduce a Jewish/Christian opposition, but a flesh/spirit opposition within the context of Christianity.

Paul's Letter to the Philippians makes clear that, at the very least, he was under the impression that the Philippians were experiencing some conflict on account of their new faith. To refer again to the Acts account as discussed in the previous section, some confusion may have arisen among the Philippian townspeople as to how they were supposed to regard Paul and his entourage. On the one hand they were clearly seen as deviants—Jews out proselytizing a widely practiced, though technically illegal, act (Sherwin-White 1964, 78)—who upset the normal rhythms of the city and were therefore justly punished—the punishment reinforces the deviant status.[57] On the other hand, they had been escorted out of the city by the city magistrates, who no longer had the power to tell them what to do; indeed, Paul does the opposite of the magistrates' requirements by not leaving the city directly, rather via Lydia's house. The Western text's version of Acts 16:39 suggests that the situation may have been rather volatile and that the magistrates were anxious to get Paul and his retinue out of the city lest the citizens band together against them in a riot similar to the previous day's. Given the possibility of this version of the circumstances and what we know of the situation as a whole, we expect that the Philippian church had a number of (non-Jewish)[58] enemies from the very beginning.[59]

As mentioned, the letter itself testifies to the presence of conflict at Philippi, both from within the church (Phil 1:27; 4:2–3; also 2:1–16) and from without (Phil 1:27–30; also 2:15). The internal conflict is hard to define since it relies so much on a few scant references in this one epistle, whereas the external conflict is defined in light of Acts and other comments by Paul both in this epistle and in his other epistles; moreover, these tend to follow a particular pattern and come as no real surprise. It is also the case that the external and internal find points along their borders at which they touch each other; thus, Paul exhorts the Philippians to "remain steadfast (στήκω) in one spirit, striving in one accord for the faith of the gospel, and not in any way being afraid of those who oppose you" (1:27b–28a). That is, the two participial clauses indicate the two sides of

---

[57] Anthropological theory has identified deviance as a status that comes into existence by infringing rules generated by social groups. That is, "the deviant is one to whom that label has been successfully applied" by previously established sociological structures (Becker 1963, 9). Thus punishment serves to reinforce the deviant status, since it reinforces the sociological structures (note Barclay 1995, 114–27, esp. 122–23; Meeks 1983, 94).

[58] It is important to note that these are non-Jewish enemies since it is almost a given in Paul's experience that he and his followers will acquire Jewish enemies as they progress with the gospel of Jesus-as-Christ.

[59] This conclusion does not rely on the validity of the Western text's account of the story, it is merely assisted by it.

what it means to remain steadfast (O'Brien 1991, 152). The exhortation in Phil 3:2–3 to "beware . . . beware . . . beware" because "we are the circumcision who worship in the spirit of God," if taken as a warning,[60] also suggests that Paul was trying to ensure that the inner state of the church was such that it could endure the attacks of those Paul refers to as "dogs," "evil workers," and the "mutilation."

Paul's exhortation in Phil 3:2 serves to create an oppositional structure that reinforces the boundaries of the Philippian church and their distinction from those outside the church, thereby facilitating a move to unity by virtue of defining their identity in terms of what they are not. Thus, "dogs," "evil workers," and the "mutilation" serve as indicators or examples of what the Philippians are not, but also as indicators of the enemy, of whom they must beware, whose presence among the Philippians would dissolve their difference from them and thus also Paul's work. That these are Judaizers is suggested, at least in part, by the reference to them as κατατομή and the subsequent oppositional concept περιτομή being used of the Philippians, who were obviously not physically circumcised.[61]

Paul is naturally inclined to the preservation of the church's identity. For this reason he is most concerned about any discord and dissatisfaction, since this leaves the church in a vulnerable state and open for enemies of their faith (theological and secular) to enter the Philippian Christian community. A challenge to the community belief system as established by Paul is a challenge to his authority and a challenge to his gospel, and Paul is always prepared to react against any alteration of, or challenge to, his gospel (see Gal 1:8). The reason for this is that the nature of the community is placed into jeopardy if its central beliefs are altered; thus, Paul's reactions are designed to preserve the group's essential nature. Importantly, "the emphasis in Paul's paraenesis, however, is not upon the maintenance of boundaries, but upon internal cohesion" (Meeks 1983, 100; see also Malina 1995, 108–9). Paul understands the internal and the external conflict at Philippi to be closely related: in order for the church to survive conflict from without, it must be at peace within, yet this inner stability requires a certain hermeneutic, which enables the Philippians to read the external conflict in a particular way so as to affirm the difference between those outside and those inside. I suggest that it is

---

[60] There is no reason to withdraw the warning dimension from Paul's βλέπετε formula as suggested in Kilpatrick 1968, 146–48; Caird 1976, 131; Garland 1985, 166; Hawthorne 1983, 124–25. For the opposite position, see Silva 1992, 172; O'Brien 1991, 354; Schenk 1984, 253; BDF, §149.

[61] Naturally, the ease with which these people are here pronounced as "Judaizers" has not been felt throughout scholarship. For a comprehensive discussion on the various positions, see O'Brien 1991, 27–35.

the affirmation and development of this hermeneutic which forms the primary interest of Philippians.

Because internal unity and cohesion around Paul's gospel is the best defense against threats from outside the church (1:27b–28a)—both theological opposition (Jews and Judaizers) and secular opposition (the citizens and government of Philippi and the Roman legal system)—Paul includes a good deal of exhortation for the Philippians to conduct themselves appropriately, to be unified and of the same mind (Phil 1:9–10, 27; 2:1–16; 4:2–3, 8). Moreover, it has been well-noted that Philippians has a high concentration of συν- compounds and friendship terms.[62] While these are without question a part of the friendship theme maintained throughout the letter, it should not go unnoticed that they also function rhetorically to encourage the assumption that the Philippians are already in the same group as Paul and not in the same group as those who oppose Paul. So, for example, when Paul uses the first-person plural personal pronoun (ἡμεῖς) in 3:2, it serves as a subtle way to keep the Philippians on Paul's side and away from his opponents—who have now also become the Philippians' opponents. Another example is the way Paul represents his own suffering and the suffering of the Philippians as connected (1:7, 29–30).[63] Paul is anxious to maintain ideo-theological solidarity with the Philippians, since he naturally assumes that his own belief system is the true one and that the Philippians will fare their best if they are in harmony with his own ideo-theological position.[64] Of course, this solidarity that Paul seeks is not a democratic common belief as such, but belief in common with Paul's own beliefs, which function as the point of cohesion. It is this kind of power structure which Paul seeks to generate in Philippians and which constitutes the structuring process in the epistle.

The immediate external conflict, at the time of writing, comes primarily from the secular quarter, the Philippian citizens and leaders, and, *secondarily*,[65] from theological interests of Judaizers, though pressure from the former group may have increased Philippian interest in the latter. However, it is only appropriate to focus on the theology of the situation,[66] if one also understands the politics of the situation to be incorporated into the theology. That is, while Paul's comparisons may indeed be a general

---

[62] See sec. 2.d. above; see also Fee 1995, 18–21.

[63] This also serves to prevent any wedge being driven between them with respect to the honor-shame issue discussed earlier.

[64] So, for example, Phil 3:17, and note also Castelli 1991, the thesis of which is that "the notion of mimesis functions in Paul's letters as a strategy of power. That is, it articulates and rationalizes as true and natural a particular set of power relations within the social formation of early Christian communities" (15).

[65] "Secondarily" because it is the *threat* of conflict and not the actuality of conflict which causes Paul concern.

[66] Gnilka, for example, argues that the point of comparison is the theological foundation of their struggle (1965, 101–2).

struggle, this generality is enabled by real specifics. One cannot dismiss the possibility that Paul was in fact referring to some specific situation(s) at Philippi, that some of the Philippians were indeed suffering at the hand of the state and were perhaps in prison, simply because it is likely the case that ἀγών also refers to the general struggle to spread the gospel.

The reference to a common struggle in Phil 1:30 (τὸν αὐτὸν ἀγῶνα ἔχοντες) is most likely a reference to oppression by secular forces:[67] Phil 1:27 is referring to a present situation, whereas, in 3:2, Paul is referring to a future possibility; the opponents mentioned in 1:27 are headed for destruction (ἀπωλεία), which in Paul is the province of non-Christians (1 Cor 1:18; see O'Brien 1991, 153). While one could postulate that in Phil 1:30 Paul was referring to Jewish-Christian oppression in Rome, it seems more probable that he was referring to the secular opposition that he was experiencing since there is no account of his suffering at the hands of the Jewish-Christians while in Philippi. There is ample evidence that he suffered at the hands of the empire while in Philippi.

Thus, it is unlikely that he is referring to any kind of theologically based challenge (from Judaizers), since the common struggle is one which they themselves had previously observed in Paul (οἷον εἴδετε ἐν ἐμοὶ) and which they now hear Paul is experiencing (νῦν ἀκούετε ἐν ἐμοί). We know of no point at which the Philippians saw Paul in conflict with the Judaizers. They certainly did see him in conflict with the state, and one assumes that this is dominant in Paul's mind as he writes of their common struggle; however, this does not then mean that Paul is only referring to imprisonment and public floggings, since one is hard-pressed to exclude all the nuances of "struggle" (ἀγών) in this context in favor of just one. We can certainly understand Paul as referring both to his present circumstances—a well-developed theme in the epistle thus far—*and* to the general struggle for the gospel in whatever circumstances, since this encompasses his present experience and that of his Philippian experience. Hence Pfitzner's claim that "the Apostle conceived of his apostolic mission as an *Agon* for the Gospel or for the faith" (1967, 127) and that this *Agon* extends "to include the activity of his coworkers, and also the members of an entire congregation under special duress (Phil 1:27ff.)" (1967, 128; also 114–29, 191–95).

As already indicated, Paul was concerned that the Philippians would also experience conflict from an alternate form of Christianity—the Jewish-Christian group or "Judaizers" (Phil 3:2; also 3:17–19?)[68]—which

---

[67] Against Phil 1:28 as a reference to secular forces, and as a reference to itinerant Jewish-Christian preachers (or "Judaizers"), anticipating the rebuke in 3:1–2, see Collange 1979, 75; Silva 1992, 92; Hawthorne 1983, 58–60; Wiles 1974, 210. On the opposing position, that Phil 1:28 refers to secular opposition, see O'Brien 1991, 152–58; Fee 1995, 167 n. 50; Martin 1976, 15, 23, 83; Gnilka 1965, 99–100.

[68] While it is generally agreed that 3:2 is a reference to Judaizers, there is some question as to whether we can classify 3:18–19 also as a reference to Judaizers. On

Paul considered to be inferior to his own since it required the adherent to assume the confines of the Jewish law and restricted the freedom for which Paul so vigorously preached and argued (note Gal 2:4). This sort of conflict seems to bother Paul the most—that is, if we take 3:17–19 to be a warning against ideo-theological challengers. The way he refers to the opponents in 1:28 is different enough from that in 3:2, 17–18 for us to be confident that he is not in 1:28 referring to Judaizers or any other ideo-theological opponents. The Philippians are not told to "beware" the secular opponents; they are simply told not to be afraid (μὴ πτυρόμενοι), and this fits an unsubtle and physical threat far better than an ideo-theological threat. The secular threat is, as mentioned, unsubtle and simple; the danger to their faith is a crude one based on fear.

The ideo-theological threat—a threat to the stability of the discourse Paul has established at Philippi[69]—is subtle and complex, entering by already established discursive openings made by Paul's own work. It bases itself not upon fear but upon security and commonality, a sort of ideo-theological Trojan horse. The Judaizers can only succeed because of the discourse Paul has already given to the Philippians: they can enter Philippi in the belly of that gift from God, the gospel, the discourse of hope in Christ *KATA PAULON*. The action of the Judaizers is to circumscribe the Christ-event with a new context that will enable it to be reread in terms of their own ideo-theological interests. Paul, therefore, preempts this move by reinforcing the discourse already in place with his thoroughly rhetorical biographical account in Phil 3. This account maintains Paul's position of superiority (superior whether Jew or Christian or both) and thus the superiority of his own ideo-theological position that he has established at Philippi.

5. Summary

On the basis of the preceding discussion, we can say that the historical context of Paul, the Philippians, and the letter is as follows. Paul was in Rome when he wrote Philippians. He penned a single letter that was designed, among other things, to inform them of certain information and to thank them for the gift, to create a Christ-centered *phronēsis* so that they would know how to act in certain situations, and to reassure the

---

this, see the bibliography in n. 53 above, but note especially the summarizing discussions in O'Brien 1991, 26–35, and Martin 1976, 22–34. For the purposes of this book the identity is not important; what is important is that Paul understands them to be an ideo-theological threat to the Philippians.

[69] The interesting thing is that it is not so much a threat to their faith as it is to their theology and as such appears more of a problem for Paul than for the Philippians, since Paul would see this sort of regression as a move away from the potential of freedom secured by the work of Christ and thus an essential regression away from Christ.

Philippians, which is the "real business" of the letter and necessarily plays a role in the other aspects of the letter's purpose. The letter is particularly intimate, and this assists in the development of ethos within the letter, enabling Paul to perform the necessary rhetorical maneuvers he needs to make. Paul's immediate context was a low-level incarceration in Rome, the nature of which suggested that the guards in charge of Paul would have expected Paul to be released. His imprisonment nonetheless plays an unfortunate social role among the Philippians, and Paul must work in his epistle to counter the problems suggested by his imprisonment. This is exacerbated by the fact that the Philippians themselves are experiencing conflict on more than one level. However, Paul attempts to help them see things from his own perspective and to enable them to interpret the situation as the noble struggle of the gospel.

3

The Socio-Philosophical Context of Paul and His Writing

1. Introduction

Paul is a man who is a part of his society and whose society was a part of him; naturally, this was also true of the Philippians. While there may have been some divergent socially discursive features within their respective experiences, it is evident that Paul is a man who attempts to engage people on their own terms. Note, for example, the claims in 1 Cor 9:19–23 in which Paul describes his practice of adapting to the needs of those to whom he is ministering.[1] Thus, I shall discuss Paul's social location in the general philosophical matrix of his society—I have in view here the general social discourse of the shared culture of Paul and the Philippians and the set of "cognitive tools" available to Paul for use in his interaction with the Philippians. In addition, I shall also discuss the historical situation of the letter in terms of ancient letter-writing practices and the ancient assumptions associated with the function of language in general. The respective discussions on Paul's philosophical location and writing practices are essentially attempts to describe some of the key cultural features that *precede* Paul's thought and expression with a view to considering the fact that such contexts not only precede Paul's thought and expression but constrain them.

---

[1] Note also Luke's telling of Paul's sermon on Mars Hill in Acts 17:22–31, in which Paul is presented as doing this very thing: contextualizing the gospel for the people to whom he is communicating.

2. The Socio-Philosophical Situation of Paul and the Philippians

In the previous chapter it was noted that the major functions generally understood to be the complex of Paul's purposes behind Philippians are (1) to respond to their gift, (2) to allay fears of his own welfare, (3) to warn of false teachers ("opponents"), (4) to exhort them to be steadfast and unified in the face of conflict. The first two of these are generally contextualized in terms of an intimate relationship between Paul and the Philippians. The latter two suggested purposes reflect the general hortatory tone of Paul's apostolate, which pervades all of his letters.

Encountering this connection in Philippians between intimacy and ethical exhortation is not entirely serendipitous. In fact, it appears that to some degree Paul subscribed to the Greco-Roman psychagogic practice in which the intimate and the hortatory are frequently, if not necessarily, found. It is not an easy task to determine the degree of Paul's confluence with Greco-Roman moral philosophical ideals and practice. There is no question *that* Paul was influenced by the culture (see Malherbe 1989, 8–9); the question has been *what* influenced him. The search for this "what" is really the impetus behind the research on rhetorical and epistolary forms in the Pauline epistles, the various metaphors and allusions Paul employs, and anything else comprising the cultural background or social world of the apostle. The enduring research on Paul is that which develops a contextual matrix that grants historical and cultural significance to specific features of Paul's life, while keeping them in balance with other features of the culture.[2]

This matrix extends into the culture as a whole, and not to the elite alone. We cannot assume that due to the comparative lack of education and literacy[3] the poorer members of, for example, the Philippian community were completely isolated from those ideals espoused among the literate 20 to 30 percent. We have to admit, nonetheless, that making claims about the worldview of the uneducated is "tantalizingly difficult," as Meeks has it (1987, 40), for no other reason than the simple fact that their illiteracy prevented them from expressing their voice in the record of human history. The significance is that the majority of any population is not the elite; rather, it is the "small community," which "has been the very predominant form of human living throughout the history of mankind" (Redfield 1955, 3).

While illiteracy silenced the hoi polloi, it would not have prevented them from having access to a largely oral-based tradition of communicating ideas. That is, while the literary form of philosophical ideas certainly

---

[2] The respective works of Nock, Cadbury, and Judge, for example.

[3] In the first century, less than 10 percent of the general empire was literate (Meeks 1987, 62). Within the Hellenistic cities it may have reached as much as 20 to 30 percent; see "Literacy" in *OCD*, 869.

bears out the "great traditions" through history, it was "by *hearing* them recited, listening to public speeches, attending lectures, hearing sermons and homilies and exhortations that one learned the tradition" (Meeks 1987, 40). Thus, when we consider those to whom Paul is writing, we can affirm Malherbe's claims that Paul's readers can be expected to have been familiar with the philosophical traditions to which Paul adhered, and that there is no reason Paul should not have drawn directly from the popular philosophical tradition (1989, 50). The following pages of this, and the next, chapter discuss what some of those philosophical traditions and conventions were and the nature of Paul's potential confluence with them. An important point is that philosophical language filtered down into the discursive structures of non-specialized educated, and possibly even uneducated, people of the Greco-Roman world and became *normative*, even required. That is, those ways of thinking that were born in the philosophical communities, and the ideals generated by those "ways of thinking," became common to the larger populace through a popularizing process. Thus, someone in Paul's position would have had available to him philosophical ways and "tools" of thinking that he brought to bear upon his apostolic activity.

2.a. *Locating Paul as a Product of His Time*

As is the case with all of us, Paul was a product of his time. This, of course, is no new claim, but the depths of its significance continue to be plumbed by scholars of the New Testament. These depths, however, have often proved difficult to fathom, leading Edwin Judge to remark that "the trouble with Paul has always been to put him in his place" (1972, 19). Although the study of *Paulus hellenisticus*, to use Malherbe's term, tended to wane during the middle of the twentieth century, it has enjoyed a recent revival of interest, which connects one branch of more recent Pauline studies with those typical of the beginning of the twentieth century. Thus, the early-twentieth-century comment by Johannes Weiss continues to ring true: "students of the New Testament should know Seneca, Epictetus, Plutarch, Lucian, Musonius, Marcus Aurelius, and Cicero intimately, and pursue the study of the New Testament with Hans von Arnim's collection of Stoic texts at their elbows" (Malherbe 1989, 3). Perhaps the only modification we would make to Weiss's comment is to increase the list of relevant Hellenistic writers to include the likes of Philodemus and Epicurus.

One of the basic goals of this book, and Pauline studies in general, is to further consider *Paulus hellenisticus* in order to further understand *Paulus christianus*—the most prominent figure in the foundation of Christian thought. Implied in this goal is the assumption that the (primarily Hellenistic) culture in which Paul lived had a significant influence on the way he thought and interpreted the world around him. It easily follows that to understand more about his relationship with that culture is to give us a clearer picture of the processes behind Paul's thinking and writing. Thus, another claim is that *Paulus hellenisticus* forms an unconscious context, or "pre-text," and foundation for *Paulus christianus*. The general interest of this book, with respect to *Paulus hellenisticus*, is the language of the moral philosophers and Paul's adaptation and use of that language for his own apostolic purposes.

There is little risk in claiming that Paul can be classified as a moral philosopher or a psychagogue. Scholars such as Abraham Malherbe have spent much of their academic lives compiling copious documentation that evidences and articulates the affinity of Paul's activity among various churches in the mid–first century C.E. with the activity of the Hellenistic moral philosophers.[4] However, my purpose here is simply to survey some of the principles held by ancient philosophers that led to the popularizing of philosophy and thus enabled philosophical concepts to enter into the social discourse of the average educated individual as "intellectual equipment"[5] or to function as "the general intellectual currency" (Judge 1972, 33)—the sort of equipment used or currency traded by Paul to establish and nurture his churches, which forms the background of his epistolary efforts, and which constrains his discourse. However, it is important to note that the existence of such "intellectual equipment" does not also mean that those who used it were conscious that it was anything more than the norm. It is possible that highly educated individuals may have been, but as these devices filtered into the popular discourse, they would have eventually lost their specialized opacity and become as transparent as the discourse itself. Yet this does not mean that the functional features of such "equipment" were lost when it entered into social discourse. The point is that social discourse would be altered by its absorption of this conceptual equipment.

More specifically, it is the presence of a social discourse behind the writing of Paul which forms the interest here, and not the philosophical discourses themselves. Understanding Hellenistic moral philosophy in relation to Paul is a matter of understanding "philosophy . . . as a phenomenon of education *and* society" (Judge 1972, 32, emphasis added).[6] Recognizing this allows us to consider a framework according to which we can put Paul "in his place" as a possible participant in this social phenomenon of increased awareness and use of moral-philosophical

---

[4] See the bibliography in Balch, Ferguson, and Meeks 1990.

[5] Miriam Griffin uses this phrase in her description of the intellectual developments of the Ciceronian age. It is helpful because it recognizes the reality that people develop principles, ideas, and categories of thought in order *to do things with them* (read "function"), in the same way that people develop equipment to achieve various tasks (Griffin 1994, 728).

[6] I add the emphasis here to draw attention to Judge's point that philosophy was a part of society, not simply education, and as a part of society it naturally influenced the construction of conventions within society.

concepts. This means locating Paul in the context of the philosophical mood of the educated classes[7] of Greco-Roman society in order to appreciate more of the nature of the social discourse according to which Paul thought, wrote, and taught.

2.b. *Locating Paul among the Philosophers*

There are a number of close parallels to Paul when we think of the various groups of moral philosophers in the Greco-Roman world. Abraham Malherbe has presented Paul in terms of the gentle Cynics; more recently, Clarence Glad has suggested that the Epicurean parallel is preferred when one considers Paul's psychagogic activity in his nurturing of the early Christian communities (1995, 4), and Troels Engberg-Pedersen has emphasized the Stoic elements in Paul's writing (1994b; 2000). Of course, it is not a matter of choosing one over another of these parallels as the diversity between the publications of these scholars demonstrates,[8] it is rather a matter of recognizing that such structures[9] were there for the using as "intellectual equipment" by moral leaders—particularly when such leaders did not see themselves as moralists first and leaders second, and had no particular allegiance to a given philosophical school.

With respect to Paul, the implication is that there were patterns or categories of thought in existence which were created by the philosophical schools over a period of time, which were subsequently integrated into the culture to the degree that someone with Paul's education and life experience would encounter them both unconsciously as cultural norm, and consciously as moral philosophy in the "classroom."[10] The result is that when Paul goes to think about how he should act toward those whom he is guiding (the Philippian Christian community, for example)—what he should say to them, how he should say it to them, the best ways to bring them around to his way of thinking, even his own sense of responsibility toward them—he will naturally be inclined to employ the rhetorical topics and strategies, and even to conceptualize these things according to what seems normal to him—what I am here calling the "discourse" of his culture. This does not deny that Paul was innovative, or that he modified Jewish and Hellenistic values in order to cultivate a "Christian morality."

---

[7] On the idea that Paul worked with the educated classes, see Judge 1960, 60; 1972, 28. More recently, Meeks (1983, 51) and Malherbe (1983a, 29) have both advocated and developed Judge's original claims; see also Cameron 1994, 36–37. All this is contrary to Deissmann 1957, 51.

[8] This is not to suggest that these scholars claim that the only way to understand Paul is according to one particular school; indeed, the opposite is true.

[9] By "structures" I mean philosophical systems *and* structures of thought that are less conscious than the formal system, but that are produced by that system.

[10] Not everything in society, of course, is encountered unconsciously. As an educated individual, it is probable that Paul was exposed to various moral philosophical treatises.

The important point is that his modification, innovation, and cultivation all begin with something which is *already* there and that the subsequent Christian discourse which developed from Paul's writings is really based on the social discourse of his culture. Indeed, Averil Cameron sees that the Christians are "reflecting and responding to the same influences that were making themselves felt on pagan discourse," and that even when we get a century or two beyond the first Christians there is still surprisingly little difference between pagan and Christian discourse and conceptual schema (1994, 7). Or as Wayne Meeks has it:

> The daily practice of most church members was doubtless indistinguishable in most respects from that of their unconverted neighbors. Differences in moral judgment and practice between one Christian, or group of Christians, and another often seem as great as or greater than differences between the Christians and the "pagans." Attempts to discover overt changes in those areas of public discourse, practice, or legislation that we would identify as morally sensitive . . . turn up embarrassingly few examples of a clear difference that could be ascribed to Christian influence. (1993, 2)

An example of both this discourse at work and its content is found in Seneca. In a discussion on the efficacy of philosophical precepts for the person progressing toward the philosophical *telos*,[11] Seneca cites some of these "brief but weighty" precepts:

> "Nothing in excess," "The greedy mind is satisfied by no gains," "You must expect to be treated by others as you yourself have treated them." We receive a sort of shock when we hear such sayings; no one ever thinks of doubting them or of asking: "Why?" So strongly, indeed, does mere truth, accompanied by reason, attract us. (*Ep.* 94.43)

The "shock" (*ictus*) to which Seneca refers is not one of incredulity toward the precepts; it is rather a reference to the weight of their perceived *veritas*. When Seneca claims that no one ever thinks of doubting the *veritas* of these precepts, he assumes the existence of a shared set of cultural norms, what he calls "mere truth" (*ipsa veritas*), without which his example has no currency. These precepts appear to have *veritas* because they are entirely confluent with the complex of cultural expectations and codes which made up the discourse of that society. They have great effect because they summarize the ideals of the culture in brief but potent linguistic structures.

3. Paul and Psychagogy

The need for a cultural matrix to offer perspective presents Greco-Roman psychagogy to us as a valuable means for understanding Paul. The importance of psychagogy is that while we may say that it is a somewhat

---

[11] Typically understood as εὐδαιμονία ("happiness") as a result of virtue.

singular feature of Greco-Roman society, it nonetheless contains within it a complex of social features which have often been linked to Paul as separate elements of his cultural context, but not necessarily as a previously established, integrated structure. For example, many of the features of Greco-Roman philosophy and morality (such as models of friendship, pedagogy, leadership, exhortation, admonition, and so forth), which have frequently been noted in Paul's letters, find a confluence in the social model of the Greco-Roman psychagogue. As we study the psychagogue we begin to give more context, and thus more significance, to some of Paul's practices which have less obviously originated in the culture of Greco-Roman philosophy.

While the relationship between Paul and moral philosophy is not a new suggestion, it has not been until more recently that the connection has been as well demonstrated as it has been by Abraham Malherbe and Clarence Glad. Glad makes the important point that "we are indeed misguided if we exclude a pedagogical passion from Paul's nurturing paternity" (1996a, 92). As with every attempt to locate Paul within his cultural environment, it is not so much that Paul *is* a psychagogue or a Greco-Roman moral philosopher, or whatever we may want to say he is, rather that such social realities and behavioral patterns were in place as a part of the social discourse, functioning as a set of options for him to utilize as the need arose on a given occasion. Thus, as Glad points out, "it is not important that we be able to classify Paul as a 'psychagogue' but rather that we recognize his participation in a widespread 'psychagogic' activity" (1996a, 60). That is, it is important that we recognize Paul's adherence to the already available social model of the psychagogue—something exemplified in the literary relationship between Seneca and Lucilius, in which Seneca assumes an authoritative posture and gently reproaches and exhorts Lucilius to spiritual and moral maturity.[12] One may even want to avoid suggesting that Paul was conscious of such adherence; nonetheless, it must be the case that when Paul understood and enacted his role among the churches, he understood and enacted that role in terms familiar to him as a member of that culture (to whatever degree we can generalize the Greco-Roman world as a unified culture) and to his readers as members of that culture. Hence Alexander's statement that

> if we have learned anything from the last twenty years of New Testament scholarship, it is that "thought" does not operate in a kind of disembodied noetic sphere independent of personal and social structuring. Thought is an activity of thinkers, and thinkers are tied in to certain patterns of behavior, restricted to certain specific forms of communication, by the society they live in. (1994, 60)

The point to be made here is that, given his role as a spiritual and

---

[12] On Seneca as psychagogue, see Hadot 1969.

moral guide, the psychagogic model, or established norm, presents itself to Paul (unconsciously, at the very least) as a prudent path to follow in his endeavor to serve as an effective leader in that society. Hence Glad's claim that "'Hellenistic psychagogy' or the 'guidance of souls' among Greeks and Romans reflects a common leadership model available to and appropriated by Paul" and was "a widespread model of spiritual and ethical guidance, used in one way or another by most moralists of the Hellenistic period" (1996a, 57). The availability of that convention is well stated by Malherbe: "[I]t was the Epicureans who had developed the system of psychagogy, but what Philodemus says in the first century B.C.E. is reflected in the writings of Seneca, Paul's Stoic contemporary, and a generation later by the Platonist Plutarch. In short, the concerns and techniques that interest us were widespread at the time Paul wrote" (1987, 84). Thus, when we speak of the "purpose" of Philippians, the social models available to Paul play a role in both the way Paul construes his responsibility to his churches and the form in which that responsibility is manifested.

If we were to summarize Paul's purposes as an attempt to maintain his relationship with the church, which assumes also the attempt to maintain the *nature* of that relationship—the maintenance of group purity, stability, and progress—then we also summarize the basic goals of any Hellenistic psychagogue. Recognizing all this, Stanley Stowers labels Philippians as either a "hortatory or psychagogic letter of friendship" (1991, 108). Stowers also notes that Paul

> describes himself as a psychagogue for the Philippians when he says "but to remain in the flesh is more necessary on your account. . . . I shall remain and continue with you all, for your progress and joy in the faith" (1:24–25). . . . Throughout the letter, Paul presents himself as a model of one who is struggling in this process. He presses on toward the goal and strains forward to the prize. (1991, 108–9)

So why is it important to observe these psychagogic issues with respect to Paul? Philippians 1:12–18 is typically read as a minor introductory section of the epistle and thus as primarily a description of Paul's historical circumstances. It is the contention of this book, however, that this section is (1) the main reason for writing, and (2) is not simply historical data, but psychagogic/friendship rhetoric employed to rectify any potential perceptions of a discrepancy between Paul's word and deed. If we read this section of the epistle in the light of the tensions in moral discourse between the conventions of word and deed, and frank speech (friend and flatterer), we begin to see how Paul's language adheres to, and is even governed by, these well-established social conventions.

3.a. *What Is* Psychagogia?

Psychagogia was originally a reference to the leading of souls through the nether world and evoking the souls of the dead.[13] It then took the more familiar, metaphorical referents of persuasion and influence through speech. Thus, Socrates defines rhetoric as an "entirely psychagogic art" (ὅλον . . . τέχνη ψυχαγωγία) which is conducted "through words" not in the public courts alone but also in private (Plato, *Phaedr.* 261A–B).[14] Along with this came both the positive connotation of influencing people for good and the negative connotation of beguilement. In the *Phaedrus*, Socrates' point is to elucidate the difference between good and bad uses of rhetoric (Isocratean rhetoric in particular)[15] and thus also the difference between the two uses of *psychagogia* (see Asmis 1986, 157).

Rhetoric, and thus *psychagogia*, had some delightfully treacherous qualities according to Plato (among others): it is the art by which one thing can be presented as just and unjust at the same time to the same people; thus it is ἀντιλογική (*Phaedr.* 261B–E) or the "art of opposition" (Asmis 1986, 155); it is the art of deception (ἀπάτη; Plato, *Phaedr.* 261E–262A); it is the beguilement of the appetites of the soul via images and phantasms (Plato, *Tim.* 71A).[16] Or, in Isocrates' view, it is the ability to beguile through poetic device (*Evag.* 10). In the Shepherd of Hermas the participle is used to explain the effects of wealth, in that it leads the soul astray (Shepherd of Hermas, *Vis.* 3.6.6).

The Epicurean Polystratus has an interesting discussion on the nature of the philosopher that also places *psychagogia* in rather bad company. He urges that the true philosopher should not proceed with syllogisms or inductions (συλλογισμοὺς ἤ ἐπαγωγάς περαίνοντας) nor become a peddler of sentences (ῥησικοποῦντας) (col. 13.26–29); rather, he should investigate nature "straightly"[17] (φυσιολογήσαντας ὀρθῶς; col. 14.27–16.8)—"in so doing,

---

[13] See LSJ, 2026. Note also the very interesting use of ψυχαγωγ- cognates in Lucian. When Lucian discourses on contemporaneous issues, he uses it as a reference to amusement (*Ver. hist.* 1.2; *Nigr.* 18, 21; *Bis. acc.* 10), but when he discourses on the ancient myths he employs the ancient referent of leading the souls of the dead (*Dial. d.* 4.1; 11.4). For a comprehensive discussion of the development of ψυχαγωγεῖν from being a reference to the leading of departed souls to the nether world, to a reference to moral exhortation, see Glad 1995, 18; see also Asmis 1986.

[14] Plato, *Phaedr.* 261 A–B; note also *Phaedr.* 271 C–D where he rather matter-of-factly says that the function of speech is to lead the soul (ψυχαγωγία).

[15] "It is evident that *those who desire to command the attention of their hearers must abstain from admonition and advice, and must say the kind of things which they see are most pleasing to the crowd*" (Isocrates, *Ad Nic.* 49 [Norlin, LCL], emphasis added).

[16] But note that it was Plato's goal in the *Phaedrus* to advocate a positive use of *psychagogia* as positive moral guidance (see *Phaedr.* 260E–272B; 277B–C).

[17] It is interesting to consider that this reference to the necessity of the philosophical investigation being conducted "straightly" (ὀρθῶς, col. 14.24) may be the

one dispels the falsities handed down through the myths and the poets; thus one also dispels every fear and empty suspicion, along with the rest of the soul's affectations (πάθη) that such falsities produce; thereby attaining the goal of the good life." He then points out that though there are those who on the one hand use syllogisms and axioms, on the other hand there are those who say the same things but whose motives are for the adulation *or* deception of their neighbors (πρὸς τὸν πλησίον ἀρεσκείας ἤ ἀπάτης),[18] who contrive to gain momentary approval and persuasion (ψυχαγωγίαν). Thus, we find this Epicurean leader associating *psychagogia* with peddling sentences, attempts to procure favor, deception, and other abuses of rhetoric. The duplicitous nature of *psychagogia* is, however, merely reflective of the duplicitous nature of all speech, namely its "pharmacological" nature.

It is therefore no real surprise that we do not see Paul or his contemporaries using this word to refer to their own moral leadership. The negative connotations evoked by *psychagogia*, and the subsequent application of the term to the flatterer (κολάξ) and the sycophant (ἄρεσκος), meant that, in the late republic and early empire, it was little used as a positive reference (Glad 1996a, 60). This, however, does not change the social reality of the psychagogue; it merely changes the way in which people referred to it.

The fact was that, during the first century, referring to someone as a "philosopher" was tantamount to referring to that person as having the basic qualities of the psychagogue. Lutz, summarizing Musonius, comments that the "primary concern of philosophy is the care of the soul. . . . [F]rom our surroundings we have become morally ill. It is philosophy alone which can cure us by its remedy of reason (27–28)." Hence we have Seneca's understanding that the philosopher is "the pedagogue of the human race" (*Ep.* 89.13) and Maximus of Tyre's understanding that care of the soul was the product of the philosopher's rational teaching (*Dissertationes* 1.2.61–63).

The desire for a moral guide is something which obviously parallels the popularizing of moral philosophy (see Malherbe 1986, 13), and "ample evidence exists for the social practice of searching for a mature guide" (Glad 1996a, 63; see also Glad 1995, 53; Galen, *On the Doctrines of Hippocrates and Plato* 2.5.3–7; *On the Passions and Errors of the Soul* 1.1; 3.6–10; Justin Martyr, *Dialogue with Trypho*, 2.3–6; Isocrates *Antid.* 290). Indeed, that the social and moral reality of psychagogy was pervasive is demonstrated in part by the number of expressions of a need for moral guidance (note Seneca, *Ep.* 52.2). In fact, the degree to which people sought some-

---

necessary complement of παρρησία, in that παρρησία is, for the most part, the communication of that investigation. Note that Polystratus then uses παρρησία soon after (in col. 16.29–17.1) as a reference to the communication of investigation (but see the rest of the Polystratus discussion for context).

[18] Note the possibility of both adulation (ἀρεσκείας) and deception (ἀπάτης) being generated by the one speech-act.

one to fulfill the role of a psychagogue was common enough for Lucian to lend the practice some satirical attention. In his *Hermotimus* he takes great delight in poking fun at a fellow who seems to be forever seeking guidance and never arriving at the point to which he is supposedly being guided. Furthermore, looking for a guide was common enough for Seneca to set down guidelines for the task (*Ep.* 52.1–9). Seneca elsewhere cites Epicurus as suggesting that we all should have a person of high character in our lives who helps govern our character (Seneca, *Ep.* 11.8–10 = Usener Frag. 210). Quintilian states that while virtue is somewhat natural, it "will require to be perfected by instruction" (12.2.1). For Plutarch, one good sign that someone was progressing toward virtue was that the person was willing to submit to someone who would determine his problems and admonish him ("Progress in Virtue" 82A). For Clement of Alexandria, the role of the psychagogue was common enough to be confluent with the role of the pedagogue, which was "both to lead and admonish the soul" (*Protrepticus und Paedagogus* 261.23–24).

It is important to recognize that the main tool of the philosopher-psychagogue was speech, yet at the same time it was the main weakness, since speech bears no marks of veracity. Thus, a basic responsibility borne by the philosopher-psychagogue was to live in a manner which validated the truthfulness of his message. The easiest way for anyone to detect a pseudo-psychagogue was to discover that what he said and what he did were at odds with each other. This is typically seen in the common, fundamental requirement for one's deeds to be confluent with one's words. Within this word-deed complex arise the common moral philosophical *topoi* of frankness (παρρησία) and flattery (κολακεία).

Furthermore, the structural relationship with friendship conventions[19] implies that for the genuine psychagogue to practice his art, he must assume a degree of responsibility toward the person(s) being guided. Without a sense of duty toward the patient, there is no impetus for genuine admonition. Even if the guide's duty were only the integrity of the philosophy, it still implies a responsibility toward the patient.[20]

An important aspect of this is the fact that the psychagogic process

---

[19] Malherbe adds to this the social convention of a "father," and of a "nurse"; see the overall discussions in Malherbe 1970; 1987. Glad also connects the father and friend conventions in Glad 1996a, 72. Note also the sentiments offered by Maximus of Tyre, who felt that the guidance philosophy offered was similar to that offered by a friend and construes philosophical teaching in terms of the role of a true friend (*Orations* 1.2 [Trapp, 7] = *Dissertationes* 1.2.60); also note Epictetus, *Diatr.* 3.13.18–23; 2.17.1–2; 2.22.7–10; Diogenes Laertius 6.30, where Diogenes compares himself to a helmsman or a physician.

[20] It was common among philosophers to assume that all people had a duty toward philosophy, which incorporated the principle that others would benefit from it. See Musonius 2.36–38; 16.104.30–32; 16.106; Seneca, *Ep.* 90.1; Diogenes 21.8–9; 35; also Heraclitus 9.210.20–21; Diogenes Laertius 10.122; 10.83, 85.

was a part of a larger, reciprocal process of mutual affection (see Malherbe 1987, 84). "Whatever the group, and however it might be structured, they shared a concern for each other. Those who led in exhorting were to do so out of friendship and a genuine desire to help" (Malherbe 1987, 88). Combining this relational structure with the previously mentioned desire to seek out a mature guide suggests that the desire itself is "not an exercise in solitude, but a true social practice" (Foucault 1986, 3:51), or even an "intensification of social relations" (Foucault 1986, 3:53). "The care of the self appears therefore as intrinsically linked to a 'soul service' [psychagogy], which includes the possibility of round exchanges with the other and a system of reciprocal obligations" (Foucault 1986, 3:54; also Glad 1996a, 74).

This reciprocal process producing obligation is of critical import to our understanding of Paul's activity in the writing of Philippians. As a psychagogue, Paul has a sense of responsibility or obligation to the Philippians. This obligation has naturally formed itself in terms of Paul's Christian gospel and manifests itself in Paul's activity as a literate apostle. That is, Paul has a specific task to perform in the Philippian community (the same specific task he has everywhere else), which is to involve them in the gospel. He is going to seek the completion of that task in the socially constructed conventions available to him; thus, psychagogy presents itself as a suitable set of conventions for our understanding of Paul's practices within that society. Furthermore, taking our leave from Foucault, we should understand this practice as an intensification of social relations between Paul and the Philippians. As their psychagogue, Paul has a special set of relations to the Philippians. As the recipients of Paul's psychagogy, the Philippians have a special set of relations to Paul. These relationships are expressed in their sense of responsibility toward each other. For the Philippians it has been their submission to Paul's authority, and their support of his mission. For Paul it has been his devotion to them as an apostle through his writing to them, sending them ambassadors, writing them letters, encouraging them in general, and, not least, his willingness to remain alive when he would prefer to die.

Paul's sense of obligation, both to his followers and to his apostolic assignment, would naturally mean that he would be willing to take up any challenges threatening either of those obligations. However, any question concerning the validity of his gospel, any questioning of the foundational subtext of that gospel (the story of Paul and the gospel), will naturally take place along socially conventional lines, and Paul's reactions are also going to be in terms of the social conventions available to him. Just how this works out in Philippians is the subject of the following chapter.

3.b. *Psychagogy and the Language of Truth and Friendship*

There is a close relationship between psychagogy and friendship. In distinct contrast to the flatterer, the psychagogue was very much a true friend. Interestingly, the manner in which the falsehood of the friend or the psychagogue was determined was primarily through the relationship between speech and action.

Seneca provides for us a model for understanding this connection which we also see in Paul; Seneca is both a psychagogue and a friend to Lucilius in a similar way that Paul is both psychagogue and friend to the Philippians. Traditionally, psychagogy was the practice of one person, a psychagogue, guiding the life, or "soul," of others. Naturally, a psychagogue would have been a person who was perceived to be superior in some way so as to be worthy of imitation.[21] But placing oneself in the hands of a psychagogue left one open to various abuses from *pseudo*-psychagogues. It was important, therefore, to establish whether a person was a genuine psychagogue or a pseudo-psychagogue.

As discussed earlier, Plato makes the point that the psychagogue conducts his business, the leading of the soul, through words[22] (ψυχαγωγία τις διὰ λόγων), and this highlights precisely the source of the problem: words themselves bear no mark as to whether they are true or false; thus, in this same work, *Phaedrus*, Plato constructs language, writing in particular, as a *pharmakon*, at once a remedy and a poison (274C–278B, esp. 274E–275A). Of course, this issue of "genuine" versus "pretext," or as we find in our passage in Phil 1:18, ἀλήθεια versus πρόφασις, was frequently the subject of philosophical and moral discourse, particularly with respect to such *topoi* as friendship, flattery, and psychagogy, not to mention those *topoi* associated with sophistry and the like.

Such conventions developed common safeguards for, in our case, protecting oneself from stumbling into the semantic snares of pseudo-psychagogues. One can tell a genuine psychagogue from a false one by observing whether his life (deeds) matched his philosophical teaching (words), and a genuine psychagogue, like a genuine friend, speaks with παρρησία.[23] Thus, in moral exhortation, or psychagogic literature, one constantly finds claims to a continuity between word and deed, and therefore to frank speech (παρρησία), for which a working definition could be: a mode of communication (speech/writing) intended to refer *by virtue of itself* to the continuity between word and deed. That is, frank speech was both word and deed.

We also find these very claims in Paul. The classic example is Paul's comments in 1 Thess 2:5–6, where he says that he and his retinue did not come with words of flattery (ἐν λόγῳ κολακείας), nor with the pretext of

---

[21] On mimesis in antiquity see Castelli 1991, 59–87; note also Castelli 1991, 21, for a discussion on how mimesis reinscribes power structures and social hierarchies.

[22] For a fuller, original discussion see Plato, *Phaedr.* 260E–272B; 277BC.

[23] Although, as we see in Philippians, even παρρησία (bold speech) was eventually mimicked further, compounding the problem of how to tell a flatterer from a friend, or πρόφασις from ἀλήθεια (see Phil 1:18).

greed (ἐν προφάσει πλεονεξίας), nor seeking the glory of men. Paul goes on to remind the Thessalonians that they themselves are aware of his labors among them; he thereby reinforces the idea that he was a genuine and not a pseudo-psychagogue, thus also contributing to a validation of his gospel. Note also 1 Cor 2:4, where Paul claims that his message and preaching were not in persuasive words of wisdom, but rather in the *demonstration* of the spirit and power (ἐν ἀποδείξει πνεύματος καὶ δυνάμεως).

As discussed earlier, by the time Paul entered into the Greco-Roman world, the term "psychagogue" appears to have fallen out of use, perhaps due to the abuses of pseudo-psychagogues.[24] A general skepticism had developed in Hellenistic culture concerning the intentions of someone who might claim to be a guide of the soul but who in fact was more interested in guiding one's money into his own purse. This is the same suspicion that we find being directed toward the sophists, and which Paul himself affirms in order to create a distinct contrast to his own rhetorical activity. Nonetheless, psychagogic activity itself was alive and well at this time, albeit operating under various other labels, and offers itself as one of the cultural analogues for our interpretation of Paul.[25]

The well-established (note Malherbe 1987, 84; Glad 1996a, 60) practice of psychagogy in the ancient world offers a set of ethico-cultural conventions according to which we could say that Paul was constrained to operate. As culturally accepted norms, these ideals provide an easily accessible structure for when one had occasion to wax eloquent on moral and ethical issues. More to the point, the structures or discourse associated with psychagogy had, by the time of Paul, entered into the wider populace as normative. Thus we hear Engberg-Pedersen suggest that Stoic ideals and structures became a part of the "ordinary discourse at a certain level" (Engberg-Pedersen 1994b, 261), that is, a part of their particular structure of codes of significance. Thus, it is not necessary to say that Paul was formally a psychagogue in order for us to accept that Paul employed structures formally associated with psychagogy.[26] Once such a structure enters into the discourse of a culture it enters into a reciprocal relationship of affirming and being affirmed by that culture.[27] Consequently, it is difficult, if not impossible, to speak of the degree to

---

[24] Note again Glad 1996a, 60–61.

[25] That is, as stated earlier, the social convention remained, what changed was the way in which people referred to it.

[26] To cite Glad again: "it is not important that we be able to classify Paul as a 'psychagogue' but rather that we recognize his participation in a widespread 'psychagogic' activity" (1996a, 60).

[27] This subscribes to fundamental human orders. Note, for example, Berger and Luckmann's discussion on social interaction and the foundation for knowledge in everyday life (Berger and Luckmann 1967, 28–34).

which Paul was conscious of the psychagogic analogue, even though his language is often rather psychagogic.

Genuine psychagogues, like genuine friends, assumed a certain responsibility toward those being led. More specifically, they were interested in the ethical or moral outliving of their discourse (their "gospel") in the lives of their followers. As a result, we find that the rhetoric of the psychagogues focuses on creating within the follower an apologetic discourse that enables the follower to deal with potential threats to the ideals of the psychagogic discourse in general. We find Paul doing this very thing in Phil 1, although it is specifically targeted toward the Christian community and participates within fundamental sociological practices of group maintenance.[28]

Paul's letter is mainly about reassuring the Philippians. He is in a negative situation, and he needs to ensure that the way the Philippians interpret his imprisonment is confluent with the gospel/discourse he has preached to them, lest there appear some anomaly between the gospel he has preached and its practical ability, that is, initially at least, between word and deed. Thus, employing common *topoi* associated with psychagogic and friendship rhetoric (such as "progress" and "frank speech"), the discourse Paul inserts into the situation works to reassure the Philippians that the situation is not a negative comment on the adequacy of the gospel he has preached. It rather becomes a positive example of its power; thus, he presents a confluence between the claims of the gospel and its power.[29] Paul's sense of responsibility to the Philippians, his pastoral need to reassure them, naturally affects his rhetoric.[30] The various *topoi* Paul employs and his disposition toward the various issues he encounters are naturally governed by his psychagogic or pastoral agenda. I would suggest that Paul's reluctance to articulate his usual theologically charged rebuke of the selfish preachers in Phil 1 is due, at least in part, to his psychagogic agenda in this reassuring section of the epistle.

What is of interest here in the first chapter of Philippians is that Paul's "detour"[31] into the discussion of the good and bad preachers is a way to

---

[28] The goal of psychagogic discourse was essentially teleological, seeking to enable the student to attain the great goals of moral philosophy: happiness, being good, and so on.

[29] Note again 1 Cor 2:4: "[M]y message and my proclamation were not in persuasive words of wisdom, rather in the demonstration of the Spirit and of power."

[30] Which is interesting in light of the moral ideal to leave speech "unaffected" (see Seneca, *Ep.* 75.1; Plutarch, "How to Tell a Flatterer from a Friend" 62C, and the citation from Euripides, *Phoen.* 469, 472; Plutarch, "On Stoic Self-Contradictions" 1047A–B, and the citation from Chrysippus, *SVF* 2.297–98). On frank speech and thus "unaffected" speech as the "new virtue," see De Witt 1935, 313.

[31] Philippians 1:12–18a is unsatisfactorily, but often, seen as an excursus by commentators. My point would be that it is not only an integral, but a central feature of the function of Philippians.

deal with the potential discrepancy between word and deed in his own situation. That is, Paul's discussion of the two preachers, and 1:18 in particular, shows that when it comes to the gospel, the Philippians are to break out of the cultural norm of evaluating discourse according to this word-deed binary structure. Paul wants them to view the gospel message as being a sort of self-validating discourse. But as I say, the discussion of the two kinds of preachers is a way of making this point, which can then bracket Paul's own imprisoned situation so that it does not affect the Philippians' evaluation of the truth of the gospel message. At the same time, Paul does not discount the value of the cultural norm, and a few verses later (1:20) makes a claim to frank speech and continuity between word and deed with respect to his own integrity. Thus, we end up with Paul claiming that, on the one hand, the truth of the gospel is not judged by human circumstances. But, on the other hand, Paul recognizes that humans themselves are still judged by the traditional word-deed structure. I shall develop this strange division in chapter 4.

3.c. *Frank Speech, the Word-Deed Convention, and Letter Writing*

Language was the well-honed instrument of the psychagogue.[32] The psychagogue applied this instrument both to speech and to writing, both treatises and letters. This also harks back to the question of the degree to which Paul's pastoral or psychagogic concerns affect his rhetoric.

Seneca, a moral philosopher, psychagogue, and Pauline contemporary, presents us with an interesting example of psychagogic ideals being represented in the form and content of his epistles.[33] He begins *Ep.* 75 with a rebuke:

> You [Lucilius] have been complaining that my letters to you are rather carelessly written. Now who talks carefully unless he also desires to talk affectedly? I prefer that my letters should be just what my conversation would be if you and I were sitting in one another's company or taking walks together, spontaneous and easy, for my letters have nothing strained or artificial about them. If it were possible, I should prefer to show, rather than speak, my feelings. . . . I should like to convince you entirely of this one fact, that I feel whatever I say, that I not only feel it, but am wedded to it.

Lucilius is shown to be entangled in concerns about formal epistolary structure, rather than paying more attention to the *function* of Seneca's letter writing. Lucilius may think he is being a superior epistolist by levelling such a critique at Seneca, but Seneca's reply invokes the established epistolary theorists when he says that he wants his letters to be like an ac-

---

[32] Note again Plato's comment that the psychagogue leads the soul through words.

[33] Note that the letters of Epicurus also provide philosophical parallels with the letters of the New Testament; see the discussion in De Witt 1954, 32.

tual conversation. D. A. Russell suggests that "Seneca's view is bound up, as the context shows, with his insistence that *res* [things] matter more than *verba* [words], and that the problem of philosophy is a matter of not only intellect (*ingenium*) but also of the soul (*animus*)" (Russell 1974, 73). Or as Seneca puts it, "let it [eloquence] be of such a kind that it displays facts and not itself. It and the other arts are wholly concerned with cleverness; but our business is the soul" (*Ep.* 75.5). And later, "Are you concerned about words [*verba*]? Rejoice this instant if you can cope with things [*res*]" (*Ep.* 75.7). Here Seneca *seemingly* drives a moral wedge between language (or *verba*) and that which it attempts to signify (*res*, real things); but, actually, he is distinguishing between two kinds of speech: artificial (in the technical sense, yet invoking its "figurative" sense) and plain or "frank" speech.

The point is that although it stood apart from what Lucilius assumed to be normal, Seneca's deviation from standard epistolary form has its roots in the fact that he values the *function* of the communication more highly than the communication itself, which perhaps we might distinguish in his terms as being the priority of the soul over mere words, which could in fact entangle the soul. This also implies that he sees language or communication as a two-tiered structure. Seneca's question "Who talks carefully unless he also desires to talk affectedly?" is very much a reflection of standard Hellenistic ideals of frank speech, that is, of παρρησία.

3.c.i. *Frank speech.* Παρρησία took on significance in Periclean Athens as the symbol of freedom, since nothing symbolized personal freedom as much as the freedom of speech[34]—a point reinforced by the fact that slaves did not have this freedom (see further Euripides, *Phoen.* 390; Radin 1927, 215–20; Bultmann 1985, 84–85). What is important for our purposes is that παρρησία was not restricted to a purely political referent. Nor did it maintain the common philosopher-versus-tyrant referent. The philosophers moved the idea of free speech, or παρρησία, from the discourse of civic freedom to the discourse of moral freedom (see Fredrickson 1996, 166).[35] Schlier notes that the original political aspect of the παρρησία had three components: the right to say anything; that the actuality of things is stated; the courage of openness (1967, 5:872–73).

The latter two of Schlier's components appear to be those which developed into the use employed by the philosophers for their moral interests. It is not difficult to imagine how "the courage to be open" could

---

[34] The reason is that it represented political openness. This of course was something in which the Greeks took great pride; see Radin 1927, 215; Humphreys 1978, 185.

[35] For the Cynics, παρρησία was a most beautiful thing, a moral virtue, a property of the wise (Diogenes Laertius 6.69). The Cynics bear out the relationship of παρρησία to truth very well.

convert into the psychagogic activity and frankness of speech employed in the pedagogy and healing of the student/patient. The idea of "the actuality of things being stated" fits easily converted into philosophy by virtue of signifying "a close relation to truth (ἀλήθεια)" (Schlier 1967, 5:873). Thus, Bultmann, recognizing the shift away from the classical usage of παρρησία, notes that Paul's use of παρρησία in 2 Cor 2:12 "is not openness toward God [a common early Christian referent], but rather the apostle's openness toward his hearers in his public activity" (1985, 85).[36]

As with Bultmann's observation, παρρησία was a symbol of truth and openness of the philosopher toward his audience and among philosophical friends. Initially, this use is most prominent among the Epicureans, for whom παρρησία was a "corollary to their cardinal principle of friendship" (De Witt 1935, 312). While prominent among the Epicureans, it was not exclusively Epicurean. Even Aristotle comments that friends should always use frankness of speech toward each other (*Eth. nic.* 9.2.9; see further Malherbe 1987, 42). It is in this environment of friendship that the definition of παρρησία undergoes development, "eventually becoming a classical topic" (De Witt 1935, 313). Contributing significantly to that development is Philodemus's own essay ΠΕΡΙ ΠΑΡΡΗΣΙΑΣ (or *On Frank Criticism*). One of the more interesting features of Philodemus's description of παρρησία is the degree to which it is to be done with gentleness (fr. 37–38), although there is, on occasion, still the need for the harsh (σκληρός) form (fr. 7, 10).

De Witt notes that "during the Augustan age the adjective *candidus*, if not the noun *candor*, took on the meaning of frank, [and] unaffected. . . . The new virtue . . . signified absolute openness of speech and conduct, without, however, implying the reproof and admonition that went with παρρησία" (1935, 313).[37] Yet παρρησία itself has not been left behind. De Witt understands that the concept of παρρησία has also developed a similar "new specialized sense."[38] This development in the use of παρρησία is where we begin to see it become a part of the psychagogic discourse. That is, the use of παρρησία as a mode of interaction within philosophical-friendship communities reintroduces the issue of responsibility. It was not outspokenness for its own sake, it was rather designed to function as a benefit for the person to whom it was directed.

This was in direct contrast to flatterers—those whose speech was de-

---

[36] Van Unnik has suggested that Christian παρρησία derives from a Semitic background. His discussion focuses on the conscious attempt by Christians to speak boldly, which is virtually the same as the classical philosopher-tyrant use of the term. I am more interested, however, in παρρησία along the lines of the "new virtue."

[37] On the virtues of *candor* see Cicero, *Amic.* 25.95.

[38] Exemplified by Varrus in Horace's *Ars poetica* (434–38); see also De Witt 1935, 313, and his discussion of Horace's *Ode to Licinius* (II, 10).

signed to procure their own interests—who tended away from bold speech so as not to destabilize their sycophantic relationship with their benefactor(s). Yet even this symbol of truth and true friendship came to be mimicked by flatterers. In fact, Plutarch is quite indignant over the fact that flatterers would dare to imitate frank speech:

> But the most unprincipled trick of all that he has is this! Perceiving that frankness of speech, by common report and belief, is the language of friendship especially (as an animal has its peculiar cry), and, on the other hand, that lack of frankness is unfriendly and ignoble, he does not allow even this to escape imitation, but, just as clever cooks employ bitter extracts and astringent flavourings to remove the cloying effect of sweet things, so flatterers apply a frankness which is not genuine or beneficial, but which, as it were, winks while it frowns, and does nothing but tickle. (Plutarch 51C–D; see also Plato, *Phaedr.* 239)

It should be made clear that this was no small issue in the ancient world. A good deal of philosophical and moral literature attempted to deal with the problem that speech can be both a poison and a remedy; it can lead the soul as well as beguile it, or according to Seneca's *Ep.* 75 it can be factual or artificial. And here is the important point; Seneca sees his freedom from form as an expression of truth, as an example of παρρησία, as a way to demonstrate the continuity between what he says and what he does. As παρρησία, freedom from formal epistolary structures can take on this definition I offered earlier, a self-reference to integrity in the attempt to become both word and deed.

3.c.ii. *Word and deed.* The relationship between παρρησία and the word-deed convention is an important one; thus, Malherbe summarizes the ancient assumption that "every philosopher's *parrēsia* should therefore be backed by character" (Malherbe 1989, 160). Plutarch states it a little more colorfully: "[T]he speech of a man light-minded and mean in character (ἐλαφροῦ δὲ καὶ φαύλου τὸ ἦθος), when it undertakes to deal in frankness, results only in evoking the retort: Wouldst thou heal others, full of sores thyself!" (Plutarch, "How to Tell a Flatterer from a Friend" 71F). In his essay on frank speech, Philodemus assumes that the teachers (pedagogue/psychagogue) who employ frank speech properly will have the deeds (ἔργων), and not just the words, to support their pedagogic and psychagogic function (fr. 16). Furthermore, the person seeking a psychagogue will seek one with both the right speech and the right practice (ἔργου) (fr. 40).

The word-deed complex is an important social convention to consider when we account for the way in which the discourse of Paul's psychagogic/apostolic activity was constrained. According to Musonius, the philosopher's "treatment should consist in showing himself not only as one who utters words which are most helpful, but as one who acts consistently with them" (Musonius 36.3–5, Lutz). As for the student, living out the philosophical teachings is the only way in which philosophy will be of any profit (Musonius 36.8–12), since, after all, "philosophy is nothing other than knowledge (ἐπιστήμη) about life" (Musonius 40.13–14, Lutz). Importantly, it even took on a theological flavor: "God is an ever present witness to our words and deeds" (Seneca, *Ep.* 83.1; *Vit. beat.* 20.5). Note also the way in which the Cynic writer Anarchasis points out that the appropriate employment of the faculty is to investigate whether one's words match one's deeds while discussing the faculty of reason the gods have afforded to the Greeks and non-Greeks alike. The important point here is that Anarchasis is not actually talking about the word-deed convention; he simply assumes it to be of valid concern to the reader (2).

In general, however, people simply expected that if someone was genuine there would be a confluence between their words and their deeds. "This was particularly applied to a philosopher who justified his exhortation by his own moral progress or attainment" (Malherbe 1986, 38), and "was generally regarded as an index to his trustworthiness" (Malherbe 1989, 57–58), or, as Glad puts it, as "two recurring prerequisites for being a psychagogue, namely self-scrutiny and consistency of word and deed" (1995, 21). Furthermore, Glad notes that the assumption was an holistic one in which speech was understood to be "an integral part of conduct" (1995, 21). For Cicero, knowledge completes itself in action, since the effect of knowledge upon one's life is the whole point of acquiring it through philosophy (*Fin.* 1.7.25; *Tusc.* 5.24–5; *Off.* 1.43.153; note further his *Acad.* 2.41.127; *Tusc.* 5.3.9; 24.69; *Fin.* 4.5.12). Indeed, Malherbe notes that "the philosopher's whole manner of life, extending in the case of the Cynics to their simple garb, could be pointed to as a deliberate demonstration of the principles they taught" (1986, 38). One need only to read through the antics of Diogenes in the *Cynic Epistles* to gain a sense of the degree to which he sought to saturate his every movement (in both senses of the word!) with his philosophical ideals.[39]

The Cynics were particularly interested in the idea of a philosopher's word being confluent with his deed. In fact, they took it so far that they practically reversed the problem; instead of privileging words, they tended to privilege deeds. Thus Crates claims that the Cynics had found some shortcut to happiness: "[T]he way that leads to happiness through words is long, but that which leads through daily deeds is a shortened regimen" (Crates 1977, 21 [Hock]; note also 13; 16; Diogenes 30). Julian, having a positive view of the Cynics, rhetorically asks: "Now what was the manner of Cynics' association with people? Deeds with them came before words." He then goes on to list a host of examples (Julian, *Or.* 7.214 B–D). For the Cynics the convention usually amounted to a sense of self-

---

[39] Though these epistles are pseudonymous, they represent the Cynic ideals of those who wrote them.

confidence in putting themselves forward as models of imitation (Lucian, *Demon.* 3; Crates 1977, 20; 21 [Hock]; Diogenes 15; 27; 29; Heraclitus 4; 7). Of course, the confluence of word and deed was not a convention peculiar to the Cynics (Malherbe 1989:57),[40] especially since the fact that Paul also adhered to this well-established and fundamental convention is all too obvious from his writings. While there are numerous examples (Rom 2:1; 15:18; 1 Cor 2:4; 1 Thess 2:5), note the interesting comment in Rom 2:24, where, after listing a set of examples (2:17–24) in which Jews failed to demonstrate confluence between word and deed, Paul then applies the Old Testament citation: "the name of God is blasphemed among the Gentiles because of you." Paul seems to employ the social standards of this convention to isolate their failure as a cause for public shame.

3.c.iii. *Letter writing.* As mentioned earlier, Seneca represents a convenient example for our understanding of Paul. To draw wide uncritical formal parallels between Seneca's and Paul's epistles would be naive. However, we can draw parallels between the similar culturally constrained motives behind each writer's relative epistolary freedom. Both writers operate with the idea that speech has a lethal dual nature and attempt to employ an openness or frankness in their writing that will demonstrate the virtue of their communication. For example, in 2 Cor 10:9–10, Paul recites a testimony by some of the Corinthians that his letters are weighty and strong, which could easily be understood as "frank"; hence Fredrickson's suggestion that "in 2 Cor 10:9–10 we learn that the severity of the so-called 'letter of tears' proved to Paul's critics in Corinth that he was capable of παρρησία" (173). It was when the Corinthians detected a difference between Paul's speech in person and the tone of his epistles that the old problem of how to tell a friend from a flatterer developed (173), that is, the issue of distinguishing between the two levels of language.[41] Moreover, Paul himself claims that his rhetorical conduct is characterized by παρρησία (normally translated in the New Testament as "boldness" or even "confidence," emphasizing a disposition of Paul's consciousness and unfortunately neglecting the rhetorical aspect of the word; Fredrickson 1996, 165), using the term itself (2 Cor 3:12; 7:4; Phil 1:20; Col 2:15; Phlm 1:8; see further Eph 3:12; 6:19; 1 Tim 3:13) and often simply employing the concept by virtue of negative reasoning; for example, in 2 Cor 2:17, Paul compares his activity to those who "peddle the

---

[40] See further examples in Cicero, *Off.* 1.65; Musonius 36.8–12; 52.8–10; Seneca, *Ep.* 108.35–38; 6.5–6; Julian *Or.* 7.214BC; Lucian, *Peregr.* 19; *Demon.* 3.

[41] This reading of 2 Cor 10:9–18 may challenge the idea that the reference in 2 Cor 10:10 to Paul's speech being "contemptible" (ἐξουθενημένος) is a comment about his inadequate rhetorical style. It would rather suggest that the problem was that what the Corinthians took to be one level of language, plain and frank speech, was actually another level, affected and artificial speech.

word of God" (καπηλεύοντες τὸν λόγον τοῦ θεοῦ), characterizing his own
activity as sincere (εἰλικρίνεια). As mentioned earlier, 1 Thess 2:5–6 is also
an important example. Paul says that he and his retinue did not come
with words of flattery (ἐν λόγῳ κολακείας), nor with the pretext of greed
(ἐν προφάσει πλεονεξίας), nor seeking the glory of men.

Paul consciously represents himself as not only characterized by
παρρησία, but also as the opposite of a flatterer. I would suggest that this
bears itself out not only in various references such as those I have mentioned, but that, as with Seneca, Paul's structuring of his epistles is
generated at least in part by this conscious activity. Not that Paul is abandoning epistolary structure; rather he employs what is necessary in order
to allow the function of communication to take place without the *apparent*
artifice of form. He is, in short, being frank, which is confluent with being
a true friend, or a genuine psychagogue. It might also be possible to go a
step further and to suggest that since, again in the vein of Seneca, Paul's
epistles go beyond the topics typically associated with letter writing and
the tradition of epistolary theory, that, as Russell says of Seneca's epistles,
they "are what Pliny calls *scholasticae litterae* . . . they belong . . . to the
philosophical line of Plato and Epicurus" (1974, 74).

4. Writing in the Greco-Roman World

Writing has been the subject of philosophical inquiry for almost as long as
there has been philosophical inquiry. While we have already discussed
the relationship of letter writing to psychagogy, in order for us to further
contextualize Paul and his epistles, it is important to investigate further
the nature and assumptions of writing in the ancient world. The study of
Paul in general, especially in theological contexts, has tended to neglect
the assumptive features of ancient writing practices. While I do not intend to discuss *all* the features of ancient writing, what I do intend to
discuss here is the fact that ancient writers understood their texts, and
language in general, to be highly functional, as opposed to simply
informational.

An example of this sort of thinking is seen in the theorist Longinus's
discussion on the sublime.[42] The real mark of good communication is "not
to persuade (εἰς πείθω) but rather transport (εἰς ἔκστασιν) them out of
themselves" (Longinus 1.4). This effect of communication upon the audience is what Longinus refers to as the "sublime" (ὕψος): "a well-timed
flash of sublimity scatters everything before it like a bolt of lightning and
reveals the full power of the speaker at a single stroke"; more important,
he compares the sublime to "the due disposal and marshalling of facts"

---

[42] Longinus is not necessarily talking about the sort of writing that Paul does,
but the point here is to observe this sense of function that good communication is
apparently supposed to have.

(Longinus 1.4). That is, it is not a benign presentation of data, but a crafted arrangement of the data for a particular purpose. Longinus assumes that the goal of the communicator is to generate an *effect* upon the audience,[43] and thus his entire work is primarily how one goes about doing precisely that (see further Atkins 1952, 2:210–53)—hence Jane Tompkins's observation that "for Longinus language is a form of power and the purpose of studying texts from the past (such as Herodotus)[44] is to acquire the skills that enable one to wield that power" (1980, 203). Thus we note, in Longinus's work, that he is clearly not interested in effect alone, but also the power of effect. So, for example, Longinus points out that one particular writer has failed because he has overdone his attempts to create effect, and the actual resulting effect is one of "confusion" and not of "intensity" (Longinus 3.1); such things are labeled as "tumors," "empty inflations, void of sincerity, as likely as not producing the opposite to the effect intended" (Longinus 3.4, Fyfe).

That we can treat Longinus as somewhat paradigmatic of a first-century understanding of literary theory is in part answered by the fact that his work was not so much an abstract theorizing of elevated literary style but a corrective response to what he observed were contemporaneous (first-century) excesses and failures (Atkins 1952, 2:213, 216). It appears that a similar document produced by Caecilius of Caleacte was the impetus for the response (Longinus 1.1; Atkins 1952, 2:213–24). However, reference to yet another theorist, Theodorus of Gadara (Longinus 3.5), suggests that Longinus (with whom Atkins believes Theodorus had a theoretical affinity) was not simply responding to Caecilius alone, rather to a general debate that extended though the first century (Atkins 1952, 2:214) between the rival schools of Theodorus and Apollodorus of Pergamum.

Going back into the tradition of communication, Tompkins further notes that "it is the consequentiality of poetry as a political force that explains Plato's decision to banish lyric and epic poets from his republic" (1980, 204). "The equation of language with power, characteristic of Greek thought at least from the time of Gorgias the rhetorician, explains the enormous energies devoted to the study of rhetoric in the ancient world" (203–4). The point of this is again well stated by Tompkins: "[A]ll modern criticism . . . takes meaning to be the object of critical investigation, for *unlike the ancients we equate language not with action but with signification*" (203, emphasis added).

When it comes to epistolary texts such as Romans and Philippians there are additional comments to be made with respect to a functional

---

[43] One criterion cited for determining whether something is "sublime" is whether the effect lasts or not (Longinus 7.3). Once again, this concept of an "effect" is understood to be the goal of the communication.

[44] See, for example, Longinus's discussion on various ancient writers in Longinus 24.

view of ancient texts. The most fundamental element of an epistle in the ancient world is a functional one in that, before anything else, the epistle is an attempt to compensate for authorial absence by creating the effect of the personal presence of the writer to the recipient. Thus Berger states that in the ancient world "letters are a substitute for presence (*Anwesenheit*)," albeit an imperfect (*unvollkommener*) substitute (*Ersatz*) (1984, 1329). Interestingly, Berger suggests that the friendship letter is not so much a type; rather, the presence of particular topics within any type can make it a "friendship" letter. In particular he cites two *topoi*: the expression of friendship, and the letter as substitute for presence (1984, 1329). Thus, one might also note that the idea of the letter as a substitute for presence should be understood as an epistolary *topos* as well as an actual function of the letter.

Koskenniemi suggests that in the ancient world "it is regarded as the most important task of letters, namely a form simply to represent this relationship (*Zusammenlebens*) during a time of spatial separation, that is, making the ἀπουσία into the παρουσία" (1956, 38). He further understands that the idea of "presence" is not only an effect upon the reader, but is something that is a part of the letter's nature, since the writer writes while experiencing the presence of the recipient as a mental reality (*geistige Wirklichkeit*) (1956, 38). This concept of presence as a "mental reality" is what Stowers later refers to as a "fictionalized personal presence" (1988, 79), and what Robert Funk believes is a highly significant structural element contributing to the function of Paul's letters (see further Funk 1967, 263–68; Beker 1984, 24).

Of course, this is not simply a Pauline matter, but a pervasive feature of Greco-Roman letters. Thraede, for example, has produced a survey of epistolary topics and their motifs from pre-Christian letters to fourth-century letters. It appears that the letter as a substitute for personal presence was quite commonplace, giving currency to Paul's attempts to invoke his authority via the letter.[45] Koskenniemi and Funk both understand that fundamental to the nature of the letter is the simple notion that it creates a way for two people or parties to compensate for the fact that they are spatially separated.

> It is in the nature of the letter that it represents not only a means for communication or a method for all that which one wants to achieve with its help, but at the same time a uniting bond, a form of spatial contact between separated people. We can also determine that the letter-writers were well aware of this significant component of the letter—and of course they needed no explanations and instructions about this on the part of the scholar. (Koskenniemi 1956, 88)[46]

---

[45] See Thraede 1970, 95–106, where he analyzes three uses of the "presence-motif" in the New Testament; see also Koskenniemi 1956, 38–42.

[46] Note also Funk's comment: "The letter is designed to extend the possibility of friendship between parties after they have become physically separated" (Funk 1967, 263–64).

In other words, it was a simple matter of course that anyone who wrote a letter assumed this to be a fundamental reality. What we want to make of these comments is to introduce a general *caveat* that we *do not allow the apparent simplicity of this assumption to belie its importance.*

Theorists like Demetrius tend not to refer directly to the concept of a fictionalized presence, but, as Koskenniemi notes, there is a definite train of thought associated with the idea (1956, 38, 40). For example, Demetrius understands the letter to be almost an "image" of the sender's soul (Demetrius, *On Style* 227). In Pseudo-Demetrius's example of the friendly letter, he writes: "Even though I have been separated from you for a long time, I suffer this only in body" (Pseudo-Demetrius, "Epistolary Types" 1.10–11, Malherbe 1988); later, in the letter of consolation, he writes: "Since I happened not to be present to comfort you, I decided to do so by letter" (Pseudo-Demetrius, "Epistolary Types" 5.16–17, Malherbe 1988). Pseudo-Libanius states that, when writing a letter, "one will speak in it as though one were in the company of the absent person" (Pseudo-Libanius, "Epistolary Styles" 2, Malherbe 1988). Cicero writes to his friend Marcus concerning a recent letter: "All of you was revealed to me in your letter" (Cicero, *Fam.* 16.16.2, Williams). Gregory of Nazianzus understands that the letter is able "to sketch an image of the writer's presence" (σκιαγραφῆσαι τὴν παρουσίαν; Gregory of Nazianzus, *Epistulae* 196.3). Especially helpful is Seneca's comment to Lucilius:

> I thank you for writing to me so often; for you are revealing yourself to me in the only way you can. I never receive a letter from you without being in your company forthwith. If the pictures of our absent friends are pleasing to us, though they only refresh the memory and lighten our longing by a solace that is unreal and unsubstantial, how much more pleasant is a letter, which brings us real traces, real evidences of an absent friend! (*Ep.* 40.1, Gummere)[47]

It was more common, however, for the ancient theorists to understand this sense of fictionalized personal presence in terms of something taking the place of personal conversation. Hence Demetrius notes that "Artemon, the editor of Aristotle's *Letters*, says that a letter ought to be written in the same manner as a dialogue, a letter being regarded by him as one of the two sides of a dialogue" (*On Style* 223, Roberts).[48] Again, Pseudo-Libanius states that "a letter, then, is a kind of written conversation with someone from whom one is separated" (Pseudo-Libanius, "Epistolary Styles" 2, Malherbe 1988), and in his example of the friendly letter, he writes that "it is a holy thing to honor genuine friends when they are present, and to speak to them when they are absent" (Pseudo-Libanius, "Epistolary Styles" 58, Malherbe 1988). Julius Victor advocates that "it is agreeable to write as though you were conversing with the per-

---

[47] Note also Demetrius, *On Style* 227.
[48] Demetrius takes slight issue with Artemon's claim in *On Style* 224.

son actually present, using expressions like 'you too?' and 'just as you say' and 'I see you smile'" (Julius Victor, "The Art of Rhetoric" 27; "On Letter Writing" 64.17–19/§448, Malherbe 1988). In a letter of recommendation, Aurelius Archelaus closes the letter with the admonition "Look upon this letter, Sir, and imagine that I am talking with you" (*Select Papyri* 1:122.31–33, Hunt and Edgar). Cicero frequently refers to letters as conversations or dialogues: "I have begun to write to you something or other . . . that I may have a sort of talk with you" (Cicero, *Att.* 9.10.1, Winstedt). In another letter he writes: "Though I have nothing to say to you, I write all the same, because I feel as though I were talking to you" (Cicero, *Att.* 12.53, Winstedt).

Stanley Stowers, in his book on Greco-Roman letter writing, consistently points out that it is upon the *function* of the epistles that we must focus our attention.

> From the modern perspective, it is natural to think about letters in terms of the information they communicate. The interpreter, however, should resist the temptation to overlook the great multiplicity of functions that letters performed and to speak only of the communication of information. *It is more helpful to think of letters in terms of the actions that people performed by means of them.* (1986, 15, emphasis added)[49]

The most important point to note here is the difference Stowers has drawn between contemporary preoccupation with "information" and the functional interests of the ancient writers. If we do have a desire to know what someone like Paul was thinking, then we are going to have to redress the imbalance caused by a tradition of focusing on "information."

5. Social Discourse as Constraint

The significance of philosophical concepts entering the discourse of Judeo-Greco-Roman society is that they become an integral feature of the conditioning process that societal discourse or cultural code places on thought and action within that society (Berger and Luckmann 1967, 47–92). This is akin to what Peter Berger is discussing when he points to a "social stock of knowledge" which governs social practices; once certain features are factored into that common stock, they are institutionalized through habitualization and become a part of the subject's impression of reality. Given the nature of Greco-Roman discourse during the first century, it is easy to imagine that someone in Paul's position could be exposed to philosophical concepts and structures of thought and use them for his own ends with no sense of being inconsistent with an insti-

---

[49] Subsequent to Stowers's exhortation to focus on function, he lists nineteen specific functions ancient letters were designed to perform upon the reader. The important point to note from Stowers's list is the transitive nature of each item; see Stowers 1986, 15–16.

tutionalized philosophical system. Indeed, this is precisely what Paul does.[50] Note for example Gnilka's suggestion that since a Christian moral structure did not exist at the time of writing,[51] Paul falls back on the use of moral philosophical terms/concepts *and traditions* already existing within his culture (*Umwelt*) (Gnilka 1968, 51).[52] More important, Gnilka points out that after Paul takes these existing concepts and traditions (*Begriffe und Traditionen*) from the culture, he moves on to use them for his own purposes and to assist in the development of his own, *Christian* system. Thus, the popular availability of moral-philosophical structures of thought gave shape to the way Paul developed a Christian moral structure of thought (Gnilka 1968, 52).[53]

The presence of philosophical concepts in the discourse of Greco-Roman society suggests that Paul would use such terms, concepts, or structures of thought both consciously *and* unconsciously.[54] As part of the social discourse, these terms or concepts form part of the way Paul constructs or articulates his world; thus, they necessarily form part of how he conveys his ideology both to himself and to others, since language is the means by which we articulate experience and thus "necessarily participates in ideology" (Belsey 1980, 42). Since language is the vehicle for ideology, and since "it is a characteristic of language to be overlooked" (Belsey 1980, 42), to remain unconscious and transparent to the subject, Paul's use of philosophical terminology to convey theological or ethical ideals—ideals being intimately tied to one's ideological structure—should not be taken to represent an entirely conscious act on his part. The implications of this are rather extensive. The primary implication is that any theological ideal being derived from Paul's writing must be qualified by an already existing (unconscious?) structure of thought that governs the way Paul is able to think about and articulate theological ideals.[55]

---

[50] This is commonly recognized by classicists and historians. See, for example, Cameron 1994, 7; Meeks 1993, 2; as well as the discussion in sec. 3 above.

[51] Perhaps we should add that it did not exist as an established authoritative system *for Paul.*

[52] The particular terms to which Gnilka is referring are ἐπίγνωσις, αἴσθησις, and τὰ διαφέροντα in Phil 1:9–10. Gnilka then goes on to suggest that Paul did not remain within the sphere of Hellenistic moral philosophy but moved on to generate an ethic—the basis for reasoning how to act—different from both the Hellenistic and the "(Hellenistic-)Judaistic" ethics to create the Christian basis for reasoning about actions: ἀγάπη.

[53] According to Gnilka, this amounts to the principle or law of ἀγάπη.

[54] Note again Malherbe's comments (1989, 50) in which he assumes Paul's adherence to the resources of the philosophical traditions.

[55] Of course, language, or the articulation of experience, will never be the same as the theological ideals toward which it makes gestures. To say it another way, theological ideals—ontological categories—cannot be reduced to the logocentric world of language.

The production of Pauline theology is immediately troubled if it does not take into consideration the presence of these underlying structures within Paul's communication. Moreover, the presence of these structures indicates that what we confront in Paul's letters, the surface level of the text, is not theology as such, but a construct produced by other conscious *and* unconscious processes. On one level we can simply say that in Paul's letters we confront language, not theology. But we already know that language is also a construct, that it cannot be reduced to the sum of its lexical parts, that it is, to invoke De Saussure (1966, 8–11), a combination of a system of potential and the realization of that potential in specific communicative events. To remain with De Saussure a little longer, the dynamic relationship between *langue* and *parole*—the former, as a system of possibilities, determines the latter, which enables the existence of the former—is the same sort of relationship we find in operation between the discourse of Paul's society (*langue*) and Paul's letter writing (*parole*).

This principle, or process, finds its primary significance in the discussion of how Paul's ideas are put into practice in the actual lives of his followers, that is, in the ethical ramifications of his central ideas. The reason for this is that the practical outliving of Paul's theology is always performed in terms of the norms and strictures of a given culture. This means that on a fundamental level Pauline ethics could be said to be the operation of one set of cultural norms and strictures (Paul's Judeo-Greco-Roman culture) upon another (any culture in which Paul's letters are read as authoritative).

We already recognize this as a problem to some degree when we acknowledge significant cultural differences between ourselves and Paul when we read, for example, Paul's claim in 1 Cor 11:5 that a woman dishonors her head if she prays without a head-covering, since it is the same as if her head were shaved. It is commonly held that this was something peculiar to Paul's culture and that a contemporary woman in Western society would not typically dishonor her head if she prayed without a hat, let alone that being the equivalent of a shaved head! The moment we acknowledge this, however, we acknowledge a fundamental structure which conditions all of Paul's discussions about ethical norms.

6. Summary

In this chapter we have continued the discussion from the previous chapter concerning the context of Paul, the Philippians, and the letter. The particular concern of this chapter has been those things which precede Pauline thought and expression. The significance of this particular context is that it had a determinative role in the way in which Paul's thoughts and, thus, expressions were formed. Understanding what Paul said is necessarily a study in how Paul came to say what he said, that is, a study in what precedes Pauline expression. Here I have sounded agreement with those who locate in the moral philosophers and their culturally adapted ideas a precedent for Paul's thought. I also suggested that the psychagogic model in particular presents itself to Paul as a viable, prior structure according to which he could have conducted his ministry in ways that would seem "normal" both to him and his followers. Another important feature of this context is the appreciation of the ancient assumptions associated with writing practices. I suggest that preceding Paul's act of writing is the assumption of a priority of language's function, not to the detriment of information, but certainly not subordinate to it.

That Paul was a product of his environment is hardly a new idea in the history of Pauline studies; nonetheless, the consequences of this fact are still being brought to bear upon the ongoing development of our understanding of Paul, his life and works. That Paul was a product of his environment also means that he was *constrained* by his environment.[56] Abraham Malherbe's comment that Paul was at once *Paulus hellenisticus* and *Paulus christianus* (1989, 8–9) is clearly a tidy way to think about this dialogue between theology/faith and culture operating within Paul to shape the man who wrote various letters of the New Testament. However, it suggests a false balance since—without denying the distinctiveness of Paul's Christianity—*Paulus christianus* is preceded and enabled by *Paulus hellenisticus*. It was not an axiom of Christianity to employ Hellenistic ideas and structures of activity; by contrast, to "Hellenize" non-Greek ideas and structures of activity was essential to the identity of Hellenism as a phenomenon.[57] Paul can only understand himself and his beliefs in terms of the cognitive, psychological, and social structures available to him, which include any religious beliefs and those structures which make up his culture, which was Hellenistic. Hellenistic structures provide the framework that locates Paul at a particular point in the fabric of human society, his structures of communication—which is that according to which he articulates and conveys his ideology—his theology, and thus also our ability to know this person.[58]

Importantly, therefore, a reference to the constraint of Paul's discourse is also a reference to the constraint of Paul's theology to more logocentric realities rather than to ontological realities. Paul's pragmatic focus on the gospel and his use of proclamation as an ethical reference point brings logocentrism to the fore as a structuring force in how we should be thinking of the nature of Paul's texts. And not simply logocen-

---

[56] Note Alexander's comment in the above citation: "[T]hinkers are *tied in to* certain patterns of behavior, *restricted* to certain specific forms of communication, by the society they live in" (emphasis added).

[57] This is a generally accepted point; however, see Hengel 1989; also Walbank 1993, 14–16, 60.

[58] Hence, not simply "pre-Christian" in Hengel's sense of the term, which amounts to the pre–Damascus Road Paul with an emphasis on his relationship to Judaism (that is, Saulus, not Paulus); see Hengel 1991.

trism as a problem with philosophy's/theology's fundamental dependence on language, but the recognition that we really do reduce everything to language, that the logocentric operation of philosophy is there because that is simply how the world works. (Thus, for the purposes of the present argument, it is important to note that references to the "logocentric" are typically references to the reality of the inability of philosophy and theology to transcend language, and the acceptance of this as normative.) The point is to allow a natural emphasis upon the etho-poetic features of the text, which are reciprocally involved with the present, this-world social code that allows the text to have a particular meaning in the first place. This naturally fails to satisfy the lust for a "theological" reading, a reading which is unconsciously metaphysical in its desires, yet always remains just that: desire for the grammatical apprehension of the metaphysical in the text, "a kind of ontological inferiority complex" (Jameson 1988, 4). Paul's concern in his epistles is primarily to perform the function of spreading his gospel. This also problematizes the development of "normative" Christian practice, or ethics based on Paul's writing, since, traditionally, Christian ethics based on Paul's writing are structured through metaphysical categories. Here I prefer to structure them along logocentric lines, by which I mean that I prefer to structure the form of Paul's ethical exhortations in terms of the socially discursive structures that constrained Paul's own discourse and thus ideology and thus theology.

4

(Dis)Closure
CLOSELY FOLLOWING PHILIPPIANS 1:1–18

1. Introduction

In this chapter, I shall closely survey the critical contours of Phil 1:12–18. My plain goal is to defamiliarize the typical readings of the passage by highlighting the textual twists that are typically ignored. I shall suggest that there are forces at work other than those which appear on the surface of the text; indeed, Phil 1:12 has already been presented as an important moment in the letter that does more than what is explicitly obvious on, but derived from, the surface of the text.[1] I further develop that theme here and suggest that Phil 1:12–13 does two things. It generates a hermeneutical framework or "reading strategy" for the Philippians that seeks (1) to reverse common assumptions about Paul's imprisonment, and (2) to define the success of Paul's program in terms of proclamation. I suggest that these activities are rhetorically closed off by Paul through the formulaic disclosure of Phil 1:12, hence (dis)closure.

I then consider the shift in Paul's focus in 1:14–18 to describe the effects of his imprisonment in terms of those within the Christian community. In 1:15, rather than going on to develop the discussion in the way we might expect him to,[2] Paul goes into further detail, with a discussion of two kinds of preachers, culminating with the extraordinary

---

[1] Note again that Alexander has suggested Phil 1:12 is perhaps the most important moment in the epistle; see ch. 2, sec. 2.b.ii.

[2] A number of scholars have pointed to this section as a deviation or an aside of some sort (e.g., Fee 1995, 124). German scholars typically tend toward the view that it was an excursus. Notable are Dibelius 1937, 65; Barth 1962, 29; Gnilka 1968, 60.

announcement in 1:18. Paul's reasons for venturing into the selfish/loving preacher discussion in 1:15–17 are not simply to expand the Philippians' knowledge of his circumstances, but to continue generating a reading strategy for the Philippians to read his situation, which, among other things, seeks to redefine evangelical success in terms of proclamation.

The matter of proclamation is perhaps the most important point around which this discussion will cohere. While on the one hand this passage (Phil 1:14–18) clearly has a lot to do with proclamation, there are elements within Paul's discussion which raise critical eyebrows. In particular, I refer to the fact that in 1:18 Paul makes an abnormal claim that resonates more with the philosophy of Austin and Derrida than with the traditional commentary on this passage.

2. Opening: Philippians 1:1–11

Philippians opens in a somewhat typical Pauline manner, insofar as Paul adapts the standard epistolary formula of his culture, intermingled with some Jewish elements (see further Schubert 1939, 19; O'Brien 1977; Reed 1996, 87–99). While studies on formal epistolary openings are essential for our understanding of the New Testament letters, the most important point for issues of New Testament analysis is Paul's *adaptation* and subordination of such norms to his particular agenda. It is in such points of difference that we discover the contours which distinguish Paul as a particular individual and his writing as a distinct object of criticism. This interest in Paul's adaptation or his difference provides an avenue through which I may further indicate something of the critical direction I wish to take.

On the one hand, we have formal approaches to Paul's epistles which marry instances of Paul's texts with instances of other, extrabiblical texts and intend to indicate that by these points of commonality there opens an aperture through which "light from the ancient East" would flow into and illuminate Pauline studies. We may readily apply Foucault's language here and refer to the structure that enables and validates this process as an "order of knowledge"[3] that seeks to reveal truth concerning Paul, or more specifically, that constructs aspects of Pauline studies in a particular way so as to discuss and critique them. But, of course, and on the other hand, there are various other "orders," processes which seek to reveal truth concerning Paul and to construct him and his work as objects of criticism. In general, these have been combined into that large mechanism of truth-revelation known as historical criticism. The title "historical criti-

---

[3] Foucault uses the phrase "order of knowledge" to refer not to an epistemological matrix per se, but to a discursive and dominating structure which itself plays out a role in line with its own interests. In short, it is a way in which an objective of criticism is *constructed as such* (see Foucault 1986, 1:54–55).

cism" refers to a way of constructing the object of criticism and not to a method or even a particular set of methods. Thus, for example, one can be "doing" historical criticism while reading for the literary aspects of a particular text because one constructs that text in a particular way as an object of criticism; conversely, one may be investigating historical information about the New Testament and be a long way from the ordering processes of historical criticism (e.g., Moore and Anderson 1998).

With respect to Paul's opening statements, it is clearly important to acknowledge and research the formulaic norms of Greco-Roman letter writing and Paul's relationship to those norms. The importance of such study, as mentioned, is that it shows us where Paul differs from his culture, or even within the domain of his own epistles. The interest of this book, however, is to question how Paul uses such differences to secure his own interests;[4] that is, to ask how alteration of epistolary form, for example, serves to facilitate Paul's position of power—the maintenance of his relationship to, or position within, a particular discourse, or set of discourses, respecting who he believes himself to be, namely a man with a divine commission to proclaim the gospel. Such an interest does not imply that the *only* function being performed by these epistolary introductions is the facilitating of Paul's power; it is rather the case that this is simply one of the functions.

The primary difference in the opening passage (Phil 1:1–11) of interest to this project is the extended thanksgiving section in 1:3–11, which differs from letters within Paul's culture (see Arzt 1994, 28–46),[5] and the section in 1:7–8 in particular, which differs from other letters within the Pauline corpus. It has been well noted that the opening section of Philippians carries a tone of personal interest on the part of Paul toward the Philippians like none of his other letters. This personal interest gives rise to the rhetorical contours of Philippians in ways different from the well-discussed, overt protestations of Paul's longing and concern for the Philippians. Paul represents himself in the epistle as having a very close relationship to the Philippians in a manner unparalleled in his other epistles, and there is no reason to contest his sincerity.

Bolstered by Paul's constant references to friendship and joy, some

---

[4] This does not imply a lack of interest in the well-being of others, rather it implies the simple point that if we say that Paul has the interest of others at heart, then it is within his "interests" to do so.

[5] For a comprehensive discussion, see O'Brien 1977. Prayers, wishes, and thanksgivings for the good health of the recipient are more the rule than the exception in ancient letters similar to Paul's letters; see, for example, White's discussion on family letters (1986, 196–97, 200–203). Yet in spite of this, we note that Paul is using his thanksgivings in a way peculiar to him. Even Schubert, who seeks to draw close to the Hellenistic parallels, acknowledges that Paul is not a slave to the Hellenistic forms (1939, 119).

critics have then gone on to read friendliness and joy as the primary mode of the epistle, with the result that we hear such claims as that made by J. M. Shaw: Philippians is "the happiest document in religious literature" (1934, 204). Though typically less jubilant, such laud of Philippians abounds in the commentaries[6] and is clearly one of the responses that Paul was attempting to achieve.

Other commentators have detected, however, a dire side to the epistle. Gnilka, for example, senses that "despite cordial agreement (*herzlichen Einvernehmens*), all is not well in Philippi" (1968, 12). The issue of the false teachers is not yet a reality, but what is a reality, suggests Gnilka, are certain events representing a breakdown of their affection (*Lieblosigkeit*) for one another (1968, 12). Similarly, Ernst claims that Paul's letter shows that the Philippians in "no way exemplify" (*demonstriert keineswegs*) unity and are not exactly a "shining example of Christian virtuousness" (1973, 74); he further suggests that Paul understands the congregation to have failings, doubts, and error (74).[7] Peterlin, whose position on the matter is similar to my own, suggests that hostile circumstances at Philippi and Paul's imprisonment forced the church to reconsider some issues that they had previously accepted uncritically: two sides form, and their respective positions harden, thereby laying siege to, and thus weakening, the church's unified front. Paul's letter is, in substantial part, a response to this threat (Peterlin 1995, 219–24).[8] Other commentators are far more bleak, and tend to see the negative aspects as the dominant mode of the epistle. Black, for example, believes the letter to reveal that the Philippians were "diseased by strife and self-interest" (1985, 303), and Blevins, who follows Lohmeyer's infamously gloomy work,[9] argues that the church has been splintered by dissension and the formation of cliques (1980, 320–21).

Gnilka's point that there is an agreeable tone that seems contrary to some of the problems actually taking place is a suggestion that there is a discrepancy between the rhetoric and the reality of the epistle. Calvin noted, somewhat earlier, that Paul expresses his particular disposition toward the Philippians "with the view of securing their confidence" (1981, 21) and, commenting on Phil 1:8: "It was . . . of advantage, that Paul's affection should be thoroughly made known to the Philippians. For it tends in no small degree to secure credit for the doctrine, when the people are persuaded that they are beloved by the teacher." Again, we observe a difference between the rhetoric of Philippians and the points being made within in it (Calvin 1981, 30).

One would be hard-pressed, however, to find support for the claim

---

  [6] See the discussion and references in ch. 2, sec. 2.d.

  [7] Like Gnilka, Ernst also points out that this is "normal" and "human."

  [8] Note Watson's claim that the main proposition of the epistle is 1:27–30 (1988, 79).

  [9] Lohmeyer understands martyrdom to dominate the tone of the epistle.

that Paul was "faking" concern in order to get his point across, but there is a degree of healthy suspicion to be cast on to Paul's language in Philippians. It is obvious that expressing genuine concern and affection does not preclude any another operation being performed by that very expression. Paul, like everyone else in the world, has specific goals he wants to meet, and he achieves these goals by means stated and unstated, even if those unstated means are not conscious movements on his part. This does not invalidate Paul's claims of affection; rather, it merely suggests that Paul's expressions of longing and concern do not cease to function as soon as he moves on to another subject, but rather reside within all that follows.

I would then suggest that Paul makes use of the residual effects of his expression of affection in order to move toward developing a way for the Philippians to understand his imprisonment; that is, he wants to create an interpretative framework or perhaps a new context for the Philippians to view his circumstances so that they read the situation *the way he wants them to read it*. Here is clearly where this element of suspicion enters the discussion—not an incredulous suspicion, rather a critical suspicion in which one wonders if there is more to Paul's comments than what appears to be the case on the surface of the text. If there is, then we may just as easily call it a "subversive movement" in Paul's text as we may call it a rhetorical movement, since the goal of such a movement is to persuade the Philippian readers *without actually saying so*.[10]

3. (Dis)closure: Philippians 1:12–13

The rhetorical move in Phil 3, mentioned above, is indicative of an unstated function of Philippians as a whole. Paul's language works to mask and influence; it masks its own rhetorical operation by leaving unstated its most important function: to give the Philippians a reading strategy that will cause them to contextualize in a manner confluent with Paul's own discourse any difference from that discourse.[11] One can put this same strategy in different and more euphemistic terms: the reading strategy will enable the Philippians to maintain their ideo-theological position in the face of conflict it will help them to keep the true faith.

This gift from Paul of a reading strategy is also something of a rhetorical Trojan horse. Paul's letter of friendship carries within the folds of its discursive form another message which operates on the Philippians while

---

[10] Some may suggest that this reduces all attempts to persuade to being subversive. This would be an appropriate conclusion when applied to texts (written or spoken or signified in any fashion) in which the function of persuasion is not the immediate and superficial activity of the text.

[11] Note Castelli, who understands 3:15–21 to be about constructing insiders and outsiders while at the same time conveniently reinscribing certain hierarchical structures that work in Paul's favor (1991, 95–97).

they enjoy the gift. Thus, the signal for disclosure in Phil 1:12, "I want you to know" (γινώσκειν δὲ ὑμᾶς βούλομαι), is at once the signal for the opening *and* the "closure" of Paul's letter, the signal for its (dis)closure: Paul's letter is perceived as open to the Philippians, as (dis)closed and (un)covered information, a window into his "real" situation, but this moment of uncovering or opening is also the moment of closure whereby the Trojan strategy comes into operation and the Philippians accept both the stated and unstated. The window becomes a rhetorical lens through which Paul allows the Philippians to see his circumstances as he wants them to see them.

Jane Schaberg, as mentioned, has noticed this same operation in the Gospel of Luke, and for this reason she interestingly suggests, though somewhat overstating the case (for rhetorical purposes one assumes), that Luke is "perhaps the most dangerous book in the Bible" (1992, 275, 286–89).[12] What she has noticed is that while Luke seems to be the most woman-friendly of the Gospels, which leads to the text's gaining a certain privilege about the status of women, and thus to an uncritical reading or acceptance, the Gospel itself uses this to "legitimate male dominance in the Christianity of the author's time" (1992, 275). The point is, regardless of whether one agrees with the "danger" element which Schaberg suggests exists, that the Gospel of Luke, while appearing to be friendly to or even to privilege women,[13] is not at all what it appears, and is in fact quite the opposite. Thus, the text of the third Gospel uses the same Trojan logic which Paul uses. It brings in the reader on a level of reassurance and uses this reassurance to enable another discourse to operate, hence Schaberg's descriptions of the Gospel: "extremely dangerous text," "most dangerous book," "it seduces the reader into uncritical acceptance of it" (1992, 275). The element of "danger" sensed by Schaberg is caused by the realization that this unstated current flows deep within the text, particularly since this unstated flow runs counter to the current of the stated textual surface.

The Trojan strategy, in which the outside or surface of the text misdirects what is on the inside, is not exactly an uncommon one. Matthew's Jesus criticized the Jewish leaders for the same thing: "Woe to you, Scribes and Pharisees, hypocrites, because you are like whitewashed tombs (τάφοις κεκονιαμένοις) which on the outside appear beautiful, but within

---

[12] Note, however, that Schaberg speaks as though Luke the man consciously commits these crimes against women. This is quite difficult to determine, and the situation in the Gospel seems more like Luke reinscribing the values of his culture into his text, and thus it is the text which gets away from him and operates on both the subsurface and surface levels.

[13] See the commentators' claims listed (Schaberg 1992, 275), which have been used to describe Luke as "a special 'friend' of women, portraying them in an 'extremely progressive' and 'almost modern' fashion, giving them 'a new identity and a new social status.'"

are full of bones of the dead and all uncleanliness" (Matt 23:27; see further Ps 5:9; Rom 3:13). The only difference here is that Jesus castigates the process, because in Matthew the claim is that these hypocrites are doing it on purpose. One must ask whether or not they really are. They obviously do not agree with Jesus' program, and they deliberately attempt to achieve their own ends through their language. So what is the difference between them and Luke and Paul? Are they not living out and trying to achieve what they believe to be right, and is this not the very thing Luke and Paul are trying to do also? The difference is, from the perspective of the New Testament, that they do not follow Jesus' program, which is said to come from God, whereas Luke and Paul are firm adherents of Jesus' program. But does this make the Trojan logic of their texts any more or less "valid"?

Returning to Philippians, we note that the break from 1:1–11, the introductory material or "exordium" (see further Watson 1988, 61–65), is signaled in 1:12 by a "disclosure formula" (γινώσκειν δὲ ὑμᾶς βούλομαι), the function of which was to introduce the primary reason for writing. As discussed earlier, Alexander suggests that the disclosed reason for writing (1:12–26) is all about reassuring the Philippians concerning Paul's situation. It is important that we recognize that the idea of "reassuring" is also an unstated one. We assume that this must be what Paul was trying to do in 1:12–18,[14] and there is no reason at all to question that this is indeed a function of the disclosure formula in 1:12, yet the conditions which enable the function of reassurance to operate also enable differently interested[15] rhetorical moves to operate in Philippians.

This is a natural feature of rhetorical communication in general. Even if we were to assume that language is concrete and has solid connections between its signifiers and signifieds, when it aims to produce an *effect*—where the relationship between a set of signifiers and their referent(s) is "metaphorical"—such as in our text, it opens itself up to a radical polyvalence which is easily (if not always) exploited for ideological purposes. This linguistic operation is, of course, an object of critical theory and is not a matter of seeing Paul as deliberately or consciously out to deceive, but recognizes that Paul's interests are not singular, but varied; that Paul was a *normal*, subjective writer whose many interests inscribed themselves in the texts he generated. As Catherine Belsey has it: "[I]deology is *inscribed in signifying practices*—in discourses, myths, presentations and re-presentations of the way 'things' 'are'" (1980, 42).

What this leads to is the realization that when we read Paul, we read

---

[14] I am aware of no commentator who does not try to represent this section as an attempt to reassure or allay the concerns of the Philippians.

[15] That is, the language of the letter is seen to operate confluently with the flow of its own argument and at the same time in a manner other than that argument.

Paul, since his bio-graphics are inscribed in everything he writes, as is the case with all of us. Paul's texts are naturally unconsciously constructed in accordance with ideo-theological interests derived from his social discourse and the terrifyingly complex psycho-social network which that includes. This problematizes readings of Paul that are designed to generate Christian ethics in particular, since all such readings must account for the constraints which precede Paul's evaluation process and govern his reactions, what he sees as normative or abnormal, what is proper and improper behavior, and so on.

A further problem that arises is that it is a feature of language to escape its origins. The result of this, to put it negatively, is that the author loses control over what he or she produces at the moment of production. To put it positively, readers produce readings of texts that are valid in and of themselves but may not have been what the author was thinking when he or she compiled the text. The only question with this is not whether or not it happens, rather whether or not one would label as "valid" a reading other than that which is entirely confluent, even identical, with the conscious mind of the author at the time of writing. It is very important, however, to recognize that this is not a hermeneutical reality simply affecting *our* contemporary reading of Philippians, in which we experience the risk of missing the author's "intended" meaning. It was, of course, also a hermeneutical reality affecting the Philippians and forms the condition according to which both the reassuring and the subversive[16] elements of Paul's text can operate. Despite all the complaints to the contrary, the author's "intended" meaning remains a possibility. The only problems are that (1) there is no guarantee that one has arrived at that reading; (2) we must assume that the author's "intended" meaning is the one foremost in his conscious mind, if such a distinction can be made (by "foremost," I only mean in the same way that a desire for salt is foremost in my mind when I ask someone to pass the salt).

Every author has varying interests derived from transparent norms and values within his or her culture which consequently constrain him or her as a subject and thus to be subjective. As such, the author is to at least some degree blind to his or her discursive practices. Nonetheless, we can claim that the "authorial" reading is a possible reading even if there are other possible readings generated by a given text. For this reason there is no harm at all in attempting to reach Paul's "intended" meaning, although "intended" must remain in quotes since it is necessary to keep in mind point 2, above, and the question of whether we can speak of a consciously unified intention present to the subject.

---

[16] By "subversive" I mean the unstated function in the letter which works to align (further) the Philippians with Paul's ideo-theological position.

In Phil 1:12, Paul makes a point of explaining that his circumstances are actually working for the advancement (προκοπή)[17] of the gospel, which we should probably take as a reference to proclamation; hence O'Brien's suggestion that προκοπὴν τοῦ εὐαγγέλιου in Phil 1:12 is not a reference to its content, rather a reference to the act of proclaiming it (1986, 223, 219–24). O'Brien also notes that Paul "goes out of his way" to show the Philippians examples of this advance by accumulating terms expressive of courage (1986, 221): "[T]he majority of the brethren have all the more [περισσοτέρως] confidence [πεποιθότας] in the Lord by virtue of my bonds to boldly [τολμᾶν] speak the word without fear [ἀφόβως]" (Phil 1:14). The significance of this explanation, that is, the significance of *including* an explanation, is that it serves to alleviate the "natural and reasonable" (O'Brien 1986, 220) expectation by the Philippians that things do not bode well for Paul and perhaps even for the gospel itself. The contrary expectation of the Philippians is probably the significance of the term μᾶλλον ("rather"),[18] which seems best read as an attempt by Paul to point out to the Philippians that the "unexpected" (Gnilka 1968, 56) has happened, that is, that *their* natural expectations—which Paul either knows from reports or assumes on the basis of cultural norms—have been confounded.[19]

As almost every commentator points out, Paul is here quite concerned to represent the gospel as something which transcends his own circumstances and the power of the Romans. A rather helpful point can be derived from a phrase used by Fee to describe the situation. Fee observes that Paul's "present focus is not so much on himself . . . as it is on *how he views* what has happened" (1995, 108). While the phrase "*how he views*" is also emphasized by Fee, I would suggest that it might be better to emphasize only the personal pronoun, so as to indicate that what is important about the explanation in 1:12, from a critical perspective, is that it is *Paul's* view. In fact, I would further suggest that we take this as not simply how *Paul* views the situation, but how he wants the *Philippians* to view the situation. Hence the well-established argument in the commentaries that Paul seeks to show that even the antagonists further his interests.

That is, 1:12 offers Paul's preferred "spin" on his present circum-

---

[17] Προκοπή is something of a technical term in Greco-Roman moral philosophy; however, it does not appear to carry this technical sense at this point. See Foucault 1986, 3:43; Epictetus, *Diatr.* 2.12–22; the essays in Dodds 1973. Also see Stählin 1968, 704–11; in the New Testament, only in Phil 1:12, 25 and in 1 Tim 4:15.

[18] For "rather," see Vincent 1897, 16; Fee 1995, 110; O'Brien 1991, 90; Collange 1979, 53; Lightfoot 1953, 87; but note BAGD, which suggests "to a greater degree" for μᾶλλον in Phil 1:12 (BAGD, 489).

[19] While Paul may have felt that the gospel had made "considerable and unexpected progress" (O'Brien 1986, 221), one suspects that the Philippians too would not have expected any advance. Indeed, they probably expected the contrary (Fee 1995, 111; O'Brien 1991, 90; Lightfoot 1953, 87).

stances. There are a number of possible reasons for this, but the one which forms a central interest of this book is simply that Paul desires (βούλομαι) to create the impression that the gospel prevails in spite of bad circumstances, and that, in accordance with the norms of popular discourse about psychagogic activity,[20] Paul's words match his deeds. Thus, "I want you to know" (1:12) becomes, functionally speaking, a covert way of saying, "this is how I want you to read the situation." The object of Paul's desire (βούλομαι) is, therefore, not the Philippians' simple, unitary cognizance of the gospel's progress (προκοπή) but the dynamic polysemy effected by the explanation. That is, the explanation in general, and the ὅτι-clause in particular, is this aforementioned rhetorical Trojan horse that functions purely and singularly on the surface, while on the inside lies the discursive complex that Paul wants to unfold and lay over the Philippians' understanding of his situation.

As mentioned, we find in 1:12–18 an attempt by Paul to counter the expectations among the Philippians that there was something untoward about Paul's message, which would be suggested by his prolonged imprisonment, and that these expectations are derived from the norms generated by Greco-Roman social discourse. Apart from the social norms of linking prison and shame, discussed earlier, there is also another very important social expectation in place and which Paul may indeed be attempting to meet in Phil 1:12–18, namely the aforementioned word-deed convention. This convention was incumbent upon philosophers and psychagogues in particular, but certainly as a standard, popular ethical convention that one's words ought to match one's deeds.

Philippians 1:12, and the rest of our passage, works to demonstrate that any potential problem based on the word-deed convention is countered by the fact that the gospel continues to progress. The problem is this: if Paul has preached the gospel at Philippi and claimed that it was the message of God by whom he has been personally commissioned to tell them these very things, and then finds himself in prison for a number of years, what does this then say to the Philippians who are already starting to falter in their unity— and to new converts in particular— about the validity of Paul's claims? Not very much.

The fabric of the Philippian Christian community's self-understanding is woven through with stories of God's demonstration of power through Paul, not the least of which would have been the divine attack on the Philippian prison while Paul was being held there. Paul's long-term imprisonment can threaten a retrospective interpretation of these previous events. Philippians 1:12–18 is a bid to prevent this: if Paul's words were thought *not* to match his deeds—his "deed" in this case is his long-term imprisonment—then he need only point out that the gospel is still

---

[20] Hence the earlier discussion on Greco-Roman philosophical conventions and psychagogy (ch. 3, sec. 3).

being spread while he is in prison. But is this enough? Perhaps Paul did not think so, because Phil 1:14–18 continues the development of his attempt to generate the right reading of his situation. It is a subtle development, but it also explains what is going on in the passage as a whole (Phil 1:12–18a), a passage in which Ralph Martin sense a "tantalizing obscurity" (1976, 70).

To take stock of the discussion, in 1:12 we find Paul sifting through the rubble of his socially degraded circumstances, which likely have relegated him to a lower stratum of an intensely class-conscious society and stripped him of any semblance of honor in an equally intensely honor/shame–driven society. In spite of these dire straits, and contrary to the natural expectations of the Philippians, he has nonetheless been able to unearth from the rubble one important rhetorical nugget: the claim that the gospel has progressed. In order to validate his claim, Paul begins in 1:13 to unpack the significance of the term "progress" (προκοπή) by giving an account of supporting evidence. He begins with a complex infinitival result clause (ὥστε . . .),[21] lasting through to 1:14, which describes or "explains"[22] his circumstances in terms of the results of the coming about of the progress of the gospel (προκοπὴν τοῦ εὐαγγελίου ἐλήλυθεν).

It is difficult to say precisely what Paul's claim is in 1:13 as opposed to the rest of the results stated in 1:14. Is he saying that he has been able to win converts among the Praetorian Guard and "all the rest"? It does not appear to be the case that he is. That he is careful to add a salutation "especially (μάλιστα) from those out of Caesar's house (Καίσαρος οἰκίας)" in 4:22 at the very last moment in the letter, before his formulaic closing, indicates that he was certainly interested in pointing out to the Philippians that he was still at work among the house churches in Rome. It is clear that there were already Christians in Rome before Paul arrived, and that the salutations are made in the way they are ("especially" [μάλιστα]) is perhaps indicative more of the fact that the saluters were already Christians of whom the Philippians were at least aware or perhaps even knew, than of new converts unknown to the Philippians. What the salutation does evidence, as indicated above, is the fact that Paul was working among the Christians in Rome. This is a point Paul is obviously keen to make sure the Philippians know in order to further develop the impression that things are going well, with respect to his ministry, in spite of the circumstances.

So, what is to be made of the claimed result in Phil 1:13? An obvious

---

[21] The use of ὥστε with the infinitive could refer to either real, potential, or intended results (BDF, §391); the present context indicates that Paul refers to actual results (see Rom 15:19; 1 Cor 5:1); see also Silva 1992, 69; O'Brien 1991, 91 nn. 18–19.

[22] On ὥστε as explicatory, see Collange 1979, 54 n. 1; also Vincent 1897, 16; Silva 1992, 69–70; Gnilka 1968, 56.

point is that it differs from the result in 1:14, insofar as 1:13 refers to the progress of the gospel outside the Christian community, as opposed to 1:14, which refers to the progress within (see O'Brien 1991, 91). One thing Paul is not claiming is that he has been able to win converts; instead, he appeals to *proclamation* as the basis of the advance, which is also the basis of the advance in the second result stated in 1:14. That is, Paul points to his achievement of spreading the "message" throughout the Praetorian Guard and all the rest with the result that they are now aware that his imprisonment is "in Christ" (ἐν Χριστῷ).[23] This raises two questions: what is meant by ἐν Χριστῷ? and what is the significance of the fact that Paul's claim of progress is based on proclamation and not upon conversion?

The phrase ἐν Χριστῷ is used seventy-six times in the New Testament, seventy-three of which are in Pauline literature, while the remaining three are located in ever so Pauline 1 Peter. It is as common in Paul as it is ambiguous, hence the frustrated tone of BDF, "the phrase ἐν Χριστῷ (κυρίῳ), which is copiously appended by Paul to the most varied concepts, utterly defies definite interpretation" (BDF, §219 [4]).[24] Here the problem has been to determine with what other phrase(s) in the clause in 1:13 (ὥστε τοὺς δεσμούς μου φανεροὺς ἐν Χριστῷ γενέσθαι) one should connect ἐν Χριστῷ, since it leaves the word order in a rather awkward or at least unexpected state.[25]

One option, typically rejected (e.g., Vincent 1897, 16), is to connect it to the phrase "my bonds" (τοὺς δεσμούς μου).[26] The problem with the resulting phrasing ("my bonds in Christ") is that it strains the Greek word order by not allowing the predicate adjective "manifest" (φανερός), which separates the two phrases, to function adequately as a modifier of the phrase "my bonds" (τοὺς δεσμούς μου). For this reason, it appears best to take the lead from the Greek word order (note Vincent 1897, 16) and to render the phrase ἐν Χριστῷ in such a way so as to link it to the entire preceding accusative construction (τοὺς δεσμούς μου φανεροὺς) (Gnilka 1968, 56 n. 11) so that it renders the dative ἐν Χριστῷ as indicative of the sphere in which the manifestation of Paul's bonds has "come about" (γενέσθαι) (note Dibelius 1937, 64). It is not quite correct, therefore, to get around the problem by rendering ἐν Χριστῷ as "for Christ" (Vincent 1897, 16; NIV; NRSV),[27] although this certainly comes close to the point.

---

[23] This assumes a certain rendering of the word order in the infinitival clause in 1:13, which I discuss below in conjunction with the meaning of ἐν Χριστῷ.

[24] For a good summary of the interpretative situation regarding this phrase in Paul, see the discussion and bibliography in Seifrid 1993, 433–36.

[25] Gnilka notes that one expects ἐν Χριστῷ to follow γενέσθαι (Gnilka 1968, 56 n. 11).

[26] Such as the AV: "So that my bonds in Christ are manifest in all the palace."

[27] Some, unwilling to trouble ἐν by rendering it as "for," have understood the phrase in an elliptical sense, rendering it as "in Christ's cause" (Kramer 1966, 154).

Neugebauer suggests that we take the phrase as an adverbial or circumstantial modification. This is helpful only if we see it as adding to the
complexity of the phrase's referents, rather than excluding the metaphorical reference to space that is inherent in the term. For this reason, the rest
of his claim, that the phrase is a temporal reference to Christ's saving activity and that therefore Paul's imprisonment was an example of that
saving activity, is harder to accept (Neugebauer 1961, 121).[28] Note, however, O'Brien's concern that "it is doubtful whether the phrase 'in Christ'
can really bear the weight Neugebauer has put on it" (1991, 92).

The phrase ἐν Χριστῷ nonetheless remains ambiguous even when we
do determine its syntactical function, or perhaps even in spite of its syntactical function. While it is probably impossible to nail one referent to the
phrase, we can of course approximate the sense of the range of referents
Paul may have intended. Seifrid notes that the expression in Paul "probably came from earlier Jewish Christianity" (1993, 435). As an example, he
points to Acts 4:2, 12 as indicators that "the earliest believers in Jerusalem
proclaimed Jesus as the decisive 'sphere' of God's saving action" (435).

The signifier "in Christ," in such cases, therefore becomes the label for
the context of work done as a result of the messianic activity of God's son.
That is, Paul assumes a certain metaphysical shift occurs when one converts and that this is a direct result of the messianic activity in which the
Christian, in this case Paul, *participates*. So, in Rom 6:3–5, Paul says that
those who were baptized into (εἰς) Christ Jesus were baptized into (εἰς)
his death, the result of which is that the Christian's activity is now recontextualized so that it is performed in this sphere of Christ: "so that we
walk in newness of life" (Rom 6:4). The result of this is that *everything* the
Christian does is in the context of "Christ," because "God has rescued us
from out of the domain of darkness (ἐξουσίας τοῦ σκότους) and trans-
ferred (μεθίστημι) [us] into the kingdom of his beloved son" (Col 1:13, also
1:22–23). The point I draw from this is that the phrase "in Christ," when
used in references to activity, is merely a way of contextualizing that activity. Thus, in Phil 1:13 Paul's point is simply that his imprisonment has
come to be understood by the Praetorian Guard and "all the rest" to be a
part of his activity as someone who has adopted Jesus Christ as his Lord
and who tries to act in accordance with the fact, namely, his *activity as a
Christian*.[29]

Paul claims that the Praetorian Guard and the others have been able
to (re)contextualize his imprisonment, not in terms of the normal social
expectations, the natural context, but in terms of his work as a servant of
Christ—not as impotence, since he is not simply thrown in prison at the
whim of the state, but as power, since his imprisonment is being used for
a higher purpose. This throws light onto the sort of critical move Paul is

---

[28] See also his more accessible, earlier article (1957–58).
[29] Note the translation in Beare 1959, 56.

making throughout this passage. He is attempting to give the Philippians a specific way of reading his situation that enables them to look
favorably on his present circumstances and, in keeping with the normal
context with which they would read anyone's imprisonment, not
unfavorably.

The second question mentioned above concerned the significance of
Paul's claim that progress is based on proclamation. Paul has attempted to
recontextualize his imprisonment by claiming that his circumstances
have, against normal expectations, brought about the progress of the
gospel. As discussed earlier, Phil 1:13 is an explanation of the claim in 1:12.
But if so, in what way does the manifestation of his bonds ἐν Χριστῷ infer
the progress of the gospel? In trying to determine just what he is claiming in his explanation of the claim in 1:13, we also confront the problem
of defining the term "gospel" (εὐαγγέλιον).

Originally, a εὐαγγέλιον was a reward for bringing good news,[30] and
then, as is presently obvious, it eventually conflated the circumstances
and was used to refer to the good news itself (see BAGD, 317; Becker 1976,
2:107; Friedrich 1964, 2:722). In the New Testament the noun is used seventy-six times, *sixty* of which are found in the Pauline epistles.[31] Partially
on this basis, some have suggested that "it was Paul who established the
term *euangelion* in the vocabulary of the [New Testament]"; not that Paul
invented the term, but rather that "he was taking over phraseology already familiar to his readers," who were already aware of the word's
content (Becker 1976, 2:110). Perhaps Paul's most explicit description of
the (semantic/kerygmatic) content of εὐαγγέλιον is located in 1 Cor.
15:1–4: "I make known to you, brethren, the gospel . . . namely that Christ
died on behalf of our sins according the Scriptures, and that he was
buried and that he was raised on the third day according to the Scriptures." To say that this statement is fundamental to all that Paul writes
rather understates the case. "The gospel" is the point of cohesion around
which crystallizes the meaning of all that Paul is and does.

Becker has pointed out that the term εὐαγγέλιον in Paul's writing
does not only refer to the kerygmatic content of the term, "but also the
act, process and execution of the proclamation" (1976, 2:111). The implication of this for our problem in Phil 1:12–13 is that when Paul claimed that
the gospel had progressed, and then points to its manifestation "in
Christ" among the Praetorian Guard and all the rest, he was not referring
to the winning of converts, but to this verbal, dynamic aspect of
εὐαγγέλιον, that is, to proclamation. According to Paul, the criterion of

---

[30] This is the sense of the substantive in its earliest known use, Homer *Odyssey*:
14.152–53; 166–67. Note that the word was still rooted in the sense of good news
εὖ + ἄγγελος, insofar as the bearer brings good news that brings relief for the recipients and for that he was subsequently rewarded (Becker 1976, 2:107).

[31] Including the disputed epistles.

progress which he meets is proclamation (or "re-iteration"); that is, the gospel has advanced because he has been able to communicate basic content concerning Christ's salvific work.

The importance of this cannot be overstated. In εὐαγγέλιον, we have all that Paul considered important, we have both "theology" and practice. Perhaps more important, I suggest that the communication of the gospel, its reiteration, is not only central to Paul's work, but that what he says elsewhere, particularly in passages affecting ethics and church polity, which I combine under the title "Christian practice," is subordinated to it. The content of the gospel is the information concerning Christ's work; the practice—that is, *Christian* practice because it is performed ἐν Χριστῷ—is all that is necessary to communicate the message of Christ's work. A primary reason that Phil 1:12–18 is so important to a "theology" of Paul is that it develops this point like no other passage. Paul is willing to allow what can only be considered in normal circumstances as unethical or inappropriate Christian practice simply because it spreads the gospel, and thus meets the very criterion he holds up for his own sense of progress. The significance of this is that it problematizes other discussions in Paul in which he discourses on appropriate Christian practice. I submit that when we encounter other discussions on Christian practice, what we see is not a discussion based on a metaphysical ethic, rather a fundamentally pragmatic, logocentric discussion that Paul believes will bring about the best circumstances for the gospel's progress.

Paul has invested a great deal in the gospel and sees himself as the spiritual father of, and thus responsible for, the Philippians. The Philippians are in conflict, experiencing pressure from within and without; the church is not as stable as it should be. Some are worried about Paul (4:10), and some are worried about themselves (1:28). The cause of all this is their adoption of the gospel. "Is it worth it?" must have been a frequent and perhaps quietly discussed question—Is it worth holding on to Paul's gospel?[32] or Is it worth holding on to any form of the gospel? Thus, Paul cannot afford his present circumstances to detract from his work at Philippi; he therefore takes special care to ensure that though he may appear to be impotent and in prison (and thus under all the social pressure and shame associated with that fact), the Philippians do not use his present circumstances as the occasion for any "retrospective interpretation"[33] of his work, and thus his message, and degrade his status to match the

---

[32] Since they could opt for the *religio licita* version in Jewish-Christianity.

[33] On the phenomenon of retrospective interpretation, see Malina and Neyrey 1991, 106–7. Basically, the point is rather simple and obvious; when someone comes to be seen in negative light, such as being in prison for several years (!), that person's past, if a positive one, begins to be re-understood in terms of that person's present negative circumstances (one assumes the opposite would be true also). This leads the observers—such as, perhaps, the Philippians—to degrade the

perceived situation. For Paul this would be disaster, both for his position at the head of the Christian community in Philippi—and thus also his ability to maintain their ideo-theological position—and for the gospel he preaches.

4. There's No Such Thing as Safe Text

"Text" is these days commonly understood to be a reference to any codified structure or semiotic system. As semiotic structures, texts are not the works themselves, to invoke Barthes, rather that which is produced when one engages the "work"; that is, the text is the "methodological field" of activity (Barthes 1977, 155–64, esp. 156–57). The problem with text, however, is that it all looks and sounds the same. Its phonetic and graphic marks bear no mark of truth value, no apparent or latent metaphysic. Truth (ἀλήθεια) and pretext (πρόφασις) easily, perhaps necessarily, cohabit the same text—not as permanent residents, though, and certainly not as innate qualities of a text's structure; they exist in the (un)conscious intentions, the prior structuring, of the signifying subject. The problem is that they remain there. The auditing subject bears the responsibility of inscribing the perceived text with his or her own intentions and interests. Basic expectations, cultural code, and common social discourse work toward enabling the communication of ideas between two subjects to function fairly smoothly.

Language, however, is never what it seems to be, because it all looks the same—not that it is not what we think it is, but rather it is always more than we think it is. It is always something else as well. Trouble arises. How is it possible that language is always more than we think it is? It is because of its iterability: its ability to be cited and resituated into new contexts; that is, its ability to be recontextualized and not necessarily into homogenous contexts (writing for writing, speech for speech), but into heterogenous contexts (culture/speech, writing/ideology). Derrida has much to say about the context in his intercourse with Austin's *How to Do Things with Words*, and in the course of this chapter we shall have further occasion to interact with this dialogue. However, we do not want simply to leave the dialogue situated on the pages of Derrida and Austin; rather, there is opportunity to re-cite the dialogue in our reading of Paul. Indeed, Paul himself has something to contribute to the discussion, for in his letter to the Philippians, Paul also saw that the problem with language was that it all sounded the same. Having recognized this, Paul decides not to write against the iterable nature of language; he rather decides to use this quality of language against itself in an attempt to halt the progress of iterability. That is, Paul produces a new context in which his imprisonment

---

previous status of the individual and to rebuild a new status that is confluent with the present reality.

and relationship to the gospel can be re-cited and thus enables the Philippians to read his situation in a manner confluent with the way he himself wants them to read it. We could hardly say that Paul is attempting to delude his readers; it is rather the case that he necessarily seeks to persuade his readers to believe what he believes to be true, even if "persuasion comes from what seems to be true, not from the truth" (Plato, *Phaedr.* 260A, Fowler; also 272D–E).

At this point, we must ask Paul to rest his pen, or at least that of his amanuensis, the "citer" of Paul, while we take stock of the situation. The present task is to investigate a problem of language, namely its iterability, repeatability, or citability and its relationship to the production of meaning, although such critical theory often finds itself as an uninvited guest at the gatherings of biblical scholars. In spite of this, we find Paul in Philippians posting an open invitation: to the Romans, a Roman; to the Greeks, a Greek; to the critical theorists, a practitioner. In his letter(s)— γραφή, γράμμα(τα), ἐπιστολή—to the Philippians, Paul pulls on his critical commentator's cloak (ἐπι-στολή) and comments upon the (metaphysical) relationship between author and message, form and essence, entity and being, letter and spirit. One can hardly reject an invitation from such a man, so we must also don our critical attire and respond. Before we go on, however, let us reread the text thus far and preempt where it will go.

We have noted that Paul glides through the standard introductory citation of the marks of ancient epistles, offering his thanks to God for the Philippians; ma(r)king some comments regarding what God will do for them; citing his own affection for them; and concluding the introduction with his prayer for them. Following this rather conventional opening, Paul begins the body of the letter with a formula not altogether common to the New Testament: γινώσκειν δὲ ὑμᾶς βούλομαι (1:12). This turn of phrase, along with other literary aspects of the letter, suggests a more intimate and informal correspondence in which Paul communicates with good friends as opposed to a group with whom he is unfamiliar. It is significant that Paul had a close relationship with the people of the Philippian church, because, as this book suggests, it plays a crucial role in the way in which he presents information to them.

After creating a sort of "just for you" ambience, he proceeds through the channels of his personal relationship with them in order to develop a "correct" interpretation of his circumstances. Paul is able to do this with a degree of ease, since the evidence of his close relationship with the Philippians also suggests that he had an established ethos (in spite of the probability that it had been damaged by virtue of his imprisonment) that would have enabled him to say a great deal without challenge from his audience. Thus, Paul applies himself to the aforementioned task of fixing an interpretive perspective from which the Philippians are supposed to view the bland historical fact of his imprisonment. He could hardly allow the fact of his imprisonment to suggest that his gospel was in some way subordinate to Roman power. Thus, while it is quite rare for commentators to venture a discussion of Paul's attempt to create an interpretive perspective for this historical event, Craddock assumes that Paul's circumstances naturally warrant his providing an interpretative perspective to prevent what could otherwise be a detrimental interpretation: that Paul's gospel is not a divine program (1985, 24). Martin also comes close when he suggests that Paul is trying to communicate that the imprisonment does not invalidate his status as an apostle, or perhaps the power of apostleship in general, as well as the fact that the gospel continues to advance in spite of various obstacles; rather, Paul's "interest focuses on giving a statement of personal vindication of his apostleship and on announcing the progress of the gospel" (Martin 1976, 71).

There is no way to know just what the Philippians thought of Paul's circumstances, apart from the fact that they must have had some concern for him.[34] But it is not so difficult to determine what Paul thought of the Philippians at this time; he was obviously concerned about them. This concern of Paul's for the Philippians is generally acknowledged to be twofold: his concern for the personal opposition experienced by the ecclesial community in Philippi (see 1:27–30) as well as the threat to Paul's established set of beliefs and principles or theology brought on by false teachers or leaders (see 1:27; 2:1–4; 3:1–3, 17–19; 4:9), which may have been the cause of some unrest.[35]

As the spiritual father of this group, and in keeping with the nature of his apostolate, Paul is naturally compelled to recontextualize[36] the situation so as to alleviate their distress and any danger that he might perceive they are in. His main tool is his rhetoric, through which he "bring[s] into existence a discourse of such a character that the audience, in thought and action, is so engaged that it becomes a mediator of change" (Bitzer 1968, 4). That is, his epistle serves as a potential "mediator of change" by virtue of its ability to "alter" the way in which the Philippians view various circumstances.[37] Paul exhorts them to "stand firm" and "strive together" in the things that they already know, and to beware of certain ones who might threaten what they know. It just so happens that the two issues going on at Philippi are similar to two issues with which he is also dealing in his imprisonment: personal suffering for his faith, and self-oriented preachers. It is reasonable to assume that a probable reason for Paul's foregrounding these two issues in Phil 1 is due to the fact that they reflect something of what the Philippians themselves are experienc-

---

[34] This is evidenced by Epaphroditus's presence as their "apostle," who meets Paul's needs on their behalf (2:25), as well as by their gifts to him (4:10, 13–18).

[35] See the discussion of these two concerns in Fee 1995, 29–34.

[36] Echoes of *Entstellung* resound through this movement (see the discussion of *Hinterfragen* above in ch. 1, sec. 2.b.).

[37] In this particular case, Paul is seeking to strengthen internal cohesion.

ing. Paul can demonstrate his own situation as a potential model for their own.[38] But he must present his imprisonment in such a way so that it really does function as a positive model and not an ominous death knell for both Paul and the power of the gospel or worse, for those at Philippi who have thrown their lot in with Paul and his gospel. After all, the power of the gospel does not appear to be all that powerful while Paul seems to be humbled by the Roman state. So, it is incumbent upon Paul to (re)present his situation to the Philippians in a way that is positive ("acceptable"),[39] so that it can slip past the Censor. He needs to persuade them to see that such opposition does not, as might be supposed or even suggested by some among them, subordinate the power of the gospel, which is the power of God to act in this world. That is, Paul must re-create their own sense of the world.

But here, in the attempt to create a new discourse to resolve a problem, in the attempt to persuade the audience to adopt a new perspective, a fissure between the bland historical event and its interpretation is exposed. The very possibility of persuasion ("interpretation") exposes an already existing split between, or a demarcation of, every event and its interpretation, an opening that never permits closure. That is, an interpretation can never achieve complete identity with its object. There is only always a cite of ongoing (re)production, because this possibility of persuasion is also the possibility of the continual citing and grafting of new iterable or repeatable structures into the context of that space.

Every event is a text open for (re)production, thus all of history is a text open for (re)production, and so, as Derrida suggests "there is nothing outside the text" (1976, 158), there is nothing which escapes text, nothing which escapes mediation.[40] As stated earlier, the result, in short, is that interpretation changes with new information. Again, the possibility of change prevents closure from ever taking place, and this possibility is also continuous because context itself is continuous. Thus to cite Derrida again, "no meaning can be determined out of context, but no context permits saturation" (1979, 81; see also 1998a, 2–3; Culler 1982, 123). That is, meaning requires a point of reference, but there can never be a final decision regarding what that point of reference might be. Thus, the context of any event is always beyond every description of it.

In Paul's discussion of his imprisonment in Phil 1, the rhetorical gestures inscribed in his letter simply offer the Philippians new information to add to their interpretive processes, their perception of a context, so that

---

[38] Indeed, it has been suggested that models are the "core" of the letter and the "key" to the "architecture" of Philippians (Stowers 1991, 117).

[39] Note the idea of "acceptable" above in ch. 1, sec. 2.b.

[40] Hart takes Derrida's comment ("*il n'y a pas de hors-texte*") to infer a virtual given in poststructural critical theory, that "there is no knowledge of which we can speak, which is unmediated" (Hart 1989, 26).

they might not perceive or interpret that his imprisonment has signaled the overpowering of the gospel, but rather that the gospel transcends even the power of the Romans, thereby providing them with a perspective from which to view their own circumstances. This information comes as the object of γινώσκειν in 1:12–14, specifically the summary in 1:12 that "my circumstances have turned out for the greater progress of the gospel," in spite of what appears to be a negative situation for him and his work, namely, his imprisonment. Immediately following this statement, Paul seeks to qualify his positive account in 1:15–18. In so doing, he exposes his assumptions about the relationship of authors to intention and meaning. This qualification consists of Paul's description of two opposing kinds of people who preach the gospel with respect to his imprisonment. He notes that on the one hand there are those who preach the gospel "through good will" and "out of love," knowing that he had been appointed for the defense of the gospel (1:15b–16). On the other hand, says Paul, there are those who preach through envy (φθόνον) and strife (ἔριν) (1:15), out of selfish ambition (ἐριθείας) and without purity (οὐχ ἀγνῶς), imagining (οἰόμενοι) that they are causing Paul further grief in his imprisonment (1:17). On the contrary, says Paul, they cause him to rejoice (1:18). But, historically speaking, Paul does not rejoice in their attitude or intentions, of which he clearly disapproves.

After suggesting to the Philippians that the latter group of preachers is a mob of sophistic, preaching-for-profit ingrates whose association with the gospel message is dubious,[41] Paul makes an interesting move. In 1:18 he suggests that whatever the motive or intention behind the preaching of this bad group, his only concern is "that in every way, whether in pretext (πρόφασις) or in truth (ἀλήθεια), Christ is proclaimed."

A couple of questions pose themselves at this point: What is the nature of the hierarchical relationship Paul creates between the two different kinds of preachers? or, what is the nature of the relationship between the opposing terms πρόφασις and ἀλήθεια? and, what are the implications of Paul's suggestion that the gospel message performs a function beyond the boundaries of what he claims are the intentions of some who preach the gospel message?

5. The Good, the Bad, and the Undecidable

Paul's discussion of the two kinds of preachers in 1:15–17 finds its inception in a complex of events and social roles which created within him a sense of lack, that is, a "want" or "desire" (βούλομαι, 1:12) that the Philippians have a certain kind of knowledge. When this absence presents itself to Paul, when he perceives his desire, he seeks satisfaction in the produc-

---

[41] They do not accept Paul's authority, they preach for personal profit. Note also the use of πρόφασις in Phil 1:18 as a reference to a "pretext for greed" and compare 1 Thess 2:5; see also BAGD, 722.

tion of his discourse that might enable the Philippians "to know" (γινώσκειν).[42] He desires them to have the correct perspective on the circumstances surrounding his imprisonment (1:12), a desire he hopes to actualize through *his* description of his circumstances, and the rhetoric that presents it. Paul thus sets out to describe the advance (προκοπή) that has come about through his imprisonment, since, as mentioned earlier, it is important for him to demonstrate that his imprisonment does not herald a weakness on the part of the gospel's ability to move forward in the face of adversity. As he works toward developing the perspective the Philippians are to have, Paul makes the claim that "the majority of the brethren in the Lord have been persuaded by my bonds to dare all the more to speak the word boldly" (Phil 1:14).

Yet Paul knows that the progress which he suggests his imprisonment has enabled has already stumbled, since some of the people who gain boldness are not only antagonistic toward him (Phil 1:15, 17), but they in fact only (ab)use the gospel to secure their own gain. These people employ the gospel in a manner quite distinctly other than that which is suggested by the very gospel being proclaimed; they do it for self-oriented reasons and have an attitude quite other than the one which Paul says Christ had and which Paul calls for his Philippian readers to have (Phil 2:5–16).[43]

The very thing which Paul says has occasioned the possibility of progress has also created the occasion for regress. Paul finds himself on the defense and seeks to re-present the situation so that his circumstances appear to be working for the advancement of the gospel. The issue here is not whether or not Paul's situation actually was advancing the gospel, it is rather how Paul's rhetoric attempts to create a particular kind of perspective, and thus not necessarily a pure and unmediated image of reality. He attempts this by drawing a line of division between the two groups in order to clarify what has happened. Then, instead of embarking on a thorough condemnation of the anti-Paul group in order to render their message as invalid—as he is wont to do with other members of the Christian group who have a perspective different from his own—he proceeds to demonstrate that the difference which constitutes this group does not in fact invalidate the gospel which they preach. The happy result is that the potentially weak point in Paul's earlier claim—that his incarceration has worked not *against* but *for* the advancement of the gospel—is now reinforced, since even these roguish sophists can be said to preach the gospel and thereby contribute to the advance of the

---

[42] This perception of an actual or potential exigence is by no means unique to Paul; it is analogous to any rhetorical situation.

[43] This is yet another example of why Philippians is sometimes seen as cohering around the presentation of good and bad models of behavior. But also see Fowl, who does not think of the Christ hymn as a "model" (1990, 85–92).

gospel. Paul takes a situation in which people are preaching in a manner that he believes is contrary to the purpose of the gospel, a situation that he cannot control, and uses it as a way to gloss over and recontextualize the impotence of his own position in prison *and* his inability to control the citation of the gospel by whomever desires to employ it for whatever reasons. By validating the preaching of the selfish preachers, Paul validates his own claim to the gospel, but at what cost?

Paul has often made overtures to possess and master the re-citation of the gospel message; yet, language's iterability has proven too slippery for him to maintain his grip. Paul discovers that Plato's problems with writing have extended to speech as well. For example, in Galatians, Paul attempts to persuade the Galatian Christians that what they have received from the Judaizers is not a gospel at all (Gal 1:6–7). Paul believes that *his* contextualization of Jesus' death, burial, and resurrection is *the* gospel and that other contextualizations of that message are only perversions. However, what makes the one a "perversion" (μεταστρέφω) and the other "truth" is the same thing: contextualization or recitation of an iterable text.

Paul's desire and lack of fulfillment is the same as Socrates' because the problem with writing is also true of speech. This is one of the insights Derrida has contributed to the philosophy of language though his critique of Western metaphysics in general, and of Plato's oppositional structure of speech and writing in particular.[44] Speech and writing meet in some primordial structure which is their common origin. Derrida refers to this structure as "archewriting" in order to represent that part of language which is at once both inside and outside of language by virtue of being prior to language. It both constitutes and signifies language. This is that quality which makes language work.[45] That is, because language can be signified and constituted by the same structure, language can therefore be repeated, and thus it enables the communication of (the father's) ideas. In short, the essence of language is communication, and communication relies upon iterability, and iterability is a quality of language which precedes both speech (phoneme) and writing (grapheme) and which is named by Derrida as this "archewriting."[46]

It is the iterability of the gospel which enables it to be communicated in a manner confluent with Paul's own ideo-theological position, but it is also iterability which enables it to be used in a different manner. The citation of the gospel has escaped Paul's mastery and is now in the hands of

---

[44] The most thorough discussion of Plato's opposition of speech and language in Derrida's oeuvre is "Plato's Pharmacy" (1981a, 61–172).

[45] Derrida chooses arche*writing* over arche*speech* since it is in writing that the iterable quality of language is most evident.

[46] Derrida discusses this at length in the chapter entitled "Linguistics and Grammatology" (1976, 27–73, esp. 44–70).

other would-be masters, who can control it no better than he, though they may re-cite it in whatever context they wish and thus for whatever purposes they wish. Paul seems to have realized this and thus also the impotence of his position. Therefore, instead of condemning what he sees as a misuse of the gospel, scheming a kidnapping, and risk exposing his impotence, he gives it his blessing. Paul thus makes a Socratic bid for paternal power over the re-citation of the gospel, but he does it in a way that masks its violence; he uses a Freudian *Entstellung* to slip it past the Censor, disguising its unacceptability.

Paul's bid for patronage of the re-citation of the gospel is a slippery one. It also causes institutional problems for the keepers of the commentaries since it creates a gap in the construction of a "Pauline theology." This in turn leads commentators frequently to take note of the fact that he stops short of the strong, excommunicative language he normally employs for such people and refer to his attitude as "large-heartedness"—the commentators do not have a problem with Paul's comments in Phil 1:15–17, where the language is typical of Pauline invective; it is the "large-heartedness" of *Phil 1:18* which pumps confusion back into the preceding verses. This break from the "norm" problematizes the assumption that Paul's ethics are based on something radically external to his own desires. Even if Paul's imperative were nonimmanent, his behavior is governed by a cohering, immanent "principle"—proclamation of the gospel *in this world*—and thus his ethics are constructed as non-metaphysical and rather based on a certain kind of desire.

The very act of labeling Paul's treatment of these people as "large-hearted" reflects the idea prevalent in biblical studies that Paul seems to break away from an assumed normal practice. Paul's "normal" behavior is to label or describe antagonists in such a way so as to place them firmly *outside* the group, in order to maintain the stability of the (Pauline) group's identity, since such people threaten the theological boundary Paul has drawn. This subsequently threatens to alter the dogma and praxis of the people within the group. Any group, in order to remain as a group, must maintain the difference between itself and the rest of the world. This is a complex process of affirming and re-affirming rules and practices consistent with the basic tenets of the group. As a leader who desires to perpetuate the group, Paul must make sure subordinate members within the group know just where the boundaries of acceptable beliefs and behaviors lie, in order that the group's members act accordingly and the group maintains its purity or difference from the rest of the world. If some within the group act and/or think like those outside the group, then, the group has lost its purity or radical difference from the rest of the world.[47]

---

[47] For fuller discussion on groups and the Pauline community, see the chapters "Formation of the Ekklēsia" and "Governance" in Meeks 1983, 74–140.

This practice of Paul is also evident in Phil 3, where Paul exhorts the Philippians to beware of people he describes as "dogs," "evil workers," "false circumcision" (3:2), and, in the latter part, as "enemies of the cross of Christ, whose end is destruction, whose god is their stomach, and whose glory is in their shame, whose minds dwell on earthly things" (3:18–19). This is harsh language whose function is excommunicative, insofar as it places such people outside of the Pauline group.[48] Thus, through the use of such language, Paul creates for the Philippians a well-defined category for them to interpret accordingly the actions of those who differ from himself. If, from the perspective that Paul has given, there be any selfishness, if there be any shame, if any dwelling on earthly things, then consider such ones as *outside* the group.

While Paul's comments are descriptive to some degree, they *perform* the function of setting up the one group as clearly other than Paul and the church at Philippi; furthermore, these comments re-mark the boundary between the inside and outside of the Christian group in general, or at least, the boundary of the Pauline Christians. Thus Barclay points out that Paul is not averse to making "proto-sociological" statements which, in our present terms, serve to "give the Christian community definition and identity" by "creating distinctions between the 'genuine' (*dokimoi*) and the 'spurious' (*adokimoi*)." Barclay then comments that, throughout Corinthians, Paul creates "insiders and outsiders on his own terms. . . . He identifies deviants in order to establish boundaries and solidify the identity of the Corinthian community. . . . It is easy to recognize here [in Corinthians] . . . that 'deviant' labels are being applied as part of a power struggle, here a fundamental battle for control of the Christian tradition" (1995, 124).

Thus, Paul's comments are to be read as *performative*, especially since they do not really fall into a positivistic true/false dichotomy. This performative aspect of language is located within the philosophy, or speech-act theory, of J. L. Austin discussed earlier. The present benefit of speech-act theory is that it exposes the functional quality of language, even language thought to be purely descriptive. More important, it exposes that functional quality to be the *primum mobile* of all "meaningful" statements. So, for example, the rhetorical value of calling people "dogs" transcends the question of its propositional truth; that is, the act of doing so is what is important. And this does not mean that it is "wrong" or philosophically ineffective to use such metaphoric language. These comments are there to *act* upon the Philippians. They perform this action by showing the Philippians that these people to whom Paul refers are not the kind of people whose example they ought to follow. These "dogs," therefore, stand in stark contrast to Paul himself (who, in the eyes of his Philippian readers,

---

[48] Hence Fee's comment that "this language ordinarily refers to those outside Christ altogether" (1995, 371).

one imagines, is clearly not a dog), whose example, it is suggested, the Philippians are to follow (see 3:17; 4:9) (note Castelli 1991, 96).

We note here that Paul's conclusion in Phil 1:18 is, by contrast to the diatribe of Phil 3, suspiciously restrained. It is necessary, then, to observe some of the differences and similarities between the two groups which may perhaps explain the difference in treatment. The group discussed in 3:2–4 is most likely a Judaistic one which accepts the work of Christ but only within the confines of Jewish custom, hence Paul's testimony and subsequent rejection of his boast in the flesh. However, the foil for Paul's handling of the non-Pauline preachers in Phil 1 is really the latter group in 3:18–19. The description in 3:18–19, in particular, is rather broad. The phrase τοὺς ἐχθροὺς τοῦ σταυροῦ τοῦ Χριστοῦ is, again, more performative than propositional and is qualified by a series of broad claims which contribute to the basic rhetorical function of the phrase: Paul equates their τέλος with "destruction" (ἀπώλεια) and says that they are selfish or serve their own desires (ὧν ὁ θεὸς ἡ κοιλία), that their glory is their shame, and that their minds dwell on earthly things (as opposed to heavenly things). This description of what constitutes an enemy of the cross is quite generic and could be made to fit almost anyone (similarly, O'Brien 1991, 454); indeed, the girth of this belly-worshiping category easily encompasses the kind of selfish preachers discussed in Phil 1. That these descriptions are more performative than descriptive is what Hawthorne is trying to say when he states that they are "short, verbless sentences; constructions that are broken off without proper completion; clipped phrases whose meaning defies precise explanation; strong words, *whose force lies not in lexical definitions*, but in the sound and suddenness with which they come" (1983, 163, emphasis added).

Given the nuances that cross through Paul's use of the word σταυρός in Phil 3, there is much debate about the identity of those whom Paul labels τοὺς ἐχθροὺς τοῦ σταυροῦ τοῦ Χριστοῦ (see further O'Brien 1989, 453). It is possible that these people either never were or no longer are members of the Christian community; thus, the label τοὺς ἐχθροὺς τοῦ σταυροῦ τοῦ Χριστοῦ would refer to a cosmic difference between these people and those within the general Christian community. It is also possible that they are Judaizers who are not, in Paul's view, crediting the cross of Christ with all that it achieved. Typically, however, these people are identified as Christians (and possibly teachers) of some sort (e.g., Martin 1976, 143). Whatever the case, it seems that Paul's problem with this group was with the way they conducted themselves: πολλοὶ γὰρ περιπατοῦσιν . . . (3:18). And this is also very close if not identical to Paul's problem with the non-Pauline preachers in Phil 1.

Paul does not mention whether he has a problem with the theology or message of the group in Phil 3; he simply focuses on their conduct as a contrast to his own conduct and that of others like him (3:17). Thus, as Fee suggests, they serve their performative purpose by "standing in sharp relief to Paul's own 'walk' . . ." (375). Indeed, one would be hard-pressed to find an occasion in which Paul criticizes someone else without his own ideas or conduct being thrown into exemplary relief. This, in fact, seems to be a given when dealing with Paul: as an apostle, he wants his followers to imitate him (1 Cor 4:16; 11:1; Phil 3:17).[49] Criticism is therefore quickly served by Paul to those who might present themselves as an example (τύπος) other than the one he has set, particularly when his own followers are concerned.[50] It also seems that this serves as the point of difference in Paul's treatment of the antagonists in Phil 3:18–19 and Phil 1. As mentioned earlier, Paul has a keen desire to serve and protect his own group of people. Some of these people, to be sure, may dispute this—the cause of a great deal of Paul's troubles—but the important thing is that Paul himself senses a psychagogic responsibility to a particular group.[51]

The significance of Paul's sense of responsibility is that it is fundamental to the fact that he feels the need to respond to certain circumstances with whatever discourse he believes may solve any exigencies he perceives. Paul's responses, however, will always be attempts to help his audience to view things from his perspective. If there were some issue about which he thought a particular group might have the wrong interpretive perspective, then his discourse will re-present the situation in such a way so as to favor the presentation of his own position. This assumes, of course, that Paul, as the rhetor responding in epistolary form, believes that his perception of reality is superior to the audience's. His epistolary discourse will therefore attempt to bring their perception of reality into line with his. Again, this is not peculiar to Paul, it is what anyone does when he or she attempts to inject a discourse into a situation in order to resolve any perceived problems.

In Phil 1, Paul has something at stake that is not at stake in Phil 3: the reputation of the power of the gospel. Paul has to re-present the circumstances surrounding his incarceration in such a way that the power of the gospel does not appear to be diminished. Given the antagonism that the Philippian Christians were apparently experiencing,[52] and Paul's own sense of responsibility to them, it was necessary for Paul to comfort them,

---

[49] Also see Phil 1:30 and 2:18, where the idea of *imitatio* is also present. For comprehensive discussion on the debate regarding the definition of συμμιμηταί μου γίνεσθε in Phil 3:17, see O'Brien 1989, 444–47. For a general description of mimesis in antiquity relevant to the present discussion, see Castelli 1991, 74–78; on mimesis in Paul, see Castelli 1991, 89; also see Fowl's discussion on mimesis and the concept of the exemplar (1998, 148–49).

[50] Commentators frequently observe this; e.g., Martin 1976, 143; Jewett 1970a, 376.

[51] Evidenced not only by the fact of his correspondence but throughout the Pauline corpus (e.g., Gal 2:7).

[52] Paul also seems concerned (Phil 3:17–21, νῦν δὲ καὶ κλαίων) that the Philippians are open to corruption by enemies.

since the continued imprisonment of their spiritual father would have been most disconcerting. However, though he may be in prison, the power of God is still greater than any other powers, implies Paul when he describes the "advancement" of the gospel in spite of what might appear to some to be a defeat. Thus, Paul presents to them a positive interpretive perspective of his circumstances, *contrary to what they might have expected* (O'Brien 1991, 36). Presenting this perspective to the Philippians also serves as an example of how to act while experiencing conflict. Insofar as the Philippians are able to see that Paul's suffering for the gospel leads to the advance of the gospel, they are then able to attribute to their own sufferings such an interpretation. Indeed, Paul attempts to create this perspective when in Phil 1:30 he suggests that their conflict is "the same" as his.

Paul even presents his opponents in a similar light; the kind of people who in Phil 3 are labeled "enemies of the cross of Christ" in Phil 1 have their motives reprimanded but their practice praised. How is it that such people can cause Paul to rejoice when everywhere else he has only contempt for them? Philippians 1:18 is a climax and a summarizing of Paul's development of the perspective from which he wants the Philippians to view his circumstances. Yet it is an odd sort of a climax and perhaps an unexpected one on behalf of the Philippians, since Paul takes the unusual step of not castigating those whom he earlier suggests are charlatans; he rather focuses on what good they do. By doing this, Paul introduces into his discourse on the non-Pauline preachers a division which glosses over itself. Moreover, his discourse in general confidently draws a line between the two kinds of preachers, but by the time we finish reading the passage 1:12–18, the line has been effectively erased and the effects of the division have gone.

What prompted Paul to say what he does about the two kinds of preachers only to end up saying that the difference is ultimately irrelevant? Perhaps it has to do with his desire to create models and demonstrate the power of the gospel in the face of adverse circumstances. This means that the passage exists for reasons other those immediately apparent by virtue of the discourse itself, and that what we are ultimately dealing with is a rhetorical construct which incorporates historical events to support its rhetorical designs.[53] Thus, the operation of another division within the passage is made apparent: the division between the rhetorical argument and the discourse which presents it. What we end up with is, on one level, a play between "valid" and "invalid" within the presentation of the self-centered preachers; that is, Paul denounces their activities and attitudes early on in the passage, but in 1:18 reaffirms the gospel they preach as valid. On yet another level, there is play between "valid" and

---

[53] However, it is not the fact of the historical events recounted which is in dispute, rather the assumption of their primary status within the discourse.

"invalid" with respect to the Paul-centered preachers and the self-centered preachers; that is, the two groups are set up as opposites in 1:15–17, but in 1:18 the oppositional structure falters as Paul unites them with regard to their evangelistic activities. On another level, there is play between the argument and the discourse; that is, the passage is both metaphoric and historic. It is an attempt at both immediacy—an attempt to recount the historical situation—and mediacy—an attempt to use the historical situation to achieve purposes beyond it.

These lines of division, which work their way through this discourse, find their epicenter at a fracture operating within the word πρόφασις (1:18). To investigate this fracturing, we must first note that the words πρόφασις and ἀλήθεια in 1:18 serve to summarize Paul's description of the two groups of which he has been speaking in 1:15–17.[54] They sum up what Paul thinks of the various speakers' relationship to the gospel that they have been proclaiming. The signifieds of these labels are not only open to semiotic influence by Paul's discussion thus far, but also by their syntagmatic relationship to each other in 1:18. Paul positions πρόφασις in an oppositional structure with ἀλήθεια; thus, the signifieds of these two labels feed off the relationship of the labels (signifiers) within the statement itself. One apparent effect of this is to suppress or regulate a certain polysemy, or fracture, operating at the cite of πρόφασις, since the word opposes within itself at least two differing concepts or possibilities for translation/substitution: it can refer to a *valid* motive or excuse, or it can refer to a *invalid* motive or excuse (BAGD, 722).[55] Thus, πρόφασις is a signifier of both truth and falsehood, the cite of the intersection of mutually exclusive signifieds, a rupture in the established continuum between signifier and signified, the point at which the προκοπή begins to falter, the epicenter of the text.

This fracturing, however, is far from being a negative aspect of the discourse as it may at first appear. Indeed, it is crucial to the discourse, if Paul's rhetoric is to work at all. The argument in 1:12–18 stretches from a typically Pauline castigation of the selfish preachers to a rejoicing in their actions. But the discourse which presents the argument does not flow so continuously and folds along the line between that which is valid and that which is invalid—the motives of the preachers are invalid but the product of those motives is valid. Thus, there is also a discontinuity between the motives and that which the motives produce. If it were not for this fracture, or space, or *différance*, or whatever else it may be called, preventing the continuous flow of presence from speaker to text in Paul's discourse, his presentation of the advancement of the gospel would al-

---

[54] That the terms represent two respective groups, see Hawthorne 1983, 36; Fee 1995, 124, against Collange 1979, 58.

[55] O'Brien recognizes this. See O'Brien 1991, 106; also John 15:22 and compare 1 Thess 2:5.

ready be defeated by the presence of the speaker's motives/intentions becoming present also in the text, thereby invalidating their gospel and thus also Paul's claim to progress. The success of Paul's argument, its design to comfort the Philippians and to present the overcoming power of the gospel in the face of adversity, depends upon this fracture. However, we note that a fracture is no more than a gap, a point of nonregulation and endless play; it (is) nothing. We discover once again that for all our talk about the discourse Paul creates to relieve tensions and alter perspectives at Philippi, we are dealing with just so much rhetoric.

Mark Brett has presented a discussion on the author's motives and intentions which attempts to delineate a difference between the two (1–16). Brett seeks to tie authorial intention to content (the "what") and to locate them together under the title "communicative intention" (1991, 5). From this communicative intention, he separates out the "motives" of an author. Commenting on and summarizing Clines, he suggests that "any given author could be driven to write by the desire for prestige or by some psychological need." He then suggests that these features of the author's psyche "apply *only* to the level of motives" (Brett 1991, 5, emphasis added), as *opposed* to the author's intentions. The reason for this is that motivation, as opposed to intention, "in no way resolves the question of what was being said" (Brett 1991, 5). Brett's project here is classificatory (note 1991, 6). He is working toward creating classes of information so that we can speak of the results in more precise terms. According to Brett, in this project we are concerned with Paul's motivations, which is something we arrive at not merely by analyzing surface level of the text, but also through "wider historical contexts" (1991, 6).

While Brett's proposal is quite helpful for classifying our analytical activities with the material text, one must wonder if Brett's dichotomy can endure the metaphysical strain it relies upon. I have in mind the proposed discontinuity between motive and intention. Brett seems to be implying, though he does not state it, that there is a causal relationship here. A motive *causes* me to communicate; my communication, then, though caused by, does not have a form determined by that motive. Thus, in Brett's view, an author's desire to amuse, using his example, has no bearing on "what" the author says when the author attempts to amuse, so that one cannot simply look at the material form of the communication and arrive back at an original motivation. I agree with Brett up to this point.

The trouble begins when we ask why intention is not also subjected to the same spacing that motive is: how is it that an "intention" and a "what" can be joined in a way that a "motive" and a "what" cannot? What is the essential difference between a motive and an intention? There does not appear to be any explanation of this problem. Brett suggests that they are "separate interpretative goals" (1991, 5), but what we actually find in the text of Brett's analysis is not a separation of motive and intention, but a separation of motive and "what." Thus, the difference between motive and "communicative intention" appears to be determined by which one is more explicit, or what "the text actually says" as opposed, one imagines, to inferences about the text.[56]

The implication is that what the author intends and what the material text actually says are the same thing. Brett himself states that "motives lie behind and are prior to communicative intentions. Motives may not come to explicit expression at all" (1991, 5). However, Brett has already opposed motives to intentions; thus, the implication of this claim is that while motives are prior and may not be explicit, intentions are not prior and are explicit. What Brett is seeking to achieve is to be able to question analyses that make claims about the "why?" of a text. He simply wants to say that we have to talk about two different things when we read texts: what the material text *actually* says, and then what we think an author wanted to generate in that material text. However, again, what the text *actually* says is an assumption already and the very point of critical analysis. While we can see which material words are being used, we cannot at the same time see the conscious intentions of the author; we infer them. How do we infer them? By the very means Brett suggests we infer motives: through analysis of "wider historical contexts" (1991, 6).

So, while I affirm Brett's distancing of motives from having a presence within the text, I also suggest that intentions are equally distanced, and that both are determined by the same means. However, I also suggest that, while distanced, an author's intention is responsible for the form of the text. Hence Derrida's statement that "the category of intention will not disappear; it will have its place, but from that place it will no longer be able to govern the entire scene and system of utterance" (Derrida 1986, 326). Thus intention, while a structural part of the material text, does not function as a determining force in its reproduction. Hence a major point of this book: the activity of the material text of the gospel message is not enabled by the respective reproductive intentions/motives of the good and bad evangelists in Phil 1:12–18; it is rather enabled by a fracture.

As mentioned, the cite of this fracture is located at the word πρόφασις. The play between its references of valid and invalid motives[57] enables the text to create a line of difference within the selfish preachers themselves by severing what they do from their motives (or "intentions") for doing so. In addition, this same fracturing works its way through the text, deconstructing one level of the oppositional structure set up within the passage by distancing the selfish preachers from Paul *at the same time* that it brings them closer to him. That is, on the one hand, the text maintains a distance from those whose example is not to be followed by describing

---

[56] See his comments on Brandon (Brett 1991, 6).
[57] For the referents of πρόφασις, see BAGD, 722.

their intentions as φθόνος, ἔρις, ἐριθεία;[58] on the other hand, the text denies the ability of those intentions or motives to be present to the actions of the subject, which enables Paul to claim the proclamation of this group as being a part of the progress which has come about though his imprisonment. And this is perhaps the most significant contribution of the fracture operating in this passage, since without it Paul cannot make the claim that the gospel is advanced by the preaching these ill-motivated preachers perform. Thus, we begin to find that the very thing which makes the argument of this text possible is the fracture between the presence and the absence of the intentions of these speakers. And, again, a fracture (is) nothing.

What happens when we apply the text's fractured treatment of the selfish preachers to its presentation of the preachers who "love" Paul (ἐξ ἀγάπης, Phil 1:16)?[59] That Paul relies on a discontinuity between the intentions or motives of the selfish preachers and their actions undermines the ontological stability[60] of the oppositional structure set up in the passage between εὐδοκία/φθόνος, ἀγάπη/ἐριθεία and ἀλήθεια/πρόφασις, and even, as some have suggested, between οἶδα/οἶμαι.[61] This is because Paul's use of the term ἀλήθεια, when opposed to πρόφασις, suggests a continuity between the motives of the good preachers and that which they preach. Thus, a conflict arises between continuity on the one hand and discontinuity on the other. If, on the one hand, we privilege continuity, then Paul cannot say that the gospel which the bad preachers proclaim is valid, which subsequently undermines the quality of his claim in 1:12 that the gospel is advanced by his imprisonment. If, on the other hand, we privilege discontinuity, then Paul has no basis (other than the straightforward desire to discredit those of whom he does not approve) for saying that one group proclaims by truth while the other by pretext. It is this confusion between discontinuity and continuity, along with the other factors mentioned in this discussion, that works to unsettle the stability of the oppositional structure operating in this passage. And, in so doing, it questions the ease and definiteness with which Paul can define the boundaries of Christian practice and thus identity. Interestingly, the purity of the presence of a unified significance, and the continuity desired by the term ἀλήθεια, cannot be said to be present within our text. What in

---

[58] Coupled with φθόνος and preceded by the διά, and used in comparison with εὐδοκία, it is easy to see why ἔρις could refer to an intention or the general motivational sphere of activity.

[59] That the object of the love is Paul and not Christ is not a disputed issue; see, for example, Hawthorne 1983, 37; Fee 1995, 120.

[60] Maintenance of the Platonic continuity between the sign and its idea that dominates Western thought and theology.

[61] For the suggestion that Paul plays on the opposition between εἰδότες (1:16) and οἰόμενοι (1:17), see, for example, Collange 1979, 57; Fee 1995, 120; O'Brien 1991, 101 (see also his n. 14).

fact we have in this text is a reflection of the undecidable tension between valid and invalid found at the cite of πρόφασις.

As with all signifiers, πρόφασις simply points to a concept (an excuse, reason, or motive), and the value of that concept (valid or invalid) must somehow be related to those conventions to which the observer conforms. So, here in Philippians, the value of πρόφασις is dependent upon Paul's observations, thus, by extension, upon his personal ideology and everything else that goes into constructing his theology. It is not hard to see what sort of value Paul wants to give πρόφασις, since he places it into an oppositional structure with ἀλήθεια in 1:18. The syntagmatic or spatial relationship of these two words is subsequently intended to establish their ontological relationship, since Paul places πρόφασις into an oppositional structure with ἀλήθεια, which has the effect of πρόφασις becoming the signifier of the absence of ἀλήθεια, and ἀλήθεια the absence of πρόφασις. Thus, Paul's argument relies on clean lines between presence and absence operating within the two words. From the very start, however, this line has already gone under erasure and appears as a mere trace, since πρόφασις already opposes within itself these same structures of true and false, valid and invalid, which already throws into question the stability of the ontological framework giving πρόφασις and ἀλήθεια their respective values as opposites. As a small example, one would simply note that πρόφασις does not signify a radical or nonmodified[62] absence of ἀλήθεια, since πρόφασις also refers to a valid motive, or, to be more relevant to this discussion, it also signifies its own opposite.

More important, however, we find that the line of difference is already fading when we consider just what the text requires to be true—when we take the opposition in 1:18 between πρόφασις and ἀλήθεια at face value—in order for the argument to be persuasive. On the one hand, the term πρόφασις foregrounds the operation of personal motives in the proclamation of the non-Pauline group. On the other hand, we have a group of preachers whose motives are glossed. This group is simply said to proclaim in truth (ἀλήθεια).[63] While Paul does not explicitly suggest that one group has motives for preaching and another group does not, the text itself, by virtue of the term πρόφασις, argues that the motives of the non-Pauline group employ the gospel message as a cover for their underlying intentions as opposed to the Pauline group whose motives for proclaiming the gospel are not foregrounded. The one group preaches from "ulterior" motives as opposed to the other group, whose motives do not seem to affect the presence of ἀλήθεια. Yet earlier in this

---

[62] On "radical" and/or "nonmodified" absence/presence, see ch. 1, sec. 3.d.

[63] The dative case of προφάσει and ἀληθείᾳ alerts us to the accompanying circumstances of the proclamation of Christ; thus, one set of circumstances is equivalent to truth while the other is equivalent to falsity.

passage, Paul seems to put both groups on equal footing by appearing to describe their motives.

The issue of motives requires some attention. After pointing out that one kind of preaching used the gospel as a mask for selfish ends, O'Brien says that "over against this there was a preaching without any unworthy personal motives whatever, and which was concerned only with the truth (ἀλήθεια)" (1991, 106). Thus he acknowledges that there were indeed motives behind the preaching of the Pauline group, but he plays down any potential problems this might suggest through the rhetoric surrounding the word "motives": "*without any unworthy personal* motives *whatever.*" They have motives, it is just that they are not deemed "unworthy." In addition, their preaching is presented as having an undiluted (perhaps ἀγνῶς; see 1:17) relationship with the "truth." Just what is assumed by O'Brien's comments here? First of all, it does not matter what value is given to the motives (worthy or unworthy), or how many qualifiers we place on the word, motives or intentions still mediate between the subject (evangelist) and object (gospel) and thus prevent an unmediated continuity between the subject and the object, which means that opposing one group to another on the basis that one group has a direct and unmediated connection to ἀλήθεια while another does not is problematic from the very start. Second, the difference between "unworthy" and "worthy" suggested here by O'Brien is a difference dependent upon the dominance of Paul's own theological system over other systems built on the basic premise of the gospel. Paul simply mentions that there is such a difference, and O'Brien is here affirming that difference as a hierarchical one. However, O'Brien attempts to make this hierarchy more pronounced by stating that the Pauline group has as the sole object of its evangelistic activity "Christ and his glory" (1991, 106), but this goes beyond what the text indicates: the differences between the motives find their exigence with respect to the evangelists' relationship to Paul.

To be sure, both groups of speakers have "motives" or "reasons" (προφασεῖς) for proclaiming Christ; thus, ultimately, both groups have as a part of the accompanying circumstances of their proclamation a reason to speak, a motive for proclaiming Christ; thus, both operate in a sphere of πρόφασις. Moreover, as mentioned, it seems that it is the preachers' relationship to Paul which establishes the value of the πρόφασις of his or her proclamation. Those who proclaim Christ through envy and strife (1:15), out of selfish ambition (1:17), and by pretext (πρόφασις) (1:18) are said to be doing so by Paul because they conflict with him: they imagine (οἴομαι) that they raise up tribulation for him in his imprisonment (1:17). Likewise, those who proclaim Christ through goodwill (1:15), out of love (1:16), and by truth (ἀλήθεια) (1:18) are labeled so because they confer with Paul— knowing (οἶδα) that he has been appointed for the defense of the gospel (1:16). Thus the classifications of πρόφασις and ἀλήθεια are dependent upon who Paul is and not upon who Christ is or what the gospel means, which consequently undermines the theological privileging of Paul's use of ἀλήθεια in 1:18 as the opposite of πρόφασις. Thus, again, the line of difference which Paul's argument has intended to draw between the two groups has been blurred by the text upon which it was drawn. The underlying ontological structures upon which Paul's theological argument rests are not confluent with that argument. What we are left with in Philippians are simply individuals who proclaim Christ for their own purposes, not metaphysical categories determining and dominating legitimacy.

6. Severing the Tie That B(l)inds

Philippians 1:12–14 draws an ironic picture: Paul is bound, but his gospel message advances freely. The perspective of the text, however, is that it is Paul's tethered circumstances that have untethered the gospel: "my 'imprisonment' has turned out for the greater progress of the gospel." The grain of the text is to present Paul as maintaining a position of influence—that is, maintaining his presence, and thus authority and power, with respect to the evangelists. The Philippians text suggests that the various products of the gospel text (at least two are mentioned) are linked back to Paul, and that Paul is still having an influence on the text *by virtue of his absence*. The evangelists are said to speak because they have gained boldness by Paul's imprisonment (1:14), some because they love Paul (1:16) and others because they imagine they will cause Paul strife in his imprisonment (1:17). The implications of this are interesting, since what is analogically true of Paul and his gospel in these circumstances is metaphysically true of authors and their texts in general. While Paul is forced into absence from the gospel text, the text itself is free to produce things he would prefer it did not produce. Every author is forced into absence by the mark of signification, since what Derrida labels *différance* functions as a metaphysical barrier imprisoning the presence of the author's consciousness.

Metaphysics is a reference to any system that employs a fundamental separation of the sensible and the intelligible and subsequently relies on the priority of the intelligible. Classically, the idea of an object has been understood as prior or superior to the thing itself which is a representative of the idea. The notion that the thing itself (the sensible) is a representation of the idea (the intelligible), which is also that which has come to be understood as presence, is fundamental to philosophy. Derrida's project, however, seeks to intervene in the difference between the sensible and the intelligible, questioning the assumed priority of the intelligible or what has come to be known as presence. Spivak therefore notes that, for Derrida, metaphysics is "shorthand for any science of presence" (xxi).

Thus the operation of Derrida's *différance* and the phenomenon of iterability, fundamental axioms of Derrida's philosophical project, prevent the author's presence or conscious will-to-communicate, or will-to-mean, from occupying the text. The intentions of the author's consciousness remain forever just that, the intentions of his or her consciousness; they cannot escape into and occupy the iterable marks of his or her text. Hence we read Barthes's claim that "linguistically, the author is never more than the instance writing, just as *I* is nothing more than the instance saying *I*: language knows a 'subject,' not a 'person'" (1976, 145). Once the signifying mark materializes, a space between the mark and the one who made the mark also materializes both spatially and chronologically. This spacing is, of course, a part of the structure of the mark without which there could be no mark, a space that is irreconcilable and without which the mark could not signify. It is this space, and thus "absence," as a necessary part of the structure of every signifying mark which enables the possibility of text to operate in the first place. And this possibility created by absence marks also the impossibility of the presence of the author's consciousness to occupy the text. This does not then suggest that absence now functions as the dominant category within the oppositional hierarchy absence/presence, but that the two infect, efface, and displace each other, calling into question the oppositional structure itself.

The forced absence of every author severs the text from its tether and thus enables it to be cited in various productive contexts; that is, forced absence enables the text to go beyond the bounds of the tether of univocality or even regulated polysemy[64] which the author's presence would attach to the text. As Barthes would say, this absence enables the text to become "writerly" (*scriptible*), to become productive rather than product, "not a line of words producing a single 'theological' meaning (the 'message' of the Author-God) but a multi-dimensional space in which a variety of writings, none of them original, blend and clash" (1976, 146). Barthes's semiotic theory, in part, works upon the difference between readerly (*lisible*) and writerly (*scriptible*) texts. Readerly texts are consumer-orientated, whereas writerly texts are typically understood to be producer-orientated. Ultimately, the distinction is not between two different kinds of texts, but different ways of constructing the text. The readerly approach is to subordinate the text to metaphysical significance or representation; the writerly approach is to disrupt the ease of generating metaphysical connections by acknowledging the resident textual folds and aporiae and seeking their logocentric performance.[65] In Philippians, Paul is caught in the difference between the gospel as writerly and as readerly.

In Philippians, it is never assumed that the text cannot continue to

---

[64] Regulating polysemy is the attempt to denote the semantic variation by naming specific semic units, in order to regulate the polysemy of the text and thus retard, or prevent, textual (re)production.

[65] For more on this, see Johnson 1978, 4; also Barthes's extended treatment in *S/Z*.

produce what Paul used it to produce. Even though Paul's hands are tied, he suggests that the hands of those citing the gospel are equally bound; they cannot control the text either. As far as Paul is concerned, the gospel text can continue to produce what he used it to produce regardless of the intentions of those who cite it. The only problem for Paul (though he does not mention it) is that the gospel text produces that and more. Again, this is true of authors and texts in general, and it is a particularly important point because the metaphysical disjunction between author and text is not a nihilistic phenomenon; indeed, it is quite the opposite. Orphaned texts (that is, *all* texts) are not doomed to a poverty of meaning; rather, their orphaned status places them in a position for continual abundance of meaning. Indeed, the very possibility of meaning is founded on the possibility of a text being able to break free from its parent, its "origins," and to become iterable. To tether the text absolutely to the consciousness or will of the author would prevent communication in the first place, since it would force texts to be subjective in the extreme, preventing them from being re-iterated in the experience of the reader/hearer. Again, for the text to operate, it must do so by being apart from the author, and thus by being reproduced or reinscribed in the wor(l)ds of other subjects (note Derrida 1986, 317).

Communication or meaning is only possible by virtue of our ability to re-cite the marks of a message in terms of our own horizon of life experience. So, unless the marks of communication can be severed from the author and his or her own subjective world, they cannot even begin to mean. Thus, every attempt to communicate or to mean is an act of disownment whereby the author disseminates, by virtue of a text, the seeds of signification in order that they might find purchase in the soil of some other subject. Thus it is by no means a nihilistic move to acknowledge the orphaned status of texts; it is rather the acknowledgment of a text's ability to produce beyond the expectations of the author, but not necessarily instead of them.

In Phil 1:18, Paul actually invokes this metaphysical separation of the message from the messenger; with his own chains he unlocks the bonds which bound intention to meaning. But can Paul have his meaning and keep it? On the one hand he attempts to inject his controlling presence into the proclamation of the gospel by claiming that various kinds of preachers preach by virtue of his own circumstances. On the other hand, he claims that the gospel message is free of the intentions of those preachers.

The graphematic gospel, the iterable mark(s) of an apostle, finds a new cite of production in the contexts brought into being by the acts of different preachers. Paul says that the message spoken by the aforementioned preachers performs, or has the potential to perform, a function or a meaning either exterior to the speaker's intention, or at least not defined by or tethered to those intentions. There are several important points to make about this critical move. We shall begin with an observation, introduced in chapter 1, of language performance in the vein of J. L. Austin, since Austin addresses the distinction between language used in normal circumstances, that is, "serious" language (requiring the comprehensive presence of the speaker's intentions), and abnormal circumstances, that is, "non-serious" language (requiring that intentions are other than that which would be present in the same text in normal circumstances).

A question to begin with is, do utterances performed under duress or in "non-serious" contexts have the same performance value or "meaning" (if we can call it that) as utterances performed in serious contexts? If an actor in a play says to another actor, "I love you," is it an expression of truth? Most people would follow Austin and answer no (1976, 22).

If it seems to us that "no" is the correct answer on both of the above accounts, why is it, then, that Paul seems to think that an utterance spoken in a "non-serious" mode (that is, from φθόνος and ἔρις, with ἐριθεία and οὐχ ἁγνῶς, and later characterized by Paul as πρόφασις) has the same value, or can mean the same thing, as one spoken in a "serious" mode (that is, through εὐδοκία, out of ἀγάπη, and in/by ἀλήθεια)? Asking this question leads us to discover that Paul is bound to a rather unexpected cellmate: Jacques Derrida. Derrida has also rewritten the distinction between the performative value of serious and nonserious language. Moreover, as we go along, we shall find that Paul has more in common with Derrida than most would care to admit.

5

Failing to Close

(RE)CITATION, (RE)ITERATION, COMMENT

The category of intention will not disappear; it will have its place, but from that place it will no longer be able to govern the entire scene and system of utterance. (Derrida 1986, 326)

1. Introduction

In this chapter, I comment on the textual contours of Phil 1:12–18 until we arrive at an undecidable point within the text, a point where its logic deconstructs (itself, since all deconstruction is already within the text). Traditional readings encounter this textual crevasse and seek to close it over, halting the natural dynamics of the text. The present rereading of this passage permits the logic to fail, and the result is found to be more fruitful and dynamic than the glossed, closed, halted version of commentary on this text.

I suggested above that Paul and Derrida had in common a willingness to accept a nondifference between utterances made in serious and nonserious contexts. At this point, I would like to investigate that suggestion and begin to read Philippians in light of the previous discussion between Austin and Derrida about contexts and intentions, and in light of the earlier discussion on *Hinterfragen*.

Before going on, it may be helpful to reiterate the basic point Paul makes in Phil 1:18. Paul is in prison, and he believes this ignited two kinds of reactions among two kinds of preachers. One kind of preacher of the gospel gains boldness because of Paul's imprisonment and preaches the gospel message from truth and love. The other kind of preacher also gains a boldness, but one that causes him to preach for his own gain while Paul is in prison, a sort of "while the cat's away the mice will play" scenario.

Paul also takes pains to point out that the preaching or intention of the latter group is self-oriented, impure, and false. Yet he does not suggest that these intentions infect the message or utterances of the gospel with their presence; rather, he indicates that the series of marks which constitute the gospel message act on their own. As discussed earlier, these marks "constitute a kind of machine that is in turn productive, that . . . [an author's] future disappearance in principle will not prevent from functioning and from yielding, and yielding itself to, reading and rewriting" (Derrida 1986, 316).[1]

It is important to recognize that the value system governing the description and distinction of these two kinds of preachers is a construct made with reference to Paul himself. He labels those supportive of him as good-willed (εὐδοκία) and those who preach from truth (ἀλήθεια), but those whom he believes are not supportive of him are selfish and impure (ἐριθεία καὶ οὐχ ἁγνῶς) and preach from falsehood (πρόφασις). Since Paul raises the issue, I shall later follow through the logic of his text and ask what the relationship is between the message and these messengers, and then what the relationship is between the two opposing kinds of messengers. For now, I turn to the treatment of this text by the commentaries on Philippians.

2. (Re)citation: Erasing the Contours of the Cite

Commentary on our passage has not really taken Paul's remarks "seriously." The tendency is to trace their discussions along the textual contours, but glossing over the metaphysical chasms. They fall precisely in line with the traditional discourse of Western metaphysics. This leads the commentaries to focus on the dynamics of the historical relationship between Paul and the preachers to whom he refers. Thus, for the commentaries, the primary critical issue associated with Phil 1:18 is the question of the identity of the bad preachers (see Michael 1928, 44–45; Beare 1959, 26; Martin 1976, 73–74; 1987, 72–75; Collange 1979, 9–10, 58; Hawthorne 1983, 35–38, esp. 37; Fee 1995, 121–24; also Jewett 1970a, 363). This is naturally followed up by an intense interest in the situation from which Paul wrote, since most theories of identity depend, to varying degrees, on determining whether Paul was in Caesarea, Ephesus, or Rome, and in or out of prison. Generally, the commentators wonder why Paul does not articulate some polemical diatribe against the selfish preachers in accordance with what is thought to be his normal practice. In other words, they see Paul's "soft" approach as abnormal. Jewett, who stands in contrast to the content of the general trend, suggests that Paul is not being soft on his antagonists, since he does cast dispersions upon the bad evangelists. The softness of Paul's comments may, suggests Jewett, derive from

---

[1] See also the earlier discussion in ch. 1, sec. 3.d.

the confusion over the fact that Paul does not label them outrightly as heretics (Jewett 1970a, 365–66).

It is no surprise to see this interest in the historical relationship between Paul and the other preachers, since it appears to be the simple perspective of the text. Paul is, after all, the one who is writing and he naturally sees the world with respect to his own experiences. Yet the "abnormality" of Paul's comments is not derived from a historical issue, but from a critical issue: the separation of author and text, intention and message, the subordination of the metaphysical to the logocentric. Furthermore, these mechanisms are hidden within the text itself; they are not brought to bear upon the text. What we find, however, is that to write about the text while glossing these aporiae is to bring something else to bear upon the text, to introduce to the text something foreign, to "distort" it, and finally to replace it, in order to make it acceptable.

To recite the text: Phil 1:13–14 is a complex result clause. The first part of the clause (1:13) focuses on the progress of the gospel outside the Christian community, the second part (1:14) refers to the situation *within* the Christian community. As a part of the same clause, Phil 1:14 continues to express the object of Paul's desire (βούλομαι, 1:12). He wants them to know that "the majority of the brethren have all the more confidence in the Lord[2] by virtue of my bonds to boldly speak the word without fear." Once again, Paul's focus is upon the re-citation of the gospel in new contexts, or "proclamation" ("to boldly speak the word[3] without fear"), which he cites as evidence of the gospel's progress. Thus, as with 1:13, 1:14 is an important contribution to Paul's rhetorical agenda to create a way of reading his situation so that the Philippians will not perceive some lack in either himself or his gospel.

As mentioned, Paul is now addressing the effect his imprisonment has had upon the interior of the Christian community. One of those effects has been to engender courage within the Christian community, and it is well noted among the commentaries that Paul is stressing this effect by piling up words which reflect this courage: πεποιθότας, περισσοτέρως, τολμᾶν, ἀφόβως. But of course, the effect is not singular; it is divided along two lines of interest, suggested initially by the comparative adjective πλείονας ("majority"; BAGD, 689), the point at which the story of another

---

[2] I have rendered ἐν κυρίῳ as a reference to the object in which the confidence is placed and treat τοῖς δεσμοῖς as the means by which the confidence is placed. As noted in O'Brien, adding "in the Lord" (τὸ ἀδελφῶν) is somewhat superfluous (1991, 94–95).

[3] The assumption here is that τὸν λόγον refers to the gospel. Apart from the fact that this is a classic New Testament reference to the message received from God (see Gal 6:6; 1 Thess 1:6–8; but note "the word of God" in Paul, 1 Cor 14:36; 2 Cor 2:17; 4:2; in early Christian use, for example, Acts 4:29; 6:2, 7; 8:4; 11:19; 13:5, 7, 44, 46; 16:32), there is a strong tradition clarifying the referent of τὸν λόγον: ℵ, A, B, (= D*), P, Ψ, et al. insert the modifier τοῦ θεοῦ; however, the more likely readings of P[46], D[2], et al. omit the phrase.

set of interests—that of the "minority"—becomes manifested within the text. One cannot help but wonder *why* Paul decided to volunteer this second story, a story of dissent and faction. The great interest of the commentaries appears to be the historical identity of the opponents;[4] however, I suggest that the "why" here is much more important than the "who," simply because what Paul is trying to do by mentioning this story of dissent is much more important *to Paul as he writes Philippians* than who is or is not dissenting. Fee is one of the few who attempts to deal with the "why" (1995, 123). He concludes that it anticipates the exhortations of 1:27–2:16 and 4:2–3. Hawthorne, somewhat defeated and more typical, states: "Why Paul felt it necessary to disclose to the Philippians the weaknesses of some of the brothers who were with him in Caesarea is a mystery" (1983, 38).[5]

2.a. *Identifying the Division*

The more substantial reference to division comes in 1:15 with the indefinite pronoun τινές ("certain ones"), which here refers to those other than the previously mentioned "majority." These "certain ones" preach Christ (Χριστὸν κηρύσσουσιν) through envy (φθόνον) and strife (ἔριν); they proclaim Christ (τὸν Χριστὸν καταγγέλλουσιν) out of selfishness (ἐξ ἐριθείας), without pure motives (οὐχ ἁγνῶς), supposing (οἰόμενοι) to raise up trouble while Paul is imprisoned. There are a number of interesting terms here, none of which, one imagines, would find a place on Paul's favorite "fruit of the Spirit" list.

In addressing the historical question of identity, the important task is to establish, at the very least, what *kind* of people they are. In fact, Fee asks this very question: "But who are these people, or at least *what kind* of people are they?" (1995, 121). The commentaries *tend* to suggest two certainties: they are brethren,[6] and they are brethren whose doctrine is no problem for Paul (among others Bockmuehl 1998, 77–78; O'Brien 1991, 103; Collange 1979, 55–56; Fee 1995, 118–23). It is this latter claim which

---

[4] An important problem which actually assists in determining the "why," though it is rarely treated as such.

[5] Note that the various arguments suggesting that this section is an excursus are by virtue of that suggestion attempting to answer the "why" of Paul's comments.

[6] There are many kinds of ἀδελφοί. The suggestions include the seemingly ubiquitous "Judaizers" (Lightfoot 1953, 88); people who were not actually opponents of Paul, but anti-imperialist Christians seeking the (eschatological) glory of persecution and martyrdom (Hawthorne 1983, 316–17); a set of circumstances based on the personal rivalry among the Roman Christians that extends itself to Paul (Cullman 1958, 104–9); Gnostics (Schmithals 1972, 65–122); Christian missionaries with a Greco-Roman divine-man view of apostleship (Jewett 1970a, 366–71); finally, Christians in Rome who did not like Paul, who were "downright antipathetic" (Bruce 1977, 390).

has the greatest interest for this book, for now we can certainly acknowledge that these preachers are indeed brethren; after all, they preach and proclaim Christ (1:15, 17), and they are the "certain people on the one hand" (τινὲς μέν) of "the majority of the brethren" who have gained confidence.

It is worth noting that involved in the discussion is Phil 2:20–21, where Paul seems to lament that no one seems to be concerned about the interests of Christ. They all seem to be preoccupied with their own interests.[7] Jewett, among others,[8] argues that we have here in Phil 2:20–21 a reference to the same group of people mentioned in Phil 1:15–17 (1970a, 369). If this is in fact the case, we have a delightful example of Paul's underlying disposition toward the "selfish" preachers surfacing only briefly, but long enough for us to begin to suspect even further the operation of 1:12–18.

2.b. Identifying Activity

On historical grounds, I would suggest that the most productive way to consider the issue is deciding what these people are actually doing or, perhaps more subtly, how one phrases what they are doing. Bockmuehl and Silva represent two of the important positions on the matter: Bockmuehl states that these self-centered preachers "smell an opportunity for self-advancement, even at the expense of causing the captive Paul distress" (1998, 76); Silva states that these people "merely pretended ... to be concerned for the gospel when their real desire was to aggravate Paul's sufferings" (1992, 72). The difference between these two scholars is how they have reconstructed the intentions of the self-centered preachers.

Bockmuehl has focused almost entirely on their personal "selfishness" (ἐριθεία, 1:17). In fact, Bockmuehl has focused on the ἐριθεία so much that the issue of deliberate antagonism toward Paul is phrased in such a way so as to suggest that it was not at all a deliberate activity but a mere by-product of seeking their own interests. In contrast, Silva has focused on their proactive antagonism, their "envy" (φθόνον), "strife" (ἔριν), and, primarily, their "supposing to raise up trouble" for Paul (οἰόμενοι θλῖψιν ἐγείρειν τοῖς δεσμοῖς μου). What this means is that Bockmuehl is going to end up saying that these people were not really opponents in the classical sense, but Christian preachers whose real problem is their selfish ambition, and who do not mind rubbing salt in Paul's wounds as they seek their own interests (see Bockmuehl 1998, 78, 80, 81). It also means

---

[7] Τὰ ἑαυτῶν ζητοῦσιν (they seek after their own things) in Phil 2:21 is easily understood as the equivalent of ἐριθεία (selfishness) in Phil 1:17.

[8] See the general acceptance in Fee 1995, 268; O'Brien 1991, 321–22; Bockmuehl 1998, 166; H. A. W. Meyer 1885, 127; against, for example, Gnilka 1968, 159, and note that a detailed description of the relationship between the two texts is found in Ollrog 1979, 193–200.

that Silva is going to cast these fellows in a much more sinister light. He asks, "[W]ould it really occur to anyone that one way of hurting the apostle was to preach precisely what Paul himself had been preaching, especially when such an activity would brand them as 'Pauline' and thus bring danger to them?" (1992, 73).

Silva supposes that "some issues of doctrinal significance must have been at stake," in spite of the fact that people were indeed being brought to a saving knowledge of Christ, which gives Paul occasion to rejoice (73). So where lies the problem? Silva suggests that it lies with this very success, that these fellows use their evangelistic success "to subvert the apostle's authority and to establish a form of Gentile Christianity that was friendlier to Judaizing influences" (1992, 73). Silva's position is most certainly aligned with the text's derision of these bad preachers to a greater degree than is Bockmuehl's, since Paul "does not treat these persons mildly at all, but casts aspersions on their tactics as well as their attitudes" (Jewett 1970a, 365). To clarify the distinction between Bockmuehl's text and Silva's text, let us consider the language Paul employs to perform the derision.

2.c. *Identifying Language*

The terms φθόνος and ἔρις, when together, make a potent pair of adjectives indicating "a need to tear down the rival teacher, to whom one feels inferior" (McEleney 1974, 211). The two terms are found partnered in biblical and extrabiblical vice lists (see further Wibbing 1959, 17, 21 n. 54, 37, 82, 77–108, 87–88). In 1 Tim 6:4, the two terms are again partnered in a classic Pauline vice list. What is interesting about this list is that it is specifically developed to describe the kind of person who teaches a different doctrine (1 Tim 6:3); still more interesting is that as the discussion develops we find that these people are also the sort of people who "think that godliness is a means of gain" (1 Tim 6:5). This text bears some interesting similarities to our Philippian passage. In Timothy we have people labeled with φθόνον and ἔριν who are using "godliness" (εὐσέβεια) as a means to profit (πορισμός), and yet are labeled as teaching a different doctrine (ἑτεροδιδασκαλέω). In Phil 1:15–17, we have people who are labeled as φθόνον and ἔριν who are using the proclamation of Christ (τὸν Χριστὸν καταγγέλλουσιν) for selfish gain (ἐριθεία).

In Titus 3:3–11, the author develops an ethical section in which he categorizes the former (pre-Christian) foolishness and unprofitability as φθόνος (Titus 3:3) and ἔρις (Titus 3:9). In Rom 2:29, those people who have failed to acknowledge God and who have been handed over to a depraved mind to do improper things (καθήκω)[9] are described as being filled with φθόνος and ἔρις, among other things. The famous vice list in Gal 5:19

---

[9] Cranfield notes that the nominal form "is especially associated with the Stoics, for whom it was an ethical technical term" (1975, 1:128–29). Thus we find both

lists ἔρις and φθόνος as "deeds of the flesh," and since the "flesh desires what is against the Spirit" (Gal 5:17), "those who practice such things will not inherit the kingdom of God" (Gal 5:21).

Even outside their partnership, the two terms are used in other contexts to describe the seedier side of life. Ἔρις, for the New Testament use of which "Paul virtually holds the copyright" (Schütz 1975, 161), in Rom 13:12–13 is cataloged as one of the "deeds of darkness," which is not the sort of activity in which one is supposed to engage during the "day" in preparation for salvation. In 1 Cor 3:3 (also 1:11), the presence of ἔρις reflects the fact that they are still "fleshly" (σαρκικός). In 2 Cor 12:20, ἔρις is listed with a set of all the bad characteristics that Paul fears might exist in the Corinthian church.

Φθόνος is found less often on its own. It is located in the Gospels with respect to jealousy of the Jerusalem leadership (Matt 27:18; Mark 15:10),[10] and, in 1 Pet 2:1, Christians are called to "put off" φθόνος and other like characteristics. Perhaps more important, φθόνος is described in classical literature in specific contrast to simple jealousy (ζῆλος), which focuses on a particular object of desire. Φθόνος appears to remove the focus from the self and to represent the desire to prevent or subvert the successes or acquisitions of another person (Trench 1978, 1:557); hence Aristotle's remark: "[E]nvy is a kind of pain at the sight of good fortune in regard to the goods mentioned . . . and not for the sake of a man getting anything, but because of others possessing it" (Aristotle, *Rhet.* 2.10.1, Freese).

The final important term employed by Paul to classify his opponents is ἐριθεία (selfishness/selfish ambition; BAGD, 309). The term is relatively new in the ancient world and found only in Aristotle prior to the New Testament period—in which case it described "the self-seeking pursuit of political office by unfair means" (BAGD, 309). In the New Testament it is located in many of the same places we find φθόνος and ἔρις, though some interesting differences exist. In James 3:16, we are told that wherever there is ἐριθεία so can be found "disorder" (ἀκαταστασία) and "every vile thing" (πᾶν φαῦλον πρᾶγμα). In James 3:14, it is associated with arrogance and lying against the truth, and we find the same idea in Rom 2:6–9, where ἐριθείας is coupled with "disobey" (ἀπειθέω) as the source of behavior which receives a strong condemnation: "God will render to each person according to his or her deeds . . . to those who are ἐξ ἐριθείας and disobey the truth, but pay heed to unrighteousness, wrath, and rage, (there will be) tribulation and calamity upon every soul of those who do evil."

Considering the nature of the language Paul employs, we can hardly take confidence in the notion that the only problem with these preachers

---

Zeno and Panaetius authoring treatises entitled περὶ τοῦ καθήκοντος. The use here in Romans clearly employs this sort of moral nuance (note Cranfield 1975, 129; Moo 1996, 118 n. 142; also see BAGD, 389).

[10] It is also listed in James 4:5 as a way to describe God's desire for us.

was their bad attitude. Furthermore, we cannot sustain the implication of Bockmuehl's commentary that the antagonism toward Paul was simply a by-product of their own selfish agenda. Rather, at the very least, we need to understand that the activity of these antagonists was designed deliberately to hurt Paul. Thus, in Paul's mind, such behavior, despite what he actually says about it (since that is the point in question), is tantamount to hurting or opposing Christ. After all, the people who "know" (Phil 1:16), as opposed to "suppose" (Phil 1:17), who Paul really is, know that he has been "appointed (κεῖμαι)[11] for the defense of the gospel." The important point to be noted about Paul's appointment is the identity of the subject of the "appointing," namely God. There is a natural positive correlation between this point and the one Paul makes in Gal 1:1, where he takes pains to point out that he is sent through Jesus Christ and God the father and not from humans—on the basis of which he can anathematize his opponents.

Both of the accounts by Bockmuehl and Silva reflect the fact that Paul understands himself to be doing God's work. To oppose Paul is to oppose that work which God is doing. Thus again, it is unlikely that Paul would construct any person deliberately opposed to him as merely having a bad attitude.

2.d. *Examples from Corinthians*

A helpful discussion on the issue of identity is the one found in 2 Corinthians, where Paul is dealing with people who are clearly involved in some sort of Christian mission. According to Paul, these fellows want to be regarded as apostles, and they seek opportunity among the Corinthians to be so regarded (2 Cor 11:12). These men are "pseudo-apostles," who "disguise themselves as apostles of Christ" (2 Cor 11:13). How does one disguise oneself as an apostle? Primarily, though not exclusively, through language; these men talk the talk, probably better than Paul does. In fact, we note that in 2 Corinthians Paul thrice appeals to the essentials of the word-deed convention (2 Cor 3:12; 10:10; 11:6), and on two of those occasions Paul is referring to an apparent lack in his speech, perceived by the Corinthians, which he seeks to counter by representing himself as more substantial in knowledge and deeds.[12] By contrast, these pseudo-apostles are not what their words make them out to be, a fact that Paul drives home when he points out that their "end will be according to their deeds" (2 Cor 11:15). Importantly, Paul highlights the separation of word and deed operative within the pseudo-apostles by virtue of the

---

[11] Serves as the passive of τίθημι (BAGD, 426): to lie, recline, etc. It has the figurative sense of "appointed, set, destined" (BAGD, 426), which is clearly the sense here.

[12] Thus invoking the word-deed convention; see discussion in ch. 3, sec. 3.c.i.

verb μετασχηματίζω,[13] which he uses three times in three verses: they *disguise* themselves as apostles of Christ (2 Cor 11:13), Satan *disguises* himself as an angel of light (2 Cor 11:14), they *disguise* themselves as servants of righteousness (2 Cor 1:15).

It would be a mistake, however, to assume that these fellows merely pretended to be apostles. It is rather more likely that they assumed that they were, which is not really a problem for Paul until the Corinthian church members also assume that they are apostles. Thus, Braumann, pointing to the inadequacy of the English word "disguise," notes that they were doing more than just pretending (1975, 1:708). Hence we find Bultmann's comment on 2 Cor 11:13 that μετασχηματιζόμενοι εἰς ἀποστόλους Χριστοῦ "certainly need not describe their subjective intent, as though these persons really did not desire to work for Christ at all; it is merely stated that they actually do not do so" (1985, 208). The probability that these fellows at Corinth assume they are apostles, and that some Corinthians assume that they are, presents us with an interesting parallel to Phil 1, which is made all the more pertinent by their identification as the "super-apostles" (ὑπερλίαν ἀποστόλων, 2 Cor 11:5).[14]

Thus again, it is too simple to dismiss Paul's magnanimity in Philippians on the basis that he is merely dealing with people who have a bad attitude. Those at Corinth who assume an apostolic posture but are in fact "pseudo," who disguise themselves as servants of righteousness in the same way that Satan disguises himself as an angel of light, represent a similar category of preacher to the one found in Philippians. That is, preaching the word does not automatically infer orthodoxy, or that these preachers are not disguising themselves. The language of the Philippians account goes too far to let these fellows be understood as merely emotionally and socially deficient, but the fact that this behavior receives severe condemnation in 2 Corinthians and only magnanimous indifference in Philippians, a "particularly striking" contrast (Schütz 1975, 168), is precisely the problem.

Second Corinthians provides us with yet another way to view Paul's opponents in Phil 1. Jewett raises the possibility that in Philippians Paul may be reacting to a "divine man" assumption about apostleship similar to the one suggested for 2 Corinthians (e.g., Georgi 1987, 230–38). The ex-

---

[13] The main concern of this word rests upon external form, rather than essential substance (Braumann 1975, 1:708).

[14] On whether the pseudo-apostles of 2 Cor 11:13 are also the super-apostles of 11:5 and 12:11, it appears to me that Paul is talking about the same people based on the fact that the entire argument from 10:12–12:13 is a discussion about the same thing: that Paul is not inferior to the newcomers. See Barnett 1997, 523; also the supportive discussions in Martin 1986, 349–50; Hughes 1962, 380, 392–93; Schütz 1975, 167–68. For the contrary position, see Bultmann 1985, 199. For a comprehensive evaluation, see Barrett 1971, 233–54.

istence of a divine-man theology within the culture is not really in dispute
(see Georgi 1987, 390–422); thus, the possibility that Paul encounters a divine-man ideal operative within Christian groups (both Jewish and
Gentile) remains a possibility. This works for Jewett because he believes
that Paul is experiencing opposition precisely *because* he is in prison
(1970a, 367), since imprisonment is hardly a demonstration of God's
power. Thus, Paul's reference to the progress of the gospel while in prison
is a counter to this accusation.

Jewett's position here is very close to my own. The text appears to
represent this sort of concern on Paul's part (a concern for an accusation
of some kind of lack); however, the very points which Jewett uses to
argue for why people at Ephesus[15] would be accusing Paul of weakness, I
have understood to be true of the Philippians. That is, the historical situation appears to me to be one in which Paul is arguing in *Philippians* for
the sake of the *Philippians*, and not for the sake of people in his present locale. Jewett argues that "the letter repeatedly makes the point that the
suffering for Christ is the epitome of Christian experience" (1970a, 367–
69). But we must ask why Paul would want to thread such an argument
throughout an epistle which is not going to be read by the people in question. Thus, I would rather suggest that the apparent theme of suffering,
along with Paul's points made in the early section of Philippians (especially Phil 1:12–18), is indicative of a problem Paul is attempting to resolve
among the readers of the epistle, and not among people who would probably never read it. However, again, I would suggest that what Jewett has
observed operating within the letter, a defense against an assumption
that his imprisonment suggests that there is something wrong with him
or even his gospel, is certainly a valid observation and one to which I myself hold, and one which is deeply implicated in my reading of
Philippians.

2.e. *An Insidious Summary*

Returning to the issue of identity, I would suggest that these people in
Phil 1:15–17 are people who in a different set of circumstances would re-
ceive the full weight of Paul's invective, but for overarching rhetorical
reasons this does not present itself to Paul as the most expedient course of
action as he writes Philippians, if he is to produce within the Philippian
church the manifestation of his own desires. If there is any patience in
Philippians, it is not with the self-centered preachers, as is typically assumed. The situation is rather that Paul is "carefully measuring"
(*Entstellung?*) his response so that in the end he maintains his position
within the life of the Philippian church.

On the matter of whether these "selfish" preachers were Christian, I

---

[15] Jewett begins with an argument for an Ephesian provenance (1970a,
363–64).

simply say that the text bears out the very fact with little or no ambiguity. As to the matter of whether they were pure in their doctrine or whether they simply had a bad attitude, the bulk of scholarship assumes the latter. This assumption is naturally based upon historical conjecture,[16] which follows a line of argument that bases itself on an idea of the Paul we have come to know everywhere else, and which *assumes* Paul simply would never have been so magnanimous with questionable doctrine. It is therefore necessary to raise the question, the *Hinterfrage*, What if their doctrine was other than Paul's? What if Paul has in fact allowed questionable doctrine to pass by unchecked? Why would he do that? What would he be hiding? What would he be distorting in an effort to bypass the Censor?[17]

Of course, these *Hinterfragen* are equally applied to the commentaries. Why make the assumption that Paul would simply not allow impure teaching to get past him? The grain of the text is well-testified among the commentaries to be a surprising one, because the Paul we experience in the New Testament is not one to be so magnanimous about opposition of any sort, let alone appear to lend some approval, as we find in Phil 1:18. Commentary which argues for the assumption, even on its own terms, fails to relate Paul's description of the preachers to the larger Pauline corpus;[18] it also tends to forget—it is the art of forgetting—that Paul specifically states that these fellows were not preaching from pure motives and that their teaching was a pretext for something else.

3. Sur-prise

Lurking within Phil 1:18a is the element of "sur-prise."[19] Philippians 1:18a is an assault, but not so much upon the text itself (Phil 1:12–17) as it is upon the presentation of that text by its readers. The fractures generated by Phil 1:18a run through the "text" as the "methodological field" of activity (Barthes 1977, 155–64, esp. 156–57). The experience of sur-prise is

---

[16] To be precise, it really is based on a way of reconstructing that history with respect to the ideological framework of the person doing the reconstructing.

[17] I think this goes beyond Silva's suggestion, because ultimately Silva is satisfied with Paul's rejoicing and sees it as pure and unaffected. It is probably the case that Paul can isolate positive points about which he can be happy, but his saying so, the reason he decides to point out his rejoicing, has more to it than the fact of his "rejoicing."

[18] Baur is so indignant toward the text's lack of confluence with Paul in general that he dismisses it as altogether non-Pauline (Baur 1875–76, 2:65).

[19] "sur- /sə:/ *pref.* [Fr. (earlier *so(u)r-* f. as SUPER-.] Used in wds adopted f. Fr. and rarely as a productive Eng. pref., in senses of SUPER-" (*OED*, 3155). "prise /prʌiz, priːz/ *n.*[1] . . . [(O)Fr., use as n. of fem. pa. pple of *prendre* take seize. . .]" (*OED*, 2358). "prise /prʌiz/ *n.*[2] . . . [f. as prec. cf. PRY *n.*[4]] 1 An instrument used for prising or levering something off; a lever. . . . 2 The action of prising something; leverage" (*OED*, 2358). "prise /prʌiz/ *v.*[1]*t.* . . . 1 Raise, move, or open by force of leverage" (*OED*, 2358).

well-attested among the commentaries, albeit in various ways. However, the most unfortunate way in which this is treated is to forget it; a review of the index in Dunn's *The Theology of Paul the Apostle* reveals that this particularly problematic statement (Phil 1:18a), which has significant implications for Pauline theology, is in fact one of eleven verses of Philippians not cited or referenced in any way in this attempt to "write" the theology of Paul the apostle (see Dunn 1998a, 794–96). This is a delightful presentation of commentary as the art of forgetting.

So how does this sur-prise come about? Fee provides us with an excellent introduction: "The surprise comes in his large-heartedness about this—not that he [Paul] could not be large-hearted, *but that he could be so toward people of a kind whom he elsewhere seems to inveigh so strongly against* (118, emphasis added; 125). A little closer to the textual production of this sur-prise we find Gnilka observing that Paul creates a fracture between Phil 1:17 and 18 by "interjecting a question" (*dazwischengeworfenen Frage*) between them; he effectively "breaks off the discussion" (*bricht . . . die Erörterung* (1968, 63). Thus Gnilka notes that Paul is heading in one direction but suddenly, when he arrives at Phil 1:18, he sur-prises our thoughts on where we imagined the discussion to be going. It is very important for us to note that the sur-prise here, Gnilka's sense of *bricht*,[20] only has currency with respect to our reading; that is, it is our impressions formed by the earlier stages of the text that make Phil 1:18 a sur-prise.

Bruce detects a difference between Philippians and other readings of Paul's epistles and notes that "Paul has mellowed" and has become more like Christ (1989, 47). Importantly, Bruce's sense of difference is based upon his *Hauptbriefe* experience.[21] Bockmuehl understands the whole passage to be "unexpected" (1998, 76) and refers to the Phil 1:18a section as demonstrating a "new attitude" (81) and a "remarkable spirit of generosity" (77). He writes that Paul's "tone does seem to have mellowed" (81). In other words, Bockmuehl has been sur-prised and notices something at odds with the way he typically assumed Paul to work, which just so happens to be based upon a reading of *Hauptbriefe* such as Galatians.[22] Barth sees a change in the apostle: "[O]ne may venture the biographical remark that we have here to do with an insight that has grown and matured in

---

[20] *Bricht* is a third-person singular present-tense form of *brechen* (to break). I am anglicizing it here as something of a noun, invoking "it breaks" within the nominal use.

[21] He begins the discussion with a reference to Paul's attitude among the Galatians, as well as comparing Paul's attitude in Philippians to 2 Corinthians (Bruce 1989, 47). Note the earlier discussion on *Hauptbriefe* and reading Paul in ch. 1, sec. 2.

[22] Bockmuehl bases his comparisons on what he believes to be true of Galatians (1998, 81).

comparison. . . ." From what standard of Pauline literature can Barth say that Paul has deviated? ". . . say, II Corinthians" of course (1962, 33).[23]

Collange reveals that the problem has "often intrigued commentators," and he himself notes a difference between the "intransigence of . . . [Paul's] other epistles" and the "'liberal' attitude" in the Philippians passage (1979, 58). Schütz (1975, 164), along with Martin (1976, 74), detects a difference in Paul's demonstration of "indifference" and labels it "curious." Hawthorne is awed by a display of "splendid magnanimity" (1983, 38), and Michael by an "amazing magnanimity" (1928, 42). Silva warms to "a remarkable passage in which the apostle lays his heart bare and reveals the deepest motives of his life" (1992, 74).

Gnilka, after observing the textual *bricht*, recites the apparent trend among scholars to ask why Paul was willing "to overlook" (*hinwegzusehen*) the agitators "so generously" (*so großzügig*), and notes the common reference made by commentators on this verse is that Paul displays *Seelengröße*, a generous spirit (1968, 64). Dibelius sees in the passage a "wonderful objectivity" (*großartige Sachlichkeit*) in which all the previous "reservations" (*Hintergedanken*) become "confounded" (*zuschanden*) (1937, 66). Similarly, Lohmeyer sees in Phil 1:18 a "beautiful testimony" (*schönes Zeugnis*) to Paul's "unselfish objectivity" (*selbstloser Sachlichkeit*) (1964, 47).

One of the more remarkable commentaries on this re-markable passage comes from Michael. In an excellent demonstration of how reading turns into writing, Michael, encountering the aporia of Phil 1:18a, delves into speculation about Paul's temperament. In commenting upon Phil 2:21, he brings Phil 1:15–17 into the discussion and claims that Paul had lost control of his temper ("temporary annoyance"); thus, "we must not attach to the words too literal and strict a meaning. Paul does not quite mean all that his words seem to mean, anymore than when he condemns the preachers in 1:15ff" (1928, 115). Returning to his commentary on Phil 1:18: "Paul is hurt. Words escape him which in a calmer mood he would scarcely have uttered. He charges them with a deliberate desire to annoy him!" (45). Paul has been royally irritated, in Michael's view, and thus when he decides to suppress his true feelings "his magnanimity is no whit less magnificent; it is even more amazing" (45). Indeed, "the irritation has produced a pearl!" (45).

There is one more comment from Michael to note. He sees that there is indeed a sur-prise operating in this text which is prising our readings out of position, seizing them, opening them. He notes that "the splendid magnanimity of ver. 18 has *blinded* us to the signs of annoyance in vers. 15 and 16" (45, emphasis added). This is indeed the nature of the sur-prise, yet we find that the sur-prise is suppressed in the final reading of the passage. What Michael does somewhat consciously, most do unconsciously;

---

[23] Again, Barth's expectations of Paul are dependent upon a privileging of *Hauptbriefe* over Philippians.

they re-cite the text so as to generate a hierarchy between Phil 1:15–17 and 1:18.

The *bricht* operating between the two passages fractures the metaphysic imposed upon the text through commentary and is necessarily dispensed with in the final presentation of the text. That is, while there is apparently a hierarchy operative within the text, this hierarchy is reversed by commentary to provide conscious acceptability of the text.

4. Commentary

The remarks of surprise and cries of magnanimity are contingent upon how one understands Phil 1:18 to relate to Phil 1:15–17. The problem is simply this: Phil 1:15–17 appears perfectly normal and consistent with how we typically read Paul, but then we read Phil 1:18. At that point, an interpretative and institutional crisis develops; its resolution is "commentary." That is, the crisis must be removed and (re)presented and (de)formed in a way that allows it to fit comfortably, safely, acceptably into our conscious impressions of Paul. The mechanism for this is almost always a rereading of Phil 1:15–17, which (re)presents these verses as not what they appear to be.

When this (re)presentation is performed on Phil 1:15–18, an important and ironic decision is masked: Phil 1:18 is allowed to govern Phil 1:15–17. In other words, what at first appears to be "normal" in Phil 1:15–17 is suddenly reconstructed in the face of Phil 1:18. *Hinterfrage*: Why? Well, if Phil 1:15–17 is allowed to pass for what it typically appears to be, then Paul in Phil 1:18 is subordinating the metaphysical (theology) to something a little more earthly: words, proclamation, logocentrism.

Further: the commentary performed through Phil 1:18 upon Phil 1:15–17 implicates itself in its own critique. It seeks to replace the text with writing, or more importantly, to fill up the logical fracture in Phil 1:15–17 caused by the shock of Phil 1:18 with more writing so as to (re)create a textual grain along the lines of which a theology can be developed. It thus also fails to generate a metaphysic of the text, making a theology *reductio ad verbum*, logocentrism, logotheology. Thus, commentary participates in the very thing that is shocking about Phil 1:18 by becoming the very thing it seeks to displace.

Further still: this (e)strange(ed) movement creates a hierarchy within the text: Phil 1:18 over 1:15–17. It thus reads against the logical grain of the text and imposes upon it a supplemental logic, without which, it is apparently assumed, the text fails to cohere. Let us briefly consider this supplement. "Supplement" (*supplément*) is an important word for Derrida, developed and derived from his interaction with Rousseau's *Essay on the Origin of Languages*. Rousseau consigns writing to a supplemental role in language, but fails to maintain the difference between writing and speech, allowing Derrida to perform one of his most erudite deconstructions of Western metaphysics.[24] The importance of this here is that the logic of supplementarity comes to bear upon the idea of the commentary: "Supplementarity, which *is nothing* neither a presence nor an absence. . . . It is precisely the play of presence and absence, the opening of this play that no metaphysical or ontological concept can comprehend" (1976, 244). And this is not to suggest that commentary is nothing, rather that its supplemental logic and the "play" invoked by it precedes the object of its force: the text.[25] Thus, like the supplement, commentary is a point of metaphysical undecidability; it seeks to be both a part of and an addition to the text; it wavers between presence and absence, never quite one or the other, never quite the text, never quite theology.

The hierarchy in Phil 1:15–18 created by commentary is supplemented to the text in order "to compensate"[26] for an apparent lacuna within the text. What is this omission? Is it power? In which case, one could say that ensuring Paul remains antagonistic to difference, through "commentary" on Phil 1:15–17, is nothing less than ensuring the institutional stability of the whole nature of Western Christian theology. Failure at this point would send shock waves throughout the entire structure. Yet we find that all this relies upon the logic of supplementarity, which is really nothing at all. Unable to escape the text, commentary invokes *Entstellung* so that other experiences of the text are not in fact of the text at all, rather of the transcription of one logocentric system in the place of another.

5. More Commentary

As discussed earlier in this chapter, what makes meaning and thus commentary possible is iterability. Yet the possibility of (re)citation already problematizes the fundamental desire of biblical commentary for the metaphysical or, as Bruner puts it, "rummaging in the thoughts and words of God" (1990, 401). It does so because the moment of the iter, in which the mark comes into existence enabling the question of meaning in the first place, is the same moment it is permanently divided from the presence which it *represents* since that which representation represents more than anything else is absence. The struggle with this absence is that which invokes the need for interpretation and commentary; it invokes

---

[24] See ". . . That Dangerous Supplement . . ." in Derrida 1976, 141–64, which itself is a supplement to "Genesis and Structure of the *Essay on the Origin of Languages*" (Derrida 1976, 165–268).

[25] See Derrida's comments on the property of man (1976, 244).

[26] From *Compensare* (*OED*, 458), infinitive of *compenso* "To balance, make good, offset (a debt, deficit . . .). 2 To counter balance, make up for (a deficiency), etc.), make good in another way, offset. . . . 3 To balance mentally, weigh (against). 4 To save, secure, obtain (at the expense of or by sacrificing something else) b. to get rid of (by exchange)" (*OLD*, 374–75).

the desire for a metaphysical presence within biblical texts, that is, "theology." As we shall see, the final resting place is an undecidable point between presence and absence, never quite the text, never quite theology.

As we have seen, commentary seeks to overcome its metaphysical lack by re-citing the text in such a way so as to enable the metaphysical to maintain its dominance. In fact, commentary is entirely and radically (re)citation, unable to prevent the relocation of the text into one contextual frame or another, thus never able to present the text as something in itself; it must always take the place of the text.

Apart from the possibility of commentary and the contemporaneous impossibility of presence, the issue of iterability is invoked once more in the analysis of the Philippians passage. However, this requires an extension of the logic required to generate the metaphysical reading of our passage into the historical activity being represented by the text. That is, as mentioned earlier, commentary on our passage attempts to reverse a hierarchical structure operating within the text. It attempts to locate Phil 1:18 over Phil 1:15–17.

I suggested earlier that the reason for this binary relocation was that if Phil 1:15–17 is allowed to dominate Phil 1:18, then Paul is subordinating the metaphysical (theology) to something a little more earthly: words, proclamation, logocentrism. Such an activity by commentary should be no surprise to us, since it is in its nature to attempt to maintain, thus to "(re)create," presence within the text. Yet the act of (re)creation is a divine act; thus, as with Watson's "theological hermeneutics," commentary is a theological activity in which the commentator must become a god in order to achieve it. This particular attempt by commentary to maintain the metaphysical within the text is actually something of a problem for the solution arrived at by that same activity. That is, when Phil 1:18 is relocated to the dominant position over Phil 1:15–17, the purpose is to ensure that doctrine remains fixed to a transcendent point of reference outside the logocentric world by making sure that Paul does not allow an erasure of the most important line of distinction, that between ἀλήθεια and πρόφασις.

But what are the consequences? If the selfish preachers are said to preach the truth (ἀλήθεια), what of πρόφασις? If Phil 1:18 is made to dominate Phil 1:15–17, then the result is that the metaphysics of presence are retained within the text of Philippians, but only if at the same time the metaphysics of presence is removed from the selfish preachers of the gospel. That is, the main way in which commentary seeks to compensate for bad intentions while assuming the bad preachers preach ἀλήθεια[27] is to point out that Paul "rejoices" in it (hence the dominance of Phil 1:18). But for the graphematic gospel to be re-cited and thus to operate *apart from* the bad intentions of the selfish preachers means that the gospel is re-

---

[27] Which could only ever be a Pauline version.

quired to perform an autonomous activity.[28] In order for Paul, then, to be able to "rejoice" at this recitation of an approved gospel, the assumption must be made that this graphematic structure bears within itself the presence of the original speaker's intentions (ἀλήθεια?), but not the intentions of those who cite it.

The result is that there is a decision to be made, albeit an entirely undecidable one: (1) accept that Paul allows for an alternative version of the gospel,[29] and thus remove the distinction between ἀλήθεια and πρόφασις and the range of possibilities that depend upon the structure; (2) allow the division of ἀλήθεια and πρόφασις to work its way back through the text and require the intentions of the preachers to be absent from the recitation of the gospel, while at the same time requiring a previous author's intentions to be present. The text remains open. . . .

6. Failure to Close:
A (Non)Serious Reading of Philippians 1:12–18

What must we do to be saved? I suggest that it is precisely the failure of the text to close that is our salvation. The aperture opened by this text provides readers and scholars of Paul with access to the logocentric mechanisms or, indeed, the "machinations" and agenda that comprise the substructure of what passes for Paul's "theology." Is this the same as Dunn's reference to "*The*" theology of Paul? I do not believe that it is, primarily because it relegates Pauline theology away from metaphysical categories, which are simply inventions of writing, and toward a productive, logocentric, ethical reality. It is even different, although much less so, from those who refer to Paul as "theologizer"[30] as opposed to "theologian," since in this case writing about theologizing is still creating a metaphysic for the text. It still seeks to produce a totalization, or saturation of presence, which subsequently is thought to govern the entire reading and recitation of the product. Does the aperture allow us to escape those things? No, because "any theology, whatever else it is, must also be a semiology" (Hart 1989, 7).

Pauline theology is troubled when it fails to take into consideration the presence of underlying social and ideological structures, because Paul's text is already constrained by them. At this point a significant crisis develops in the dependence upon the text for metaphysical significance,

---

[28] Not a few authors argue the point that the gospel has its own "objective force" (e.g., Collange 1979, 58; Gnilka 1968, 64). There are others who simply argue that it is God's message and thus imply that God's presence is a part of the gospel text (e.g., Fee 1995, 125–26).

[29] For example, Silva suggests a version is being preached in which the preachers are presenting a more Jewish-friendly version (1992, 73).

[30] Note especially Roetzel (1999, 93–134), who has an excellent description of the questions this raises for such things as the privileging of Romans (93).

since socially and ideologically constrained structures of thought precede the text; indeed, they themselves are the means by which the author conceives of a text. Thus, as stated in chapter 3, in Paul's letters we confront not theology but a construct produced by a complex of conscious and unconscious processes, namely language. Bringing this to bear upon our reading of Paul is more than simply acknowledging the need for background information on Paul's text; it means that we subordinate our reading of Paul to the cultural constraints present to him. These constraints are "present" because they were a part of who Paul was; they are a part of both his unconscious and conscious mind, and thus they precede and are required by the iteration of his thought.

In chapter 3, I suggested that there is an important need for a cultural matrix to grant us the necessary dynamic context. This need presents Greco-Roman psychagogy to us as a viable social structure, since this one social structure contains within it a much larger complex of the relevant social structures that have been used to identify features of Paul's thought and practice. A couple of key features stand out: the cultural requirement for a confluence of word and deed, and the psychagogic sense of responsibility. In addition to these cultural precedents to Paul's thinking, I have also already discussed in both chapter 1, and the present chapter, the problematic nature of commentary's habit of glossing the text as it seeks the metaphysical within it. The problem here is located in that which prevents the metaphysical from operating within the text, namely the citationality, or iterability, of text as discussed in chapter 1.

If we bring all those things to bear upon the present conversation we discover an interesting, and I think highly productive reading, of Phil 1:12–18. We start back in Phil 1:12. Paul begins with a disclosure: the gospel has progressed during his imprisonment. Paul affirms this by pointing to a couple of successes: (1) the guards know that he is there for the sake of the gospel, and (2) people have been emboldened to preach the gospel. At this point, as mentioned earlier, success for Paul is measured by the gospel's progress (yet another social ideal). Interestingly, this did not mean acceptance of the gospel; progress was, instead, contextualized by the activity of proclamation, that is, of re-iteration. Already we can see Paul starting to displace certain traditional hierarchies by virtue of relegating evangelistic success ("progress") to the deeply logocentric activity of proclamation, thereby resting it upon iterability.

The importance of the gospel is its ability to be reiterated. Thus the next thing we encounter in Philippians is that very thing: a story about re-iteration, yet one which divides itself along the contours of two different contextualizing forces operating upon that reiteration—contextual forces which fail to totalize or saturate the iterable gospel text with their presence and thus fail to govern its usage (a point of success for Paul, but failure for commentary). In the face of these two sets of evangelistic iterations, and with respect to Paul's claim of success, I cite Derrida: "[W]hat is a success when the possibility of infelicity[31] continues to constitute its structure?" (1998b, 15). This is the very question that comes to bear upon commentary on Philippians that elects to privilege Phil 1:18 over Phil 1:15–17. When the possibility of communication in general—namely iterability—permanently divides the speaker and text, and at the same time erases any metaphysical marks from the text, what is it that makes one evangelistic re-iteration be considered successful or ἀλήθεια, if the other is said to forestall the presence of the speakers' intentions by the activity of πρόφασις? Nothing at all. And Paul seems to have recognized this, or at least he invokes it. Thus the logic of our text is one that disrupts itself, and prevents metaphysical commentary.

Is this disruption deliberate? In chapter 3, I argued that the disclosure formula is ultimately (dis)closure; it appears to be the avenue through which one can experience Pauline presence, but the moment in which that is accepted by the reader the text is suddenly closed. I referred to this as a sort of "Trojan logic" which was placed into operation by Paul to achieve goals not immediately apparent to his Philippian readers. I suggested that the need for such a logic is represented by both the text and the standard social norms. Essentially, the reason amounts to Paul's attempt to alleviate the socially constructed, "natural and reasonable" expectations of the Philippians that there is a problem with Paul (due to his imprisonment) and thus also with his gospel. This is also suggested by the grammar of μᾶλλον in Phil 1:12, which suggests that Paul is attempting to counter the "natural and reasonable" expectations by arguing that the unexpected has occurred. What has in fact occurred is then constructed as wholly positive: evangelistic reiteration, presented as "progress," as opposed to the expected "regress."

The natural expectation that his imprisonment demonstrates that there is something fundamentally wrong with Paul is something against which the full complement of his social faculty rises. Paul's apostolically charged psychagogic disposition, which extends its activity to both Paul and the Philippians, requires him to engage the Philippians, at least at first, on the very grounds which cause this "natural and reasonable" expectation. That is, Paul has to engage the Philippians on entirely socially constructed grounds. Since Paul's letters are all radically logocentric, constrained by the discursive structures of his culture, this should not be a surprise. It appears that Paul calls upon a certain cultural ideal to demonstrate his personal validity and thus also the validity of his gospel. Paul's commentary on his experience provides a way for the Philippians to reconstruct his situation in terms which are acceptable to their social sensibilities. The first and primary way in which he seeks to achieve this

---

[31] By "infelicity," Derrida refers to Austin's idea of the "parasitic" use of language, that is, the abnormal use of language such as in movies and plays which requires the existence of normal use in order to work (see Austin 1976, 14).

is through a demonstration that his gospel (words) is in no way compromised by his imprisonment (deeds).[32] In so doing, Paul conforms to the most basic of psychagogic ideals.

Paul's desire to demonstrate success in the standard social terms, which I am suggesting is by virtue of his employment (conscious or unconscious) of psychagogic ideals, means that he specifically argues for a *performance* of language which manifests both of the ideals embedded within the word-deed convention. It is on the basis of this that Paul then tells a story of two (re)iterations in Phil 1:15–17, and then deliberately problematizes the two stories when, in Phil 1:18, he suggests that, whether the evangelistic reiteration is labeled as ἀλήθεια or as πρόφασις, he remains happy.

This final maneuver (which ultimately becomes the "first" maneuver) is a crucial process to Paul's own activity in his apostolate and the subsequent development of "Pauline theology": Paul deliberately writes himself out of the gospel. That is, Paul dislocates the gospel from the presence of the speakers with his disruption of the ἀλήθεια/πρόφασις opposition in Phil 1:18, effectively rendering the gospel a radically logocentric structure, open for re-citation. If the gospel is *not* subordinated to the presence of the speaker, then whatever is going on with Paul's imprisonment, whatever natural and reasonable expectations that people may have had about Paul, can no longer be said to be present in the (graphematic) gospel.

Paul has done two things and in the process masterfully salvaged the gospel from potentially devastating circumstances. First Paul went about representing himself in cultural terms as above-reproach with his claim to progress and his adherence to basic expectations placed upon psychagogues. Second, Paul removed himself, *and everyone else*, from the re-citation of the gospel so that whatever might be said about the speaker, the gospel remains absent from that person's presence and, thus, intentions.

After the text's self-deconstruction, through the flotsam rises a single, intact ethical imperative: *proclamation*. While the gospel for Paul is merely language, entirely semiological, it is also a device, an apparatus, which he employs to bring about the manifestation of his ideological agenda. The precise nature of that agenda is another story altogether. I will, however, suggest this: proclamation as an activity can be argued to be the central point of reference for everything that we read in Paul. That is, what has come through this text is that which is central to Paul's own sense of the world, and the suggestion is that perhaps this needs to be a critique of how we have read Paul. It may be necessary to radically subject all of Paul's statements to the performative logic of proclamation and in the process to uncover a different Paul: Paul the pragmatic proclaimer.

---

[32] It is important to note that I am confining myself to this particular aspect of Paul's attempt to use Philippians in this way.

Works Consulted

Abel, Lionel. 1974. Jacques Derrida: His "Difference" with Metaphysics. *Salgamundi* 25 (Winter): 3–21.

Aland, Kurt. 1979. Die Entstehung des Corpus Paulinum. Pages 302–50 in *Neutestamentliche Entwürfe*. Theologische Bücherei 63. Munich: Kaisen.

Aland, Kurt, and Barbara Aland. 1989. *The Text of the New Testament: An Introduction to the Critical Editions and to the Theory and Practice of Modern Textual Criticism*. Translated by E. F. Rhodes. 2nd ed. Grand Rapids: Eerdmans.

Alexander, Loveday C. A. 1989. Hellenistic Letter-Forms and the Structure of Philippians. *JSNT* 37:87–101.

———. 1992. Schools, Hellenistic. *ABD*. 5:1005–11.

———. 1994. Paul and the Hellenistic Schools: The Evidence of Galen. Pages 60–83 in *Paul in His Hellenistic Context*. Edited by Troels Engberg-Pedersen. Edinburgh: T&T Clark.

Arzt, Peter. 1994. The "Epistolary Introductory Thanksgiving" in the Papyri and in Paul. *NovT* 36:28–46.

Asmis, Elizabeth. 1986. Psychagogia in Plato's Phaedrus. *ICS* 11:153–72.

Atkins, J. W. H. 1952. *Literary Criticism in Antiquity: A Sketch of Its Development*. 2 vols. New York: Peter Smith.

Austin, J. L. 1976. *How to Do Things with Words*. 2nd ed. Oxford: Oxford University Press.

Balch, David L., Everett Ferguson, and Wayne Meeks, eds. 1990. *Greeks, Romans, and Christians: Essays in Honor of Abraham J. Malherbe*. Minneapolis: Fortress.

Barclay, John M. G. 1995. Deviance and Apostasy: Some Applications of Deviance Theory to First-Century Judaism and Christianity. In *Modelling Christianity: Social-Scientific Studies of the New Testament in its Context*. Edited by Philip F. Esler. London: Routledge.

Barnett, Paul. 1997. *The Second Epistle to the Corinthians*. NICNT. Grand Rapids: Eerdmans.

Barrett, C. K. 1971. Paul's Opponents in II Corinthians. *NTS* 17:233–54.

Barth, Karl. 1962. *The Epistle to the Philippians*. London: SCM.

Barthes, Roland. 1974. *S/Z*. Translated by Richard Miller. New York: Hill and Wang.

———. 1977. *Image Music Text*. Translated by Stephen Heath. New York: Hill and Wang.

Bateman, Herbert W., IV. 1998. Were the Opponents at Philippi Necessarily Jewish? *BSac* 155 (January–March): 39–61.

Baur, F. C. 1875–76. *Paul, the Apostle of Jesus Christ: His Life and Work, His Epistles and His Doctrine. A Contribution to the Critical History of Primitive Christianity.* Translated by Eduard Zeller and Rev. A. Menzies. 2nd ed. 2 vols. London: Williams and Norgate.

Beare, F. W. 1959. *A Commentary on the Epistle to the Philippians.* HNTC. New York: Harper & Brothers.

Bearn, Gordon C. F. 1995. Derrida Dry: Iterating Iterability Analytically. *Diacritics* 25 (Fall): 3–25.

Becker, Howard Saul. 1963. *Outsiders: Studies in the Sociology of Deviance.* New York: Free Press.

Becker, U. 1976. "Gospel, Evangelize, Evangelist." Pages 107–15 in vol. 2 of *New International Dictionary of New Testament Theology.* Edited by Colin Brown. 3 vols. Grand Rapids: Zondervan, 1975–78.

Beker, J. Christiaan. 1984. *Paul the Apostle: The Triumph of God in Life and Thought.* Philadelphia: Fortress Press.

Belsey, Catherine. 1980. *Critical Practice.* London: Routledge.

Berger, Klaus. 1984. "Hellenistische Gattungen im Neuen Testament." *ANRW* II.25.2:1031–432.

Berger, Peter, and Thomas Luckmann. 1967. *The Social Construction of Reality: A Treatise in the Sociology of Knowledge.* New York: Anchor Books.

Bible and Culture Collective, The. 1995. *The Postmodern Bible.* New Haven: Yale University Press.

Bitzer, Lloyd F. 1968. The Rhetorical Situation. *Philosophy and Rhetoric* 1:1–14.

Black, D. A. 1985. Paul and Christian Unity: A Formal Analysis of Philippians 2.1–4. *JETS* 28:299–308.

Blevins, James L. 1980. Introduction to Philippians. *RevExp* 77:311–25.

Bloom, Harold. 1986. From J to K, or the Uncanniness of the Yahwist. Pages 19–35 in *The Bible and the Narrative Tradition.* Edited by Frank McConnell. New York: Oxford University Press.

Bloom, Harold, et al. 1979. *Deconstruction and Criticism.* New York: Continuum.

Bockmuehl, Markus. 1998. *The Epistle to the Philippians.* BNTC. N.P.: Hendrickson.

Bornkamm, Günther. 1971. *Paul.* Translated by M. G. Stalker. New York: Harper & Row.

———. 1995. The Letter to the Romans as Paul's Last Will and Testament. Pages 16–28 in *The Romans Debate.* Edited by Karl P. Donfried. Rev. ed. Peabody, Mass.: Hendrickson.

Braumann, G. 1975. "Form, Substance." Pages 703–14 in vol. 1 of *New International Dictionary of New Testament Theology.* Edited by Colin Brown. 3 vols. Grand Rapids: Zondervan, 1975–78.

Brett, Mark G. 1991. Motives and Intentions in Genesis 1. *JTS* 42:1–16.

Brown, Colin., ed. 1978. *New International Dictionary of New Testament Theology.* 3 vols. Grand Rapids: Zondervan.

Brown, Raymond E. 1996. *An Introduction to the New Testament.* Anchor Bible Reference Library. New York: Doubleday.

Bruce, F. F. 1977. *Paul: Apostle of the Heart Set Free.* Grand Rapids: Eerdmans.

———. 1981. St. Paul in Macedonia 3. The Philippians Correspondence. *Bulletin of the John Rylands University Library of Manchester* 63:260–84.

———. 1989. *Philippians.* NICB. Peabody, Mass.: Hendrickson.

Bruner, F. Dale. 1990. The Why and How of Commentary. *ThTo* 46:399–404.

Bultmann, Rudolph. 1951. *Theology of the New Testament.* 2 vols. Translated by Kendrick Grobel. New York: Scribner's.

———. 1985. *The Second Letter to the Corinthians.* Edited by Erich Dinkler. Translated by Roy A. Harrisville. Minneapolis: Augsburg.

Caird, G. B. 1976. *Paul's Letters from Prison.* Oxford: Oxford University Press.

Calvin, John. 1981. *Commentaries on the Epistles to the Philippians, Colossians, and Thessalonians.* Vol. 21 of *Calvin's Commentaries.* Grand Rapids: Baker.

Cameron, Averil. 1994. *Christianity and the Rhetoric of Empire: The Development of Christian Discourse.* Sather Classical Lectures 55. Berkeley: University of California Press.

Carson, D. A., Douglas J. Moo, and Leon Morris. 1992. *An Introduction to the New Testament.* Grand Rapids: Zondervan.

Castelli, Elizabeth A. 1991. *Imitating Paul: A Discourse of Power.* Literary Currents in Biblical Literature. Louisville: Westminster John Knox Press.

Cavell, Stanley. 1995. *Philosophical Passages: Wittgenstein, Emerson, Austin, Derrida.* Oxford: Blackwell.

Chaplin, J. P. 1985. *Dictionary of Psychology.* 2nd ed. New York: Laurel.

Clines, D. J. A. 1976. Theme in Genesis 1–11. *CBQ* 38:483–507.

Collange, Jean-François. 1979. *The Epistle of Saint Paul to the Philippians.* Translated by A. W. Heathcote. London: Epworth Press.

Cook, D. 1981. Stephanus Le Moyne and the Dissection of Philippians. *JTS* 32:138–42.

Craddock, F. B. 1985. *Philippians.* Interpretation. Atlanta: John Knox.

Cranfield, C. E. B. 1975. *The Epistle to the Romans.* 2 vols. ICC. Edinburgh: T&T Clark.

Culler, Jonathan. 1982. *On Deconstruction: Theory and Criticism after Structuralism.* London: Routledge.

Cullman, Oscar. 1958. *Peter: Disciple, Apostle, Martyr. A Historical and Theological Essay.* Translated by Floyd V. Filson. New York: Meridian Books.

Dalton, W. J. 1979. The Integrity of Philippians. *Biblica* 60:97–102.

Deissmann, Adolf. 1909. *Licht vom Osten: Das Neue Testament und die neuentdeckten Texte der hellenistisch-römischen Welt.* Tübingen: J. C. B. Mohr (Paul Siebeck).

——— . 1957. *Paul: A Study in Social and Religious History.* 2nd ed. Translated by W. E. Wilson. New York: Harper.

———. n.d. *Light from the Ancient East: The New Testament Illustrated by Recently Discovered Texts of the Greco-Roman World.* Translated from the 1909 2nd German edition by Lionel R. M. Strachan. New York: Hodder and Stoughton.

Derrida, Jacques. 1976. *Of Grammatology.* Translated by Gayatri Chakravorty Spivak. Baltimore: Johns Hopkins University Press.

——— . 1979. Living On: Border Lines. Pages 74–176 in *Deconstruction and Criticism.* Edited by Harold Bloom et al. New York: Continuum.

——— . 1981a. *Dissemination.* Translated by Barbara Johnson. London: Athlone Press.

——— . 1981b. *Positions.* Translated by Alan Bass. Chicago: University of Chicago Press.

——— . 1985. *Ear of the Other: Otobiography, Transference, Translation.* Translated by P. Kamuf and A. Ronell. Edited by C. V. McDonald. New York: Schocken Books.

———. 1986. Signature, Event, Context. In *Margins of Philosophy.* Translated by Alan Bass. Chicago: University of Chicago Press.

——— . 1988 Letter to a Japanese Friend. Pages 1–5 in *Derrida and Différance*. Edited by David Wood and Robbert Bernasconi. Translated by David Wood and Andrew Benjamin. Evanston, Ill.: Northwestern University Press.

——— . 1998a. *Limited Inc*. Edited by Gerald Graff. Translated by Samuel Webber and Jeffrey Mehlman. Evanston, Ill.: Northwestern University Press.

——— . 1998b. Signature, Event, Context. Pages 1–23 in *Limited Inc*. Edited by Gerald Graff. Translated by Samuel Webber and Jeffrey Mehlman. Evanston, Ill.: Northwestern University Press.

De Saussure, Ferdinand. 1966. *Course in General Linguistics*. Edited by Charles Bally and Albert Sechehaye, with Albert Reidlinger. Translated by Wade Baskin. New York: Philosophical Library, 1959. Repr., New York: McGraw-Hill.

De Witt, Norman. 1935. Parrhesiastic Poems of Horace. *CPh* 30:312–19.

——— . 1954. *Epicurus and His Philosophy*. Minneapolis: University of Minnesota Press.

Dibelius, Martin. 1937. *An die Thessalonicher I, II; an die Philipper*. Handbuch zum Neuen Testament 11. Tübingen: J. C. B. Mohr (Paul Siebeck).

Dodds, E. R. 1973. *The Ancient Concept of Progress and Other Essays*. Oxford: Clarendon Press.

Droge, A. J. 1988. *Mori Lucrum*: Paul and Ancient Theories of Suicide. *NovT* 33:263–86.

——— . 1989. Did Paul Commit Suicide?. *BibRev* 5:14–21.

Droge, A. J., and J. D. Tabor. 1992. *A Noble Death: Suicide and Martyrdom among Christians and Jews in Antiquity*. San Francisco: Harper.

Dunn, James D. G. 1978. Caesar, Consul, Governor. Pages 269–70 in vol. 1 of *New International Dictionary of New Testament Theology*. Edited by Colin Brown. 3 vols. Grand Rapids: Zondervan.

——— . 1993. Letter to the Romans. Pages 823–50 in *Dictionary of Paul and His Letters*. Edited by Gerald Hawthorne and Ralph Martin. Downers Grove, Ill.: InterVarsity.

——— . 1998a. *The Theology of Paul the Apostle*. Grand Rapids: Eerdmans.

——— . 1998b. Whatever Happened to Exegesis? In Response to the Reviews by R. B. Matlock and D. A. Campbell. *JSNT* 72:113–20.

Engberg-Pedersen, Troels. 1993. Proclaiming the Lord's Death: 1 Corinthians 11:17–34 and the Forms of Paul's Theological Argument. Pages 103–32 in *Pauline Theology: 1 and 2 Corinthians*. Vol. 2. Edited by David M. Hay. Minneapolis: Fortress Press.

——— . 1994a. *Paul in His Hellenistic Context*. Edinburgh: T&T Clark.

——— . 1994b. Stoicism in Philippians. Pages 256–90 in *Paul in His Hellenistic Context*. Edited by Troels Engberg-Pedersen. Edinburgh: T&T Clark.

——— . 2000. *Paul and the Stoics*. Louisville: Westminster John Knox Press.

Ernst, Josef. 1973. Anfechtung und Bewahrung: Das Bild einer Christlichen Gemeinde nach dem Philipperbrief. In *Das Evangelium auf dem Wege zu Menschen*. Edited by Otto Knoch, Felix Messerschmid, and Alois Zenner. Frankfurt: Knecht.

Fee, Gordon. 1995. *Paul's Letter to the Philippians*. New International Commentary on the New Testament. Grand Rapids: William B. Eerdmans.

Foucault, Michel. 1986. *The History of Sexuality*. Translated by Robert Hurley. 3 vols. London: Penguin.

Fowl, Steven E. 1990. *The Story of Christ in the Ethics of Paul: An Analysis of the Func-

tion of the Hymnic Material in the Pauline Corpus. JSNTSup36; Sheffield: Sheffield Academic Press.

———. 1998. Christology and Ethics in Philippians 2:5–11. Pages 140–53 in *Where Christology Began.* Edited by Ralph P. Martin and Brian J. Dodd. Louisville: Westminster John Knox Press.

Fredrickson, David E. 1996. ΠΑΡΡΗΣΙΑ in the Pauline Epistles. Pages 163–84 in *Friendship, Flattery, and Frankness of Speech: Studies on Friendship in the New Testament World.* Edited by John T. Fitzgerald. NovTSup 82. Leiden: E. J. Brill.

Freud, Sigmund. 1937. Wenn Moses ein Ägypter war . . . *Imago: Zeitschrift für Psychoanalytische Psychologie, Ihre Grenzgebiete und Anwendungen* 23:387–419.

———. 1951. *Moses and Monotheism.* Translated by Katherine Jones. International Psycho-Analytical Library 33. London: Hogarth, and the Institute of Psycho-Analysis.

Friedrich, Gerhard. 1964. "εὐαγγελίζομαι, εὐαγγέλιον, προευαγγελίζομαι, εὐαγγελιστής." Pages 707–37 in vol. 2 of *Theolgical Dictionary of the New Testament.* Edited by G. Kittel and G. Friedrich. Translated by G. Bromiley. 10 vols. Grand Rapids: Eerdmans, 1964–76.

———. 1990. Der Brief an der Philipper. Pages 125–75 in *Die Briefe an die Galater, Epheser, Philipper, Kolosser, Thessalonicher und Philemon,* by Jürgen Becker, Hans Conzelmann, and Gerhard Friedrich. NTD 8. Göttingen: Vandenhoeck & Ruprecht.

Funk, Robert W. 1967. The Apostolic Parousia: Form and Significance. Pages 249–68 in *Christian History and Interpretation: Studies Presented to John Knox.* Edited by W. R. Farmer, C. F. D. Moule, and R. R. Niehbuhr. Cambridge: Cambridge University Press.

Furnish, Victor Paul. 1964. The Place and Purpose of Phil III. *NTS* 10:80–88.

———. 1989. Pauline Studies. Pages 321–50 in *The New Testament and Its Modern Interpreters.* Edited by Eldon Jay Epp and George W. MacRae. Atlanta: Scholars Press.

Gadamer, Hans-Georg. 1975. *Truth and Method.* New York: Seabury Press.

Garland, David E. 1985. The Composition and Unity of Philippians: Some Neglected Literary Factors. *NovT* 27:141–73.

Georgi, Dieter. 1987. *The Opponents of Paul in Second Corinthians.* Studies of the New Testament and Its World. Edinburgh: T&T Clark.

Glad, Clarence E. 1995. *Paul and Philodemus: Adaptability in Epicurean and Early Christian Psychagogy.* NovTSup 81. Leiden: E. J. Brill.

———. 1996a. The Significance of Hellenistic Psychagogy for Our Understanding of Paul. Pages 57–93 in *The New Testament in Its Hellenistic Context.* Studia Theologica Islandica 10. Edited by Gunnlaugur A. Jónsson, Einar Sigurbjörnsson, and Pétur Pétursson. Reykjavík: Guðfræðistofnun-Skálholtsútgáfan.

———. 1996b. Frank Speech, Flattery, and Friendship in Philodemus. Pages 21–60 in *Friendship, Flattery, and Frankness of Speech: Studies on Friendship in the New Testament World.* Edited by John T. Fitzgerald. NovTSup 82. Leiden: E. J. Brill, 1996.

Gnilka, Joachim. 1965. Die antipaulinische Mission in Philippi. *Biblische Zeitschrift* 9:258–76.

———. 1968. *Der Philipperbrief.* HTKNT 10.3. Freiburg: Herder.

Goldenson, Robert M., ed. 1984. *Longman Dictionary of Psychology and Psychiatry.* New York: Longman.

Grayston, K. 1986. The Opponents in Philippians 3. *ExpTim* 97:170–72.

Griffin, Miriam. 1994. The Intellectual Developments of the Ciceronian Age. Pages 689–729 in *The Cambridge Ancient History*. 2nd ed. Vol. 9. Cambridge: Cambridge University Press.

Gunther, J. J. 1973. *St. Paul's Opponents and Their Background*. NovTSup 35. Leiden: Brill.

Hadot, I. 1969. *Seneca und die griechisch-römishe Tradition der Seelenleitung*. Berlin: de Gruyter.

Hart, Kevin. 1989. *The Trespass of the Sign: Deconstruction, Theology, and Philosophy*. Cambridge: Cambridge University Press.

Hawthorne, Gerald F. 1983. *Philippians*. Word Biblical Commentary 43. Waco, Tex.: Word Books.

Heidegger, Martin. 1962. *Being and Time*. Translated by John Macquarrie and Edward Robinson. New York: Harper & Row.

Hemer, Colin. J. 1990. *The Book of Acts in the Setting of Hellenistic History*. Edited by Conrad H. Gempf. Winona Lake, Ind.: Eisenbrauns.

Hendriksen, William. 1962. *Philippians*. NTC. Grand Rapids: Baker.

Hengel, Martin. 1981. *Judaism and Hellenism*. Translated by John Bowden. 1974. Repr., London: SCM.

———. 1989. *The Hellenization of Judaea in the First Century after Christ*. Translated by John Bowden. Philadelphia: Trinity Press International.

———. 1991. *The Pre-Christian Paul*. Translated by John Bowden. London: SCM.

Holladay, Carl R. 1969. Paul's Opponents in Philippians 3. *RestQ* 12:77–90.

Hughes, Philip Edgecumb. 1962. *Paul's Second Epistle to the Corinthians*. NICNT. Grand Rapids: Eerdmans.

Humphreys, S. C. (with A. Momigliano). 1978. The Social Structure of the Ancient City. Pages 177–208 in *Anthropology and the Greeks*. London: Routledge & Kegan Paul.

Iser, Wolfgang. 1978. *The Act of Reading: A Theory of Aesthetic Response*. Baltimore: Johns Hopkins University Press.

Jameson, Fredric. 1988. Metacommentary. Pages 3–16 in *Situations of Theory*. Vol. 1 of *The Ideologies of Theory: Essays, 1971–1986*. Minneapolis: University of Minnesota Press.

Jewett, Robert. 1970a. Conflicting Moments in the Early Church as Reflected in Philippians. *NovT* 12:362–90.

———. 1970b. The Epistolary Thanksgiving and the Integrity of Philippians. *NovT* 12:40–53.

Johnson, Barbara. 1978. The Critical Difference. *Diacritics* 8:2–9.

Judge, Edwin A. 1960. *The Social Pattern of Christian Groups in the First Century*. London: Tyndale.

———. 1972. St. Paul and Classical Society. *JAC* 15:19–36.

Kamuf, Peggy, ed. 1991. *A Derrida Reader: Between the Blinds*. New York: Columbia University Press.

Käsemann, Ernst. 1968. A Critical Analysis of Phil 2:5–11. *JTC* 5:45–88.

———. 1969. *New Testament Questions of Today*. Translated by W. J. Montague. New Testament Library. London: SCM.

———. 1984. *Perspectives on Paul*. London: SCM.

Kennedy, George A. 1984. *New Testament Interpretation through Rhetorical Criticism*. Studies in Religion. Chapel Hill: University of North Carolina Press.

Kennedy, H. A. A. 1903. The Epistle to the Philippians. Pages 397–473 in *Expositor's Greek Testament*. Vol. 3. London: Hodder & Stoughton.

Kilpatrick, G. D. 1968. BLEPETE, Philippians 3:2. Pages 146–48 in *In Memoriam P. Kahle*. Edited by M. Black and G. Fohrer. BZAW 103. Berlin: Töpelmann.

Kim, Young Kyu. 1988. Palaeographic Dating of P[46]. *Biblica* 69:248–57.

Klijn, A. F. J. 1965. Paul's Opponents in Philippians iii. *NovT* 7:278–84.

Koester, Helmut. 1961–62. The Purpose of the Polemic of a Pauline Fragment (Philippians III). *NTS* 8:317–332.

Koperski, V. 1993. The Early History of the Dissection of Philippians. *JTS* 44:599–603.

Koskenniemi, H. 1956. *Studien zur Idee und Phraseologie des griechischen Briefes bis 400 n. Chr*. Annales Academiae scientiarum fennicae: Series B, vol. 102.2. Helsinki: Suomalaisen Kirjallisuuden Kirjapaino.

Kramer, W. 1966. *Christ, Lord, Son of God*. Translated by Brian Hardy. London: S.M.C.

Kümmel, Werner Georg. 1975. *Introduction to the New Testament*. Translated by Howard Clark Kee. Rev. ed. Nashville: Abingdon.

Kümmel, Werner Georg, Paul Feine, and Johannes Behm. 1965. *Einleitung in das Neue Testament*. Heidelberg: Quelle & Meyer.

Le Moyne, Étienne. 1685. *Notae et Observationes, Varia Sacra*. 2 vols. Leiden: Daniel Gaesbeeck.

Lightfoot, J. B. 1953. *Saint Paul's Epistle to the Philippians*. Rev. ed. London: MacMillan, 1913. Repr., Grand Rapids.

Loh, I-Jin, and Eugene A. Nida. 1977. *A Translator's Handbook on Paul's Letter to the Philippians*. Helps for Translators. Stuttgart: United Bible Societies.

Lohmeyer, Ernst. 1964. *Der Brief an die Philipper, an die Kolosser und an Philemon*. Göttingen: Vandenhoeck & Ruprecht.

Lutz, Cora E. 1947. *Musonius Rufus: "The Roman Socrates."* Edited by Alfred R. Bellinger. Yale Classical Studies 10. New Haven: Yale University Press.

Malherbe, Abraham J. 1970. "Gentle as a Nurse": The Cynic Background of 1 Thess ii. *NovT* 12:203–17.

———. 1982. Self-Definition among Epicureans and Cynics. Pages 46–59 in *Jewish and Christian Self-Definition*. Edited by Ben F. Meyer and E. P. Sanders. Self Definition in the Greco-Roman World 3. London: SCM.

———. 1983a. *Social Aspects of Early Christianity*. 2nd ed. Philadelphia: Fortress.

———. 1983b. Antisthenes and Odesseus, and Paul at War. *HTR* 76:143–73.

———. 1983c. Exhortation in First Thessalonians. *NovT* 25:238–56.

———. 1985. Paul: Hellenistic Philosopher or Christian Pastor? Pages 86–98 in *Summary Proceedings of the Thirty-ninth Annual Conference of the American Theological Library Association*.

———. 1986. *Moral Exhortation, a Greco Roman Sourcebook*. Philadelphia: Westminster Press.

———. 1987. *Paul and the Thessalonians: The Philosophic Tradition of Pastoral Care*. Philadelphia: Fortress Press.

———. 1989. *Paul and the Popular Philosophers*. Minneapolis: Fortress Press.

Malina, Bruce J. 1995. Early Christian Groups: Using Small Group Theory to Explain Christian Organizations. Pages 96–113 in *Modelling Christianity: Social-Scientific Studies of the New Testament in its Context*. Edited by Philip F. Esler. London: Routledge.

Malina, B. J., and J. H. Neyrey. 1991. Honor and Shame in Luke-Acts: Pivotal Values of the Mediterranean World. Pages 25–65 in *The Social World of Luke-Acts: Models for Interpretation*. Edited by J. H. Neyrey. Peabody, Mass.: Hendrickson.

Marshall, John W. 1993. Paul's Ethical Appeal in Philippians. Pages 357–74 in *Rhetoric and the New Testament: Essays from the 1992 Heidelberg Conference*. Edited by Stanley E. Porter and Thomas H. Olbricht. JSNTSup 90 Sheffield: Sheffield Academic Press.

Martin, Ralph P. 1976. *Philippians*. New Century Bible. London: Oliphants.

———. 1986. *2 Corinthians*. WBC. Waco, Tex.: Word Books.

———. 1987. *The Epistle of Paul to the Philippians*. TNTC. Grand Rapids: Eerdmans.

———. 1993. The Center of Paul's Theology. Pages 92–95 in *Dictionary of Paul and His Letters*. Edited by Gerald Hawthorne and Ralph Martin. Downers Grove, Ill.: InterVarsity.

Matlock, R. Barry. 1998. Sins of the Flesh and Suspicious Minds: Dunn's New Theology of Paul. *JSNT* 72:67–90.

McEleney, Neil J. 1974. The Vice Lists of the Pastoral Epistles. *CBQ* 36:203–19.

Meeks, Wayne A. 1982. The Social Context of Pauline Theology. *Interpretation* 36:266–77.

———. 1983. *The First Urban Christians: The Social World of the Apostle Paul*. New Haven: Yale University Press.

———. 1987. *The Moral World of the First Christians*. London: SPCK.

———. 1990. The Circle of Reference in Pauline Morality. Pages 305–17 in *Greeks, Romans, and Christians*. Edited by David L. Balch, Everett Ferguson, and Wayne Meeks. Minneapolis: Fortress Press.

———. 1991. The Man from Heaven in Paul's Letter to the Philippians. Pages 329–36 in *The Future of Early Christianity: Essays in Honor of Helmut Koester*. Edited by Birger A. Pearson et al. Minneapolis: Fortress Press.

———. 1993. *The Origins of Christian Morality: The First Two Centuries*. New Haven: Yale University Press.

Mengel, Berthold. 1982. *Studien zum Philipperbrief: Untersuchungen zum situativen Kontext unter besonderer Berücksichtigung der frage nach der Ganzheitlichkeit oder einheitlichkeit eines paulinischen Briefes*. WUNT 2.8. Tübingen: J. C. B. Mohr (Paul Siebeck).

Meyer, H. A. W. 1885. *Critical and Exegetical Handbook to the Epistles to the Philippians and Colossians*. Translated by J. C. Moore and W. P. Dickson, with supplementary notes by T. Dwight. New York: Funk & Wagnalls.

Meyer, P. W. 1995. Pauline Theology: Some Thoughts for a Pause in Its Pursuit. Pages 688–703 in *Society of Biblical Literature 1995 Seminar Papers*. Edited by Eugene H. Lovering Jr. Atlanta: Scholars Press.

Michael, J. Hugh. 1928. *The Epistle of Paul to the Philippians*. Moffat New Testament Commentary. London: Hodder and Stoughton.

Moo, Douglas J. 1996. *The Epistle to the Romans*. NICNT. Grand Rapids: Eerdmans.

Moore, Stephen D., and Janice Capel Anderson. 1998. Taking It Like a Man: Masculinity in 4 Maccabees. *JBL* 117, no. 2: 249–73

Müller, Jac J. 1991. *The Epistle of Paul to the Philippians*. NICNT. *The Epistles of Paul to the Philippians and to Philemon*. NICNT. 1955. Repr,. Grand Rapids: Eerdmans.

Müller-Bardorff, J. 1957–58. Zur Frage der literarischen Einheit des Philipperbriefes. *WZUJ* 7:591–604.

Mullins, T. Y. 1964. Disclosure: A Literary Form in the New Testament. *NovT* 7:44–50.

Neugebauer, F. 1957–58. Das Paulinische "in Christo." *NTS* 4:124–38.

———. 1961. *In Christus: Eine Untersuchung zum Paulinischen Glaubensverständnis.* Göttingen: Vandenhoeck & Ruprecht.

Nietzsche, Friedrich. 1910. *The Joyful Wisdom.* Translated by Thomas Common. Vol. 10 of *The Complete Works of Nietzsche.* Edinburgh: T. N. Foulis.

———. 1911. *Dawn of the Day.* Translated by J. M. Kennedy. Vol. 9 of *The Complete Works of Friedrich Nietzsche.* Edinburgh: T. N. Foulis.

———. 1954–56. *Werke in drei Bänden.* Edited by Karl Schlechta. 3 vols. Munich: Carl Hanser.

Norris, Christopher. 1982. *Deconstruction Theory and Practice.* New Accents. London: Routledge.

O'Brien, Peter T. 1977. *Introductory Thanksgivings in the Letters of Paul.* NovTSup 49. Leiden: Brill.

———. 1986. The Importance of the Gospel in Philippians. Pages 213–33 in *God Who Is Rich in Mercy: Essays Presented to D. B. Knox.* Edited by Peter T. O'Brien and David G. Peterson. Grand Rapids: Baker.

———. 1991. *The Epistle to the Philippians.* New International Greek Testament Commentary. Grand Rapids: William B. Eerdmans.

O'Brien, Peter T., and David G. Peterson, eds. 1986. *God Who Is Rich in Mercy: Essays Presented to Dr. D. B. Knox.* Edited by Peter T. O'Brien and David G. Peterson. Grand Rapids: Baker.

Ollrog, Wolf-Henning. 1979. *Paulus und seine Mitarbeiter: Untersuchungen zu Theorie und Praxis der paulinischen Mission.* Neukirchen-Vluyn: Neukirchener.

Patte, Daniel. 1988. Speech Act Theory and Biblical Exegesis. *Semeia* 41:85–102.

Perkins, Pheme. 1990. Commentaries: Windows to the Text. *ThTo* 46:393–98.

Peterlin, Davorin. 1995. *Paul's Letter to the Philippians in the Light of Disunity in the Church.* NovTSup 79. Leiden: Brill.

Peterman, G. W. 1997. *Paul's Gift from Philippi: Conventions of Gift-Exchange and Christian Giving.* SNTSMS 92. Cambridge: Cambridge University Press.

Peterson, Eugene, H. 1990. Preface: Symposium: On Writing Commentaries. *ThTo* 46:386.

Pfitzner, V. C. 1967. *Paul and the Agon Motif.* NovTSup 16. Leiden: Brill.

Plevnik, Joseph. 1989. The Center of Pauline Theology. *CBQ* 51:461–78.

Pollard, T. E. 1966. The Integrity of Philippians. *NTS* 13:57–66.

Radin, M. 1927. Freedom of Speech in Ancient Athens. *AJP* 48:215–20.

Rahtjen, B. D. 1959–60. The Three Letters of Paul to the Philippians. *NTS* 6:167–73.

Ramsay, William M. 1912. Roads and Travel (in NT). Pages 375–402 in *A Dictionary of the Bible: Dealing with Its Language, Literature, and Contents, Including Biblical Theology.* Edited by John Hastings. Extra volume. New York: Scribners.

Rapaport, Herman. 1995. Deconstruction's Other: Trinh T. Minh-ha and Jacques Derrida. *Diacritics* 25, no. 2: 98–108.

Rapske, B. 1994. *The Book of Acts and Paul in Roman Custody.* Vol. 3. The Book of Acts in Its First Century Setting. Grand Rapids: Eerdmans.

Redfield, Robert. 1955. *The Little Community: Viewpoints for the Study of a Human Whole.* Comparative Studies of Cultures and Civilizations. Chicago: University of Chicago Press.

Reed, Jeffrey T. 1996. Are Paul's Thanksgivings Epistolary? *JSNT* 61:87–99.

———. 1997. *A Discourse Analysis of Philippians: Method and Rhetoric in the Debate over Literary Integrity.* JSNTSup 136. Sheffield: Sheffield Academic Press.

Reicke, Bo. 1970. Caesarea, Rome, and the Captivity Epistles. Pages 277–86 in *Apos-*

tolic History and the Gospel: Biblical and Historical Essays Presented to F. F. Bruce on His Sixtieth Birthday. Edited by W. Ward Gasque and Ralph P. Martin. Grand Rapids: Eerdmans.

Ricoeur, Paul. 1973. Two Essays by Paul Ricoeur: The Critique of Religion and The Language of Faith. *USQR* 28:202–24.

Roetzel, Calvin. 1999. *Paul: The Man and the Myth.* Minneapolis: Fortress Press.

Russell, D. A. 1974. Letters to Lucilius. Pages 70–94 in *Seneca.* Edited by C. D. N. Costa. Greek and Latin Studies: Classical Literature and Its Influence. London: Routledge & Kegan Paul, 1974.

Russell, R. 1982. Pauline Letter Structure in Philippians. *JETS* 25:295–306.

Saller, Richard P. 1982. *Personal Patronage under the Early Empire.* New York: Cambridge University Press.

Schaberg, Jane. 1992. Luke. Pages 363–80 in *The Women's Bible Commentary.* Edited by Carol A. Newsom and Sharon H. Ringe. Louisville: Westminster John Knox.

Schenk, Wolfgang. 1984. *Die Philipperbriefe des Paulus* Stuttgart: Kohlhammer.

Schleiermacher, Friedrich. 1977. *Hermeneutics: The Handwritten Manuscripts.* Edited by Heinz Kimmerle. Translated by James Duke and Jack Forstman. AARTTS 1. Missoula, Mont.: Scholars Press.

Schlier, Heinrich. 1967. "παρρησία, παρρησιάζομαι." Pages 871–86 in vol. 5 of *Theolgical Dictionary of the New Testament.* Edited by G. Kittel and G. Friedrich. Translated by G. Bromiley. 10 vols. Grand Rapids: Eerdmans, 1964–76.

Schmithals, Walter. 1957. Die Irrlehrer des Philipperbriefes. *ZThK* 54:297–341.

———. 1972. *Paul and the Gnostics.* Translated by John E. Steely. Nashville: Abingdon.

Schubert, Paul. 1939. *Form and Function of the Pauline Thanksgivings.* BZNW 20. Berlin: Töpelmann.

Schütz, J. H. 1975. *Paul and the Anatomy of Apostolic Authority.* Cambridge: Cambridge University Press.

Schweitzer, Albert. 1967. *The Mysticism of Paul the Apostle.* Translated by William Montgomery. London: Adam & Charles Black.

Scott, E. F. 1955. The Epistle to the Philippians. *The Interpreter's Bible.* Edited by G. A. Buttrick et al. Vol. 11. New York: Abingdon.

Searle, John. 1977. Reiterating the Differences: A Reply to Derrida. *Glyph* I: 198–208.

Seifrid, M. A. 1993. In Christ. Pages 433–36 in *Dictionary of Paul and His Letters.* Edited by Gerald Hawthorne and Ralph Martin. Downers Grove, Ill.: Inter-Varsity.

Shaw, J. M. 1934. Philippians. *ExpT* 45:203–09.

Sherwin-White, A. N. 1964. *Roman Society and Roman Law in the New Testament.* Oxford: Clarendon.

Sherwood, Yvonne. 1996. *The Prostitute and the Prophet: Hosea's Marriage in Literary-Theoretical Perspective.* JSOTSup 212; Gender, Culture, Theory 2. Sheffield: Sheffield Academic Press.

Silva, Moisés. 1992. *Philippians.* BECNT. Grand Rapids: Baker.

Sontag, Susan. 1997. Against Interpretation. Pages 249–55 in *Aesthetics.* Edited by Susan L. Feagin and Patrick Maynard. New York: Oxford University Press.

Spivak, Gayatri Chakravorty. 1976. Translator's Preface. Pages ix–lxxxviii in *Of*

Grammatology, by Jacques Derrida. Translated by Gayatri Chakravorty Spivak. Baltimore: Johns Hopkins University Press.

Stählin, Gustav. 1968. "προκοπη." Pages 703–19 in vol. 6 of *Theolgical Dictionary of the New Testament*. Edited by G. Kittel and G. Friedrich. Translated by G. Bromiley. 10 vols. Grand Rapids: Eerdmans, 1964–76.

Staten, Henry. 1984. *Wittgenstein and Derrida*. Oxford: Basil Blackwell.

Stowers, Stanley K. 1986. *Letter Writing in Greco-Roman Antiquity*. LEC 5. Philadelphia: Fortress Press.

———. 1988. Social Typification and the Classification of Ancient Letters. Pages 78–90 in *The Social World of Formative Christianity and Judaism*. Edited by Jacob Neusner et al. Philadelphia: Fortress Press.

———. 1991. Friends and Enemies in the Politics of Heaven: Reading Theology in Philippians. Pages 105–22 in *Pauline Theology I: Thessalonians, Philippians, Galatians, Philemon*. Edited by Jouette M. Bassler. Minneapolis: Fortress Press.

———. 1994. *A Rereading of Romans: Justice, Jews, Gentiles*. New Haven: Yale University Press.

Swift, R. C. 1984. The Theme and Structure of Philippians. *BSac* 141:234–54.

Tajra, H. W. 1989. *The Trial of St. Paul: A Juridical Exegesis of the Second Half of the Acts of the Apostles*. WUNT 2.35. Tübingen: Mohr (Paul Siebeck).

Tellbe, Mikael. 1994. The Sociological Factors behind Philippians 3.1–11 and the Conflict at Philippi. *JSNT* 55:97–121.

Thraede, Klaus. 1970. *Grundzüge griechisch-römischer Brieftopik*. ZETEMATA: Monographien zur klassischen Alterumswissenschaft 48. Munich: C. H. Beck.

Tompkins, Jane P. 1980. The Reader in History: The Changing Shape of Literary Response. Pages 201–32 in *Reader Response Criticism: From Formalism to Poststructuralism*. Edited by Jane P. Tompkins. Baltimore: Johns Hopkins University Press.

Trench, R. C. Envy. 1978. Pages 557–58 in vol. 1 of *New International Dictionary of New Testament Theology*. Edited by Colin Brown. 3 vols. Grand Rapids: Zondervan.

Tyson, J. B. 1976. Paul's Opponents at Philippi. *Perspectives in Religious Studies* 3:82–95.

Van Unnik, W. C. 1980. The Semitic Background of ΠΑΡΡΗΣΙΑ in the New Testament. *Sparsa Collecta*. NovTSup 30. Leiden Brill.

Vincent, Marvin R. 1897. *Critical and Exegetical Commentary on the Epistles to the Philippians and to Philemon*. ICC. Edinburgh: T&T Clark.

Walbank, F. W. 1993. *The Hellenistic World*. Rev. ed. Cambridge: Harvard University Press.

Wansink, Craig S. 1996. *Chained in Christ: The Experience and Rhetoric of Paul's Imprisonments*. JSNTSup 130. Sheffield: Sheffield Academic Press.

Watson, Duane F. 1988. A Rhetorical Analysis of Philippians and Its Implications for the Unity Question. *NovT* 30:57–88.

Watson, Francis. 1997. The Scope of Hermeneutics. Pages 65–80 in *The Cambridge Companion to Christian Doctrine*. Edited by Colin E. Gunton. Cambridge: Cambridge University Press.

Weiss, Johannes. 1908. *Die Aufgaben der neutestamentlichen Wissenshaft in der Gegenwart*. Göttingen: Vandenhoeck & Ruprecht.

White, John L. 1972. *The Form and Function of the Body in the Greek Letter: A Study of* the Letter-Body in the Non-literary Papyri and in Paul the Apostle. SBLDS 2. Missoula, Mont.: Scholars Press.

———. 1986. Light from Ancient Letters. FFNT. Philadelphia: Fortress Press.

Wibbing, Siegfried. 1959. Die Tugend- und Lasterkataloge im Neuen Testament; und ihre Traditionsgeschichte unter besonderer Berücksichtigung der Qumran-Texte. BZNW 25. Berlin: Alfred Töpelman.

Wiles, G. P. 1974. Paul's Intercessory Prayers: The Significance of the Intercessory Prayer Passages in the Letters of St Paul. SNTSMS 24. Cambridge: Cambridge University Press.

Winter, J. G. 1927. In the Service of Rome: Letters from the Michigan Papyri. CPh 22:237–56.

Wittgenstein, Ludwig. 1953. Philosophical Investigations. Translated by G. E. M. Anscome. New York: Macmillan.

Wrede, William. 1962. Paul. Translated by Edward Lummis. Lexington, Ky.: American Theological Library Association Committee on Reprinting.

Ancient Authors, Texts, and Translations

Alciphron. *The Letters of Alciphron, Aelian and Philostratus*. 1990. Translated by Allen Rogers Benner and Francis H. Fobes. LCL. Cambridge: Harvard University Press.

Anarchasis. Epistles of Anarchasis. 1977. Translated by Anne M. McGuire. Pages 35–52 in *The Cynic Epistles: A Study Edition*. Edited by Abraham Malherbe. SBLSBS 12. Missoula, Mont.: Scholars Press.

Aristotle. *The Art of Rhetoric*. 1991. Translated by John Henry Freese. LCL. Cambridge: Harvard University Press.

———. *The Nicomachean Ethics*. 1982. Translated by H. Rackham. LCL. Cambridge: Harvard University Press.

Cicero. *Letters to Atticus*. 1918. Translated by E. O. Winstedt. 3 vols. LCL. London: William Heinemann.

———. *De Senectute, De Amicitia, De Divinatione*. 1923. Translated by William Armistead Falconer. LCL. Cambridge: Harvard University Press.

———. *De Natura Deorum; Academica*. 1933. Translated by H. Rackham. LCL. London: William Heinemann.

———. *De Finibus*. 1971. Translated by H. Rackham. LCL. London: William Heinemann.

———. *Tusculan Disputations*. 1971. Translated by J. E. King. LCL. London: William Heinemann.

———. *The Letters to His Friends*. 1972. Translated by W. Glynn Williams. 4 vols. LCL. London: William Heinemann.

———. *De Officiis*. 1975. Translated by Walter Miller. LCL. London: William Heinemann.

Clement of Alexandria. *Clemens Alexandrinus: Protrepticus und Paedagogus*. 1972. Die Griechischen Christlichen Schriftsteller: Der Ersten Jahrhunderte. Otto Stählin. Berlin: Akademie.

Crates. Epistles of Crates. 1977. Translated by Ronald F. Hock. Pages 53–90 in *The Cynic Epistles: A Study Edition*. Edited by Abraham Malherbe. SBLSBS 12. Missoula, Mont.: Scholars Press.

Demetrius. *On Style*. 1982. Translated by W. Rhys Roberts. LCL. Cambridge: Harvard University Press.

Diogenes. The Epistles of Diogenes. 1977. Translated by Benjamin Fiore, S.J. Pages 91–184 in *The Cynic Epistles: A Study Edition*. Edited by Abraham Malherbe. SBLSBS 12. Missoula, Mont.: Scholars Press.

Diogenes Laertius. *Lives of Eminent Philosophers.* 1925. Translated by R. D. Hicks. LCL. London: William Heinemann.

Epictetus. *Epictetus.* 1985. Translated by W. A. Oldfather. 2 vols. LCL. Cambridge: Harvard University Press.

Euripides. *Euripides.* 1978. Translated by Arthur S. Way. 4 vols. LCL. Cambridge: Harvard University Press.

Galen. *On the Passions and Errors of the Soul.* 1963. Translated by Paul W. Harkins. Columbus: Ohio State University Press.

———. *On the Doctrines of Hippocrates and Plato.* 1980. Translated by Phillip De Lacy. Corpus Medicorum Graecorum 5, 4, 1, 2. Part 2. Berlin: Akademie-Verlag.

Grant, Robert M. 1946. *Second-Century Christianity: A Collection of Fragments.* London: SPCK.

Gregory of Nazianzus. "Epistulae." 1999. TLG E. University of California Irvine.

Heraclitus. The Epistles of Heraclitus. 1977. Translated by David. R. Worley. Pages 185–216 in *The Cynic Epistles: A Study Edition.* Edited by Abraham Malherbe. SBLSBS 12. Missoula, Mont.: Scholars Press.

Homer. *The Odyssey.* 1994–95. Translated by A. T. Murray. Revised by George E. Dimock. 2 vols. LCL. Cambridge: Harvard University Press.

Horace. *Odes and Epodes.* 1914. Translated by C. E. Bennett. LCL. Cambridge: Harvard University Press.

———. *Satires, Epistles, and Ars Poetica.* 1926. Translated by H. Rushton Fairclough. LCL. Cambridge: Harvard University Press.

Hunt, A. S., and C. C. Edgar, trans. 1959. *Select Papyri.* 5 vols. LCL. Cambridge: Harvard University Press.

Isocrates. *Isocrates.* 1986. Translated by Larue Van Hook. 3 vols. LCL. Cambridge: Harvard University Press.

Josephus. *Jewish Antiquities.* 1958. Translated by Ralph Marcus. LCL. Cambridge: Harvard University Press.

Julian. *The Works of the Emperor Julian.* 1980–93. Translated by Wilmer Cave Wright. 3 vols. LCL. Cambridge: Harvard University Press.

Pseudo Demetrius. Epistolary Types. 1988. Pages 30–41 in *Ancient Epistolary Theorists.* Translated by Abraham J. Malherbe. SBLSBS 19. Atlanta: Scholars Press.

Pseudo Libanius. Epistolary Styles. 1988. Pages 68–81 in *Ancient Epistolary Theorists.* Translated by Abraham J. Malherbe. SBLSBS 19. Atlanta: Scholars Press.

Longinus. *On the Sublime.* 1982. Translated by W. Hamilton Fyfe. LCL. Cambridge: Harvard University Press.

Lucian. *Lucian.* 1968. Translated by K. Kilburn. 8 vols. LCL. Cambridge: Harvard University Press.

Malherbe, Abraham, ed. 1977. *The Cynic Epistles: A Study Edition.* SBLSBS 12. Missoula, Mont.: Scholars Press.

———. 1988. *Ancient Epistolary Theorists.* SBLSBS 19. Atlanta: Scholars Press.

Maximus of Tyre. *Maximus Tyrius: Dissertationes.* 1994. Edited by M. B. Trapp. Stuttgart and Leipzig: B. G. Teubner.

———. *Maximus of Tyre: The Philosophical Orations.* 1997. Translated and annotated by M. B. Trapp. Oxford: Clarendon Press.

Musonius Rufus. 1947. Translated and edited by Cora E. Lutz. *Musonius Rufus: "The Roman Socrates."* Yale Classical Studies 10. New Haven: Yale University Press.

Philodemus. ΠΕΡΙ ΠΑΡΡΗΣΙΑΣ (PHerc 1471). 1914. Edited by Alexander Olivieri. B. G. Teubner.

———. *On Frank Criticism*. 1998. Introduction, translation, and notes by David Konstan et al. Society of Biblical Literature Text and Translations 43. Graeco-Roman 13. Atlanta: Scholars Press.

Plato. *Theaetetus. Sophist*. 1921. Translated by H. N. Fowler. LCL. Cambridge: Harvard University Press.

———. *Lysis. Symposium. Gorgias*. 1925. Translated by W. R. M. Lamb. LCL. Cambridge: Harvard University Press.

———. *Timaeus, Critias, Cleitophon, Menexenus, Epistles*. 1981. Translated by Rev. R. G. Bury. LCL. Cambridge: Harvard University Press.

———. *Euthyphro, Apology, Crito, Phaedo, Phaedrus*. 1982. Translated by Harold North Fowler. LCL. Cambridge: Harvard University Press.

Pliny, the Elder. *Natural History*. 1949. Translated by H. Rackham. LCL. 10 vols. Cambridge: Harvard University Press.

Plutarch. *Moralia*. 1927. Translated by Frank Cole Babbitt. 17 vols. LCL. London: William Heinemann.

Polybius. *Polybius: The Histories*. 1979. Translated by W. R. Paton. 6 vols. LCL. Cambridge: Harvard University Press.

Polycarp. *Philippians*. 1919. In *Apostolic Fathers*. Translated by Kirsopp Lake. 2 vols. LCL. New York: G. P. Putnam's.

Polystratus. *On the Irrational Contempt of the Popular Opinions. Pherc 336/1150*. 1978. In *Sul Disprezzo Irrazionale delle Opinioni Popolari*. Edited by Giovani Indelli. Vol. 2. Istituto Italiano per gli Studi Filosofici: La Scuola di Epicuro. Naples: Bibliopolis.

Quintilian. *The Institutio Oratoria of Quintilian*. 1968. Translated by H. E. Butler. 4 vols. LCL. London: William Heinemann.

Select Papyri. 1959. Translated by A. S. Hunt and C. C. Edgar. 5 vols. LCL. Cambridge: Harvard University Press.

Seneca. *Ad Lucilium Epistulae Morales*. 1930. Translated by Richard M. Gummere. 3 vols. LCL. London: William Heinemann.

———. *Moral Essays*. 1970. Translated by John W. Basore. 3 vols. LCL. London: William Heineman.

Shepherd of Hermas. 1965. In *The Apostolic Fathers*. Translated by Kirsopp Lake. 2 vols. LCL. Cambridge: Harvard University Press.

Thucydides. *Thucydides*. 1975. Translated by Charles Forster Smith. 4 vols. LCL. Cambridge: Harvard University Press.

Index of Biblical References

Index of Ancient Authors

Alciphron
Ep. 19   38

Anarchasis
Ep. 2   90

Aristotle
Eth. nic.
9.2.9   88
Rhet.
2.101   145

Cicero
Acad.
2.41.127   90
Amic.
25.95   88
Att.
9.10.1   96
12.53   96
Fam.
16.16.2   95
Fin.
1.7.25   5, 90
4.5.12   90
Off.
1.43.153   5, 90
1.65   91
Tusc.
5.3.990
5.24–65, 90
5.24.69   90

Clement of Alexandria
Protr.
261.23–24   81

Crates
Ep. 13   90
Ep. 16   90
Ep. 20   91
Ep. 21   90, 91

Demetrius
Style
223   95
224   95
227   95

Demetrius (Pseudo)
Ep. Types
1.10–11   95
5.16–17   95

Diogenes (Pseudo)
Ep. 15   91
Ep. 21.8–9   81
Ep. 21.35   81
Ep. 27   91
Ep. 29   91
Ep. 30   90

Diogenes Laertius
Lives
6.30   82

Index of Modern Authors